CW00417796

£20

Music and the Celtic Otherworld

Music and the Celtic Otherworld

From Ireland to Iona

Karen Ralls-MacLeod

POLYGON
AT EDINBURGH

© Karen Ralls-MacLeod, 2000

Polygon at Edinburgh
An imprint of Edinburgh University Press Ltd
22 George Square, Edinburgh

Typeset in New Baskerville
by Bibliocraft Ltd, Dundee, and
printed and bound in Great Britain by
The Cromwell Press, Wiltshire

A CIP record for this book is available from the British Library

ISBN 1 902930 09 6 (paperback)

The right of Karen Ralls-MacLeod
to be identified as the author of this work
has been asserted in accordance with
the Copyright, Designs and Patents Act 1988

Contents

Preface and Acknowledgements

The mysterious dimension of the Celtic Otherworld is often referred to in the early sources of Ireland, Scotland and Wales, with many descriptions of the enchanting music of the fairy harp, the mermaid's song, the joyful chants of the choirs of angels and so on. The spiritual dimension of music is a subject that has long fascinated many throughout history, from Pythagoras in early Greece to Ficino in the Renaissance and on down to more modern times. Today, composers, philosophers and scientists continue to study music and analyse its effects. As a young classically-trained musician, I also became interested in why certain music seemed to have certain effects on the listener, and in the various beliefs about music and its perceived powers.

Later, while researching the Celtic aspects of this universal phenomenon as a PhD student at the University of Edinburgh, I studied the early Celtic texts and extracted from them any references to music in an overall effort to assemble a collection of them. It seems as though the early Celts were certainly highly aware of music in general, and of its effects on the listener in particular, which modern scientific and medical research is now beginning to verify. There has always been something unique about the effects of certain types of music, and in the early medieval Irish sources, for example, the enchanting music of the fairy harp is referred to by St Patrick as having a suspicious 'twang of the fairy spell', as it lulled the clergy into a trance-like sleep state, such was its power.

I have many individuals to thank in Scotland for their help during the many stages of this project: Professor James Mackey of New

College (Divinity), University of Edinburgh, for his inspiring role as PhD supervisor and advisor; the late Dr Alan Bruford, of the School of Scottish Studies, University of Edinburgh, for his tremendous enthusiasm for this subject and great encouragement; Professor William Gillies, of the Celtic Department, University of Edinburgh, for his thought-provoking insights and discussions, classes in Old Irish, overall encouragement of this project and love of music. Dr Ian Bradley, of St Andrews University, also saw this project in its earlier stage as a PhD thesis and offered many valuable insights about Celtic spirituality in particular. To Dr Frank Whaling, New College (Divinity), for his time and encouragement through the years regarding valuable insights on Interfaith spirituality and music; to Noel O'Donoghue, for his great dedication to Celtic spirituality and inspiring classes; to the Rev. Dr Gordon Strachan, for his stimulating evening classes and discussions through the years; and to my colleagues in Celtic spirituality, Dr Tom Clancy, Fr Gilbert Markus, Dr Mary Low and Dr Clare MacRae, a big thank you for your inspiring works to date on this subject. Also thank you to Eri Ikawa, Nagoya, Japan, for her knowledge of Orkney, Shetland and Japanese folklore; and a big thank you to all at the School of Scottish Studies, for all your help and encouragement through the years. I also specially thank Mr Robert Brydon, FSA Scot, for his encouragement and highly specialist knowledge regarding early Scottish history and archaeology. A special thank you to the families and custodians of the various private libraries, archives and special collections I have consulted.

A special thank you to the late Anne Macauley, Honorary Fellow, Music Department, University of Edinburgh, for her encouragement, help, time and tremendous insights through the years, especially regarding the history of the lyre, Apollo and early megalithic Britain. Her pioneering research will be edited by academic experts and issued as a series in the forthcoming year. I have been asked to edit the second volume, entitled *Apollo's Lyre*, a musicological analysis of the early history of the guitar and lyre in the British Isles. Thank you also to Arnold Myers, Curator, Edinburgh University Collection of Historical Musical Instruments, for his encouragement to both the late Anne Macauley and myself. Great appreciation and thanks also to the librarians and archivists at the National Library of Scotland, University of Edinburgh Library, Glasgow University library, West Register House, National Archives of Scotland. Thank you to Niven Sinclair for his overall encouragement regarding my research, and thank you also to the former curator of Rosslyn Chapel, Judith Fisken. Thank you to Dr Peter Cooke, retired professor of Music at the University of Edinburgh, and to all other friends and colleagues, who are too numerous to name here.

In Ireland, many thanks to those at the UC Dublin Folklore Archive, the Dublin Institute for Advanced Studies (DIAS), the National Library of Ireland, Trinity College library, and the National Writer's Museum Library for your help and encouragement. Thank you to Dr John Carey, UC Cork, for insightful articles on the Otherworld. To Dr Breandan O'Madagain, thank you for his work on the effects of music and the lullaby, and for being a great inspiration to us all. A further thank you to Dr Daithi O'hOgain, UC Dublin, and Dr Maire Herbert, for continuing to inspire and challenge a new generation of scholars. Thank you also to the experts in heraldry and genealogy at Dublin Castle, and to the hospitality and expertise of the curators and staff at the National Museum of Ireland.

In England, many thanks to: the professors, librarians and experts at the National Library and National Sound Archive; the Warburg Institute (London); the Ethnomusicology library of the School of Oriental and African Studies (SOAS), University of London; Dr Keith Howard (SOAS) for his valuable insights; Dr Peggy Morgan, Westminster College, Oxford, for her encouragement, and to all at the Sir Alister Hardy Society and the Religious Experience Research Centre (RERC) Oxford, and to the librarians of the Bodleian Library, Oxford, and to Dr Anne Buckley, Cambridge University, for her excellent research on the early Irish timpan. Thank you to Dr Howard Brooks-Baker and his staff of *Burke's Peerage*, London, for their expertise and advice on genealogical and historical matters.

In Wales, thank you to Dr Robin Gwyndaf, Professor and folklore expert of the Welsh Folk Museum, Amgneffdu Werin Cymru, at St Fagin's, near Cardiff, for his most inspiring work on Welsh fairy lore and folklore classification. Thank you to the librarians at the University of Wales, Aberystwyth, for answering further enquiries about music.

In the United States, thank you to the Harvard University Divinity School and the Celtic Department faculty, for encouragement regarding music and the early Celtic saints' lives; thank you also to the Harvard University Center for the Study of World Religions, for their overall interest in the spiritual dimension of music in particular. Thank you to Dr G. B. Dixon for encouragement and help regarding Celtic spirituality, and to Dr Norma Goodrich of Claremont, California, for her knowledge and research regarding Celtic history and genealogy. Thanks to Howard and Margo Fish, Lake Placid, NY, for their encouragement and enthusiasm for Celtic research and that of Iona in particular. Thank you also to John and Diane Dosier, Mr Tom Pennington and Mr Gil Silva, for encouragement in music.

Finally, this book, especially in its final stages, would not have been completed without the encouragement and support of my husband, Jon, who through it all managed to maintain a good sense of humour and a genuine interest in music and Celtic folklore.

Dr Karen Ralls-MacLeod
Edinburgh, February 1999

Special Tribute to the late Dr Alan Bruford

School of Scottish Studies, University of Edinburgh

It is a rare opportunity indeed to have had the privilege and honour of knowing the late Dr Alan Bruford, internationally renowned folklore scholar, while attending the University of Edinburgh as a PhD student. This book is a further exploration of the subject of the spiritual dimension of music in the Celtic sources, which initially began as a PhD thesis with Dr Bruford, of the School of Scottish Studies, as one of the supervisors.

Dr Alan Bruford was one of Scotland's most dedicated and respected scholars and teachers, and was also archivist of the School of Scottish Studies. Through his pioneering efforts, he devised a classification system which gives access to one of the largest archives of folklore material in the world. He was a collector himself, recording many songs, tales, storytelling repertoires and details of the folklife in many parts of Scotland. In 1971 he founded *Tocher*, the School of Scottish Studies publication, which features reproducing archive materials, tales, songs, customs and beliefs, place names, and so on. He 'put Scotland on the map' in the world of international folklore scholarship through a wealth of conference papers and numerous publications, and inspired many students both here and abroad. He convened the Scottish Oral History Group from 1987 to 1993 and the legal and ethics committee of the International Association of Sound Archives. His books *Gaelic Folk-Tales and Medieval Romances* and *The Green Man of Knowledge and Other Scots Traditional Tales* have inspired many, and his most recent work, edited with Donald Archie MacDonald, is entitled *Scottish Traditional*

Tales. Today, the School of Scottish Studies continues to carry on his vision and many researchers from around the world come to the archives and library there to conduct further research.

His sudden death in May 1995 came shortly before my final PhD oral examination, so I would like to dedicate this book to him and his tremendous knowledge and enthusiasm for this subject, and that of 'fairy music' folklore in particular. A good musician and story-teller himself, he was very encouraging about further research being conducted in these areas. The day before he died, we had a meeting about folklore classification systems and how best to classify and archive the various accounts of 'fairy music' I had collected. I will never forget how, in the middle of this meeting with its many complex details, he suddenly 'became a storyteller' himself, and launched into several fascinating Scottish versions of the tale 'the Piper in the Cave', to illustrate a point. We then simply resumed our conversation about classification systems as if this magical interven-tion had never occurred, something that had happened many times before. His loss will long be keenly felt by many, and this writer is certainly no exception.

Dr Karen Ralls-MacLeod
Edinburgh, February 1999

Abbreviations

AIP	*Selections from Ancient Irish Poetry*, ed. K. Meyer
AIT	*Ancient Irish Tales*, eds T. Cross and C. Slover
BL	*Bealoideas*
CM	*A Celtic Miscellany*, ed. K. Jackson
CMCS	*Cambridge Medieval Celtic Studies* (from 1993,*Cambrian Medieval Celtic Studies*)
DIAS	Dublin Institute for Advanced Studies
EC	*Etudes Celtiques*
EIL	*Early Irish Lyrics*, ed. G. Murphy
EIMS	*Early Irish Myths and Sagas*, J. Gantz
ITS	Irish Texts Society
LSBL	*Lives of the Saints from the Book of Lismore*, ed. W. Stokes
MD	*Metrical Dindshenchas*, ed. E. Gwynn
PPCP	*Pagan Past, Christian Present*, K. McCone
RC	*Revue Celtique*
RIA	Royal Irish Academy
SC	*Studia Celtica*
SG	*Silva Gadelica*, ed. S. H. O'Grady
SH	*Studia Hibernia*
TLS	Todd Lecture Series
TLP	*Tripartite Life of St Patrick*, ed. W. Stokes
ZCP	*Zeitschrift für Celtische Philologie*

1

Introduction

F ROM THE BEAUTIFUL, ENCHANTING music of the fairy harp to the sacred singing of the choirs of angels, Celtic literature has many references to a spiritual or supernatural dimension of music. This sacred dimension is called the Celtic Otherworld, in which music is often prominently featured. For instance, there are many examples of fairy harpers, the songs of mermaids, the power of the saint's bell, the singing of angels in Heaven, musical trees, and so on. Connections between music and the Otherworld abound in Celtic literature, and especially that of early medieval Ireland.

The enchanting music of the Celtic Otherworld is portrayed as being heard from a dimension not of this world, that is, as something beyond ordinary reality and one's normal, everyday, mundane experience here on earth. There are many descriptions in Celtic literature of music having a powerful effect on the listener, often in a highly unusual way. These descriptions of music are found in references with both Christian and primal (pre-Christian) contexts from various Celtic sources.

One example of a gifted fairy harper, featured in a Christian context, is from the fifteenth-century *Acallam na Senorach* (Colloquy of the Ancient Men). Here, the fairy musician Cascorach puts St Patrick and his clergy to sleep with his sweet, beautiful music. Upon awakening, a lively debate takes place between St Patrick and his clergy, with St Patrick commenting on the power of this music to his fellow clergyman, Brogan:

'A good cast of . . . art was that . . . ,' said Brogan. 'Good indeed, it were,' said Patrick, 'but for a twang of the fairy spell that infests it; barring which nothing could more nearly than it resemble Heaven's harmony'. Says Brogan, 'if music there be in Heaven, why should there not be on earth?, . . . as it is not right to banish away minstrelsy.' Patrick answered: 'neither say I any such thing, but merely inculcate that we must not be inordinately addicted to it.'

St Patrick seems to be acknowledging the great beauty and power of the bewitching fairy music, yet also cautioning the others about it as well, implying, in his view, a possible danger inherent in the 'twang of the fairy spell'.

Many of these references have been gathered by the author into a collection about music and the Celtic Otherworld. These are primarily from the Old and Middle Irish literature of early medieval Ireland. (For an overall bibliography of literature that was examined for this collection, see the Bibliography.) This book will use selected references from the collection, like the above excerpt about Cascorach and St Patrick, to portray specific examples of music and the Celtic Otherworld. But, due to space considerations, the entire collection itelf cannot be included here.

This book will explore *the spiritual dimension of music from a Celtic perspective*. It is an interdisciplinary study in the phenomenology of religion, with music as its focus, rather than a study from the perspective of a Celtic folklorist. The references here are taken from written sources from the medieval Irish period. No oral folklore narratives from more modern times are included, as this would clearly warrant an entirely separate study. This book is representative of some of the most poignant examples of music and the Celtic Otherworld; it is by no means an attempt to be totally comprehensive, largely due to space considerations.

The sheer quantity of references to a spiritual dimension of music in the Celtic sources certainly ought to be noted, and may have quite important implications concerning the worldview of early Celtic society. But one must be mindful of the danger of needlessly romanticising this material and relegating it to the fringes of the 'Celtic Twilight', to use W. B. Yeats' well-known term. As Celtic Professor Kenneth Jackson stated about the various Celtic literatures: 'their most outstanding characteristic is rather their astonishing power of imagination'.[1] And music, it would seem, is portrayed as one of the most potent forces of the Celtic imagination.

The references to music and the Celtic Otherworld appear to reflect a worldview more widely held in earlier times, when music was viewed as an integral part of the universe. It is well documented that many cultures throughout history have made reference to a spiritual or supernatural dimension of music, and it appears that Celtic literature is no exception.

Many cultures have believed music to have a profound effect on humans, to be an embodiment of the celestial harmony which reflected the diversity and complexity of man and the universe. It is possible that what later became the theory of the 'music of the spheres' existed in earlier times. From Pythagoras to the Romantics, music was perceived to have a role which far surpassed its modern status as mere 'entertainment' or art form. It was not until the nineteenth century, when a more materialistic paradigm came to predominate, that this profound shift in perspective regarding music occurred in western culture.

Great writers and philosophers have addressed the overall issue of music in the universe and the role of humans in it. Marsilio Ficino, the fifteenth-century Renaissance physician and humanist of Florence, attributed a magical power to music in his *De vita coelitus comparanda* ('On Obtaining Life from the Heavens'). But from ancient times, the concept of the fundamental importance of sound, music and vibration in the universe has been examined by some of western civilisation's greatest philosophers:

> *Socrates* invokes music as a primary model for justice and 'the mean'. For him, as *Plato* gives him voice in *The Republic*, the musical scale is where moderation reigns in a demonstrable way, and, therefore, the musical scales model the virtues – especially distributive justice – which allow all people to 'sing the same chant together'. (*Republic* 331e–432a). In Book III of his *Elements of Harmony*, *Ptolemy* organises his zodiacal calendar of time as well as his influential physics of space according to the tones of two-octave musical scales ... *Kepler* stated 'The movements of the heavens are nothing except a certain everlasting polyphony.' ... *Sir Isaac Newton*, genius of enlightenment physics and mathematics, remained dedicated throughout his life to the fundamental musico-theological proposition that (in his own words): ... 'The soul of the world, which propels into movement this body of the universe visible to us, being constructed of ratios which created from themselves a musical concord, must of necessity produce musical sounds ...'[2]

More recently, anthropologist Claude Lévi-Strauss, in his four-volume work entitled *Mythologiques: An Introduction to the Science of Mythology,* also examines these issues, taking inspiration from Plotinus and Arnold Schoenberg. Schoenberg's famous comprehensive

mystico-mathematical theory of music was largely based on his
devout religious beliefs, as was that of Emmanuel Swedenborg. Other
theorists with clear agnostic or atheistic leanings – like Arthur
Schopenhauer, who strongly maintained that music is 'supreme of
all the arts' – still held that music has a key role in the universal
scheme of things. The Church Fathers, too, acknowledged music and
its role in the cosmos. So throughout history, scientists, philosophers, theologians and others have all grappled with the ultimate
mystery, meaning and purpose of music.

The desire to hold music fundamental to the creation of the
universe and the human being's role in it, is not only a theorising
impulse of western culture. Guy L. Beck has evaluated a spectrum of
Hindu sectarian developments in his *Sonic Theology: Hinduism and
Sacred Sound*. In this work, Beck finds common to them all a basic
commitment to configurations of sacred sound. According to Harvard Professor Lawrence Sullivan, Beck

> discloses the central role of sonic cosmologies and meditations, of
> mystical analyses of internal language, and of acoustical embodiments
> of divine beings. According to Beck, even Hindus whose traditions had
> distinct and irreconcilable theological aims agree that sonority inaugu-
> rates and sustains the soteriological quest toward the desired god,
> goddess, or condition. Sound is, at its base, sacred in origin; and
> sacrality, in its root expression, is sonorous.[3]

With its Celtic focus, this book investigates the content and meaning
of a particular people's religious and spiritual language, expression
and behaviour, as it relates to music. In this case, the culture in
question is primarily that of early medieval Ireland. Some selected
references from Scotland and Wales are also included, but mainly
for comparative purposes, due to space considerations and the fact
that further research into these areas would certainly warrant
separate studies of their own.

The overall focus of this book is on music – but not on the actual
music itself as performed as this has been largely lost to us. So the
primary perspective here is not that of a musicology or a music
history analysis; instead, this book will examine what the early Irish
seem to say or imply about music as revealed in their surviving
literature. This book will examine, as best we can in the late twentieth century, how music is thought to represent the people's experience and vision of reality, especially its sacred dimensions or
otherworldly aspects.

The term 'Otherworld' is used here to mean what it basically implies – that is, 'not of this world', something beyond one's ordinary everyday, mundane experience. In the Celtic literature, mention of such an otherworldly realm is often referred to by many names and subdivisions, such as the Old Irish *tir tairngiri* ('The Land of Promise'), *mag mell* ('The Pleasant Plain'), *tir na nOg* ('The Land of Youth'), the Welsh *Annwn* and so on.

The mysterious, sacred dimension of a people's culture and experience are most often described in terms of their religious beliefs and rituals, but various art forms can also be used to show this, including music. It seems as though many of these experiences are of a non-verbal nature, and that music can serve as an important communicative or expressive medium.

From a careful examination of the sources, it appears that the early Celts believed that music can give access to reality in both everyday, mundane and otherworldly contexts. There is even a great range in the mention and use of music in everyday situations, such as at fairs and festivals, at monasteries with the singing of hymns and psalms, or while working in the fields, for example. The great number of references to the importance of music in everyday life indicates, at the very least, that music seems to have been highly appreciated and enjoyed in society, from the music of the swords in battle, to the sounds of the fishing nets at sea.

There is also a broad range of the use of music in some kind of Otherworldly context. Examples here include references to mysterious music heard at a saint's birth or death, portrayals of the music of angels in Heaven, or of the music of the *sidhe* (fairies), for example. Clearly, music is presented in a wide range of contexts in early Irish society, both in everyday, mundane life and in more Otherworldly contexts.

The accomplished Northern Irish playwright Stewart Parker stated that 'play is how we test the world and register its realities. Play is how we experiment, imagine, invent, and move forward. Play is above all how we enjoy the earth and celebrate our lives upon it.' He further adds:

It is no accident of etymology that this fundamental ... self-sufficient force shaping the very evolution of human society, should share its name with those works of fiction which are presented by actors before an audience – the stage play, the screenplay, the radio and television play – these are merely particular and local forms of the play-force, consciously shaped, fashioned by human imagination, and usage into a highly sophisticated kind of game, the rules of which have remained surprisingly constant for well over two thousand years.[4]

And don't forget the sound track, he might have added. To play music, to compose it, and to enjoy listening to it is to also partake of this creative dynamic that Parker is referring to. Music is also a type of creative play, which humans throughout history have always experimented with, imagined, invented reality in, and moved forward from.

But the vexing question is: *how* exactly does music 'register reality' and affect the listener? That music somehow *does* affect the individual listener, especially emotionally, is almost universally acknowledged. But even today, professionals are divided as to how exactly this process occurs. We will now take a brief look at several theories from research being done today regarding this issue.

Musicologist Deryck Cooke, in his important work *The Language of Music*, discusses how music is an investigative and expressive language. In this work, Cooke determines to make a case that music is a language capable of expressing certain very definite emotions. He does not believe that this concept is a mere 'romantic aberration', but instead, he claims it has been the unconscious assumption of composers for at least the past five centuries. His study is confined to the Western European harmonic period and to music written in a specific key, as opposed to modern atonal music.

In presenting his case, Cooke begins by discussing the various means of expression available to a composer, the various procedures in the dimensions of time, pitch and volume, and attempts to look at what emotional effects these procedures can produce. More specifically, he tries to pinpoint the inherent emotional characters of the various pitch intervals of the major, minor and chromatic scales and of certain basic melodic patterns which have been used throughout our music history. He calls these patterns a music 'vocabulary'.[5]

Cooke examines the question of exactly how musical notes relate to each other. He asserts that it is the tensional relationships between various pitches that are the essence of how the language of music gets conveyed to the listener. Cooke thinks that music naturally has its own technical laws, concerned with the organisation of notes into coherent forms. But he believes that, considered as expression, it has three separate aspects, which are form, tone-painting/mood-colouring and the creation of an emotional statement.

Cooke believes that a language of music is built out of the tensions between notes, set up through time, pitch and volume, 'fine-tuned' by the composer and/or performer adding what he calls the 'characterizing agents' of tone colour, which affects mood, and the texture of the music (that is how it is harmonised and so on.) So depending on exactly how all of these various attributes are combined, different emotional subtleties are created.

He also discusses the natural phenomenon known as the harmonic series, stating that 'in nature itself, a single note sets up a harmony of its own ...'[6] The triad (1-3-5 pattern) was to become the basis of our western harmony, based on the natural harmonic series.

The introduction of the major third interval, as part of this triad, was revolutionary in music history, as it completely changed the emotional ambience of the modes then in use. In 1322, Pope John XXII was so angered by the 'corrupting' sound of the major third that he issued a decree to forbid its use. He felt it secularised the ecclesiastical modes, making it difficult to distinguish between them. The major third interval was later used in troubadour songs, and is generally thought to be a 'happy' or 'joyful' sound to the ear of the listener, even to this day. The Major third and the 1-3-5 Triad are still used in many popular songs, conveying a feeling of pleasure and joy.

Cooke notes that with the introduction of accidentals – flats, naturals, and sharps – to correct an inherent flaw in the natural harmonic series, there came far-reaching implications. As is well-known in music theory, the interval of the diminished fifth sounds 'incomplete' and 'unresolved' to the ear. Even the ancient Greeks acknowledged this.

In medieval times the first accidental, B-flat, was introduced to help correct this situation, as the diminished fifth interval, also called the Tritone, was considered to have a 'demonic' effect on listeners. Cooke says that 'clearly, our tonal system is the product of Western Europe's individual reaction to the "flaw" in the natural harmonic series: the key-system corrects it.'[7] The Greeks called this flaw the 'Pythagorean Comma'. As a result, the old modes were altered, with the Greek Lydian mode becoming what we now call the 'key of F-major'. Cooke then describes specific notes in our tonal system, and how these pitches tend to behave in our system of harmony, an example being the joyful and stable effect of the major third.

Contrast the joy of the major third with the minor sixth, which has consistently been associated with 'acute anguish' to the ear of the listener. Many composers and performers have used this interval in funeral pieces, for example. The minor sixth sounds to nearly everyone that hears it, as though it 'wants' to 'resolve' itself into a happier, more stable sound. In western music theory, the minor sixth usually 'resolves' down to the dominant, the fifth – a much 'happier' result in its effect on the ear.

Cooke maintains that the differences between various composers' usage of the same tonal tensions is due to their adding 'vitalizing agents' of time, volume and pitch. These determine exactly *how* a particular phrase will 'end up emotionally' to the ears of the listener. Of course, composers and performers have their own unique individual styles of using such vitalizing agents. They can fine tune, say, the emotional response of the minor sixth in a particular phrase by using different combinations of pitch, time and volume. This determines exactly what type of grief or joy the composer or performer wants to convey. Cooke feels that these emotional subtleties are largely what the language of music is all about, and states that this comes about by the use of tensional relationships between pitch – his main point – and the additional vitalizing agents of time and volume.

Not only do certain notes express a consistent emotional response in listeners, but specific melodic phrases do as well. Cooke calls this a musical 'vocabulary'. He then leads us to the question of exactly how these particular phrases illustrate certain feelings, and how they have consistently done so throughout western musical history. He gives examples showing how different classical composers have often not only used the same tendencies to convey an emotion, but often the same identical notes. However, he says each composer uses the vitalising agents of time, pitch and volume to put his own stamp of individuality onto the phrase in question, creating a very specific subtlety of emotion.

Cooke sees a composer's 'inspiration' as an unconscious reshaping of already existing material in his or her mind; the creative process of making music is an attempt to create an overall form. This form, the final piece of music, is an overall emotionally expressive statement. As a listener, then, we make direct contact with the mind of a great artist, interpreting his expression of emotion. His critics contend that it is difficult to tell whether this is merely our own subjective states superimposing themselves onto a given piece of music. Cooke counters by saying that many times the listener will feel as he has never felt before, and sometimes, feelings aroused by music can persist in a listener's mind for days afterwards, indicating to Cooke that it is a new feeling altogether that the listener experiences. Further, groups of people will often be affected in a similar way to a certain piece of music, lending credence to the theory that music is somehow a type of expressive language. But exactly how it all works still remains a mystery.

Finally, he briefly mentions the possibility of music conveying spiritual or mystical intuitions, but he believes that if so, it must be through the emotional terms of musical language. But he then adds, 'with a metaphysical insight into music, we should undoubtedly experience these terms with a different kind of feeling: they would be revealed as the same, but also something other'.[8] Music, he believes, is primarily a language of the emotions, through which we directly experience the fundamental urges that move humanity, without the need for additional ideas, images, words or pictures. As such, music is 'pure', as it conveys emotion directly to us.

So music may be an expressive language through working on human emotions, and may be seen to 'test the world and register its realities' to the extent that human emotions themselves can be deemed to be cognitive, that is a means of knowing our world. This is not the place for a philosophical discourse to 'prove' such a point – namely, that the way we react emotionally to the various aspects of our everyday world enables us to know a great deal about its prospects and dangers, and hence about its nature and destiny. But regarding emotions and music, there is evidence which we shall examine shortly, which regards the pivotal use of music in the mother's teaching of the new-born baby to engage in its first attempts to test the world and learn about its complex, interpersonal reality.

A dangerous art music can be, and was recognised as such by Plato, Tolstoy and some of the Church Fathers, for example, all of whom wished to control, limit and confine the uses of certain music. This might not be at all different from various modern parents' groups trying to ban certain rock music and its lyrics from their children's ears. All attest to some power, however mysterious, of music to reach us at the deepest level, for good or ill. Even in the Bible (Joshua 6), the walls of Jericho were destroyed by the sound of music.

For Cooke and others, music is the most articulate language of the unconscious; music has been termed the 'Queen of the Arts', and for good reasons. He maintains that music is a report on human experience, especially the emotions, and that it should be analysed as such. One is here reminded of the oft-quoted phrase of Dryden, 'What passion cannot Music raise and quell?' So music is seen by many as an especially effective way to register the reality of human experience; it is a commentary made by a particular people or culture.

New research has shown that in mother/infant communication, music can also serve as a universal expressive language, one that is understood by an infant under six months of age. There seems to exist an inherent musicality in the human infant, no matter what the native culture or language. Dr Colwyn Trevarthen, University of Edinburgh Professor of Psychology, states in his ground-breaking research on mother/infant play:

> We have found that most mothers begin to sing traditional nursery songs and to perform traditional action games or dances with the baby after three months. Remarkably, the temporal or musical form of these 'baby songs' and 'baby dances' appears to be essentially the same in very different cultures, regardless of their different languages. What the mother is doing is finding for herself an effective part in a performance that is prescribed by the infant's playfulness. She supports an inherent musicality, finding the beat and she varies the rhythm and expression to challenge the infant's interest and anticipation for the rise and fall of initiative in their engagement ... Mother's songs are typically made up of simple verses, usually of four lines, lasting 10–15 seconds. They follow a beat interval centered on moderato and ranging from about 750 msec (andante) to about 450 msec (allegro). Lines of the song have regular changes of pitch that raise and lower the expectation of a listener/ actor. ... we can see the mother who is singing a baby song outlining for us the three basic structural levels of at least the three macro-functions: she articulates clear phonological components in a singing voice on a regular beat, with pitch lifting or falling at specific points; she composes a verse of simple separate phrases; and she makes a whole 'text' with socio-dramatic development building to a climax which the infant is expected to anticipate and meet with excitement and happiness ... A song was sung by the mother to her twenty-week-old daughter; then a minute later she invited the child to 'do it to me' and she held her palm up. The baby looked eagerly at her mother's face, moving fingers on the palm while the mother gently recited the first line. The baby continued moving, the mother watching with a smile. Microanalysis of the video-tape showed that in the next ten seconds the infant made small movements of arms and hands that reproduced the action of the game–on the

10

beat! At precisely the right moment, the baby concluded with a vocalization that matched her mother's laugh when the song was first performed. This is proof that the infant had internalized a memory of the whole song, unfolding in time. It confirms other observations of the aptitude of infants under six months for learning to anticipate rhythmic patterns of sound ... [9]

So it appears that the dynamics of a 'baby song' can be internally represented in the mind of an infant at this early age, says Dr Trevarthen. He believes this indicates an inherent musicality in the baby, and the researchers' fascination with the baby's ability to follow pitch, its loudness or softness, and respond to rhythm seems to confirm this. It is interesting to note that these correspond exactly to the three 'vitalizing agents' of Cooke, which are pitch, volume, and time. Regarding the issue and importance of play, Dr Trevarthen comments that 'all play is metacommunication, in the sense in which Gregory Bateson used this term to describe animal play.'[10] It would appear from this research that 'baby music', like music in general, is a type of creative play, in which we experiment, imagine, invent and move forward.

Cooke, while acknowledging these various points about music, suggested that future work in the area of a possible language of music 'will probably *not* be in the area of philosophical discussions of conceptual arguments, or in 'digests' of the 'meanings' of specific works – rather, since music can only express feelings, it is thought they will probably be in the nature of interpretations of emotional attitudes.'[11] This would, in his view, most likely involve an examination of the 'images' used in the music, and an interpretation of their emotional and psychological connotations.

A new field of music theory called music signification is interesting to note. This involves looking at the meaning of a piece of music as well as the mechanics of it. Up until the 1960s, most people in western society thought of music as an abstract art that could only be analysed in its own terms. With advances in linguistic theory, music has begun to be looked at in terms of subconscious codes or signifiers, as well as its overall structure. This has brought in new contributors to the field of music theory, including experts in opera, computer analysis, cognitive science, psychology, sociology and mathematics.

Music signification, for example, might study why so few people who initially listen to the soothing music of the well- known popular ABBA song 'Fernando' seem to realise it is actually a tragic song about war in South America! How, or why, is it that the music itself soothes and pleases the listener, yet the lyrics speak of treachery and war? This again gets into the complex area of human emotions and the reactions of the listener to music.

The ability of music to 'register reality' as an expressive language is also an issue that physicians and medical scientists are examining today, especially in terms of rhythm, the human body and the pulse. The exploration of pulse is of interest to musicians, and it is important in Oriental medicine. But it is only recently that it has attracted scientific appraisal. David Epstein, conductor and Professor of Music at the Massachusetts Institute of Technology (MIT) has researched how these underlying rhythmic systems are expressed in music and why these tempo relationships affect us so profoundly. He concludes that the simple tempos we prefer in music are intrinsically compatible with our neurological and biological make-up. In fact, they reflect the way we process time at the most fundamental level.[12]

The link between physical gesture and musical expression is being explored further at the Health Center in San Antonio, Texas, where neuroscientist Peter Fox is examining the issue of the brain waves of performing musicians. As explained in an article entitled 'Music of the Spheres' (May 1996) in the British newspaper *Independent on Sunday*, Fox

> uses PET (positron emission tomography) scanners to provide visible cross-sections of blood flow within the brain. These scans reveal not only the activity of the motor function centres that control and remember the body movement involved in playing, but – even more remarkably – the areas of the brain that experience or create musical meaning. By comparing differences in brain activity when performing music – in this case Bach – and when playing scales, Fox and his team are getting close ... to the cutting edge of musical science.[13]

One prominent ear specialist has proven that certain frequencies of Gregorian chant actually 'charge' the human brain in a positive manner. Alfred Tomatis conducted his landmark work at a Benedictine monastery in France just after the Second Vatican Council in the early 1960s, when there was some discussion as to whether the Latin language should be retained for daily worship or whether the vernacular French, which was encouraged by the Council, should be adopted. Katherine Le Mee, musicologist, in reporting on Tomatis' research states:

Also under consideration was whether chanting should be continued or abandoned in favor of other activities thought to be more useful. The final outcome was the elimination of chant from the Divine Office. Before long a change took place in the community. Monks who previously had been able to survive rather well on the customary three or four hours sleep a night became extremely tired and prone to illness. Thinking that too little sleep might be the cause of their malaise, the abbot allowed more, but this did not help. The more the monks slept, the more tired they became. Even a change in diet was attempted–to a meat and potatoes regime, after vegetarianism had been the rule of the community for 700 years – but this too had no positive result. The situation grew worse and worse until February 1967 when Dr. Tomatis was invited back again ... when he arrived, he reported 'seventy of the ninety monks were slumping in their cells' ... Upon examination, he found that the monks were not only tired but their hearing was not as good as it should have been. His solution was to use a device called the Electronic Ear to increase the monks' auditory sensitivity over a period of several months. The Electronic Ear, developed by Tomatis, is a cybernetic device with two channels joined by a gate which gives the patient sounds as normally heard on one side and, on the other side, the same sounds filtered to allow an improved audition, particularly of high frequencies. Changing channels from one side to the other exercises the muscles of the inner ear and makes it possible for the patient to regain auditory acuity and sensitivity. The other aspect of Dr. Tomatis's treatment was to have *the daily chanting brought back immediately into the life of the monastery*. [emphasis mine]. Within nine months the monks had experienced an extraordinary improvement, both in their ability to hear and in their general sense of health and well-being. Most were able to return to the way of life that had been normal in their community for hundreds of years.[14]

When interviewed about this research, Tomatis explained the vital role played by the ear in stimulating the brain's activity; in particular, it serves to charge the cerebral cortex with electrical potential. A well-tuned ear is able to stimulate the brain, but this is not all.

Modern research identifies two kinds of sounds, known as 'discharge' sounds, which tire and fatigue the listener, and 'charge' sounds, which give energy and health and which have the power, like the Electronic Ear, to re-awaken the hearing and recharge the mind and body with energy. Charge sounds are rich in high frequencies, whereas discharge sounds are of low frequency.[15]

Music and sound can be used for either good or ill. Tomatis, in his book *The Conscious Ear*, states that putting an oscilloscope to the sounds of Gregorian chant reveals that it contains all the frequencies of the voice spectrum, roughly 70 to 9,000 hertz, but with a very different envelope curve from that of normal speech. The monks sing in the medium range, that of a baritone, but due to the unity and resonance of the sound, their voices produce rich overtones of higher frequency. It is these higher tones, mainly in the range of 2,000 to 4,000 hertz, that provide the positive charge to the brain.

When the monks were not chanting, they were missing their daily dose of energy. It is not difficult to understand the feeling of fatigue that they experienced.[16] The way the monks receive energy through the complex organisation of the body and its energy fields serves to reorganise the energy distribution in all 21 of the body centres. It seems that these higher frequencies, and especially those in the Gregorian range listed above, are literally 'good' for the body as well as the spirit. One may recall the great surprise of the music industry in the early 1990s with the No. 1 best-selling album of Gregorian chants by the monks of Silos, Spain. It is said that even the monks themselves were rather surprised by the tremendous public response to their sacred music.

Some individuals believe the natural world should be viewed as a gigantic symphony, composed of innumerable instruments. US medical doctor Larry Dossey suggests that

> instead of sitting imperiously atop the evolutionary chain, we might see ourselves as simply occupying the 'first chair', dependent on our colleagues to flesh out the score and enrich the performance. We might even begin to think of the Absolute not as a blind watchmaker who fashioned a mindless machine, but as the Maestro who wrote the melody and interwove all the harmonies.[17]

It is here that we may be reminded of the worldview of the early medieval Irish. They clearly did not see the Absolute as a mere blind watchmaker, but, instead, largely appear to have viewed life and the cosmos as having a unity, giving a meaning to their lives. Even in later times, regarding the function of folk song in nineteenth-century Ireland, Breandan O'Madagain states that

> song was an integral part of a whole culture which embraced the life of the community in all its facets, giving it an artistic dimension so that 'art was a part of life, not separated from it.' It has been said that everywhere 'music transforms experience': for the Irish folk mind in the nineteenth century, song had esoteric powers of transforming any situation.[18]

This has been but a very brief selection of the various theories scientists and others are considering today which seek to explain how music, like creative play, affects human beings. These various theories illustrate how integral music is to every level of our common interpersonal engagement in this complex universe, from the physical and chemical level to the most spiritual.

I am certainly not suggesting that the early Celts anticipated any of these theories of music, nor even that they had an explicit theory like Cooke's, Trevarthen's or that of the ancient Greek Pythagoreans. What I am proposing is that it clearly seems that they perceived music as having a key role in encounters with all levels of reality and human experience. References to music from the collection consistently connect music with the Otherworld and the major emotions that dominate and affect human life, for good or ill, and they do so in both the primal and the Christian contexts.

But the focus of this book is on those aspects of reality which are considered to be *sacred* or *otherworldly*, and their relationship to music. For the purposes of this book about early Irish society, it is important to consider that under the correct circumstances, music has the special potential to carry us to the highest, even supernatural, heights, whether this is portrayed in the Christian Heaven, or the magical, elusive Otherworld of the fairies. Music is seen as a universal 'connector' to the Otherworld, and as an especially effective link between this world and the Otherworld.

References to music in the major sources of early Irish literature

The sources for this book refer to the era of early medieval Ireland, generally considered by scholars to be up to approximately the end of the twelfth century. Its focus is that literature written in the Irish language referring to this period. This takes many forms, such as poetic verse, law tracts, hagiography (saints' lives), the Mythological cycle, the Ulster cycle, the cycles of the kings literature, folklore, place-lore and so on. I have selected eight major categories of early medieval Irish literature from which the references to music are drawn for this collection.

Mythological cycle tales and sagas

This is a collective term applied to the stories in Irish literature which primarily describe the activities of otherworldly personages. Daithi O'hOgain states:

> The basis for the cycle is ancient Celtic myth, and many of the characters are Irish manifestations of a Celtic pantheon of divine beings. The central story of the cycle was concerned with a battle between two supernatural groups. This theme is found in other Indo-European sources – such as the conflict between the Devas and Asuras in Vedic literature, between the Aesir and Vanir in Norse, and between Zeus' family and the Titans in Greek. In Irish myth this conflict was between the divine *Tuatha De Danann* and the demonic *Fomhoire*, and, based on this ancient lore, an account of their struggle was written down in the 8th c. A.D.[19]

This account situated the battle at Mag Tured (Moytirra, near Lough Arrow in Co. Sligo). The primary tales from this cycle that have music references in them, and are therefore relevant in this book, are: *Cath Maige Tured I*, ('The First Battle of Moytura'), *Cath Maige Tured II*, ('The Second Battle of Moytura'), *Tochmarc Etaine*, ('The Wooing of Etaine') and *Lebor Gabala Erenn* ('The Book of Invasions of Ireland').

Dindshenchas (place-lore poems)

The name *Dindshenchas* means 'history or lore of prominent places'.[20] The learned *fili* (poets) of early Ireland were generally responsible for the preservation of place-lore, among many other functions. By the ninth century onwards,

> we have a series of onomastic poems ... and by the early 12th-century these poems were brought together in one great unit known as the *Dindshenchas*. There is no full surviving manuscript of this work, but in all there were nearly three hundred poems, many accompanied by a prose synopsis. Each poem has the heading of a particular place name, and it then relates a story which purports to explain the origin of that toponymic.[21]

The writers of the *Dindshenchas* drew on many sources for their material, such as the earlier mythological, Ulster and Fianna tales, as well as oral tradition. As well as factual historical material, folklore and legends regarding specific place names were also used, so a fair number of the place names include purely legendary material. A second version of the *Dindshenchas* was compiled about a century later, in which many of the verse-texts are repeated, but its prose adds length to the stories and variety to the interpretations. O'hO-gain states that 'a great deal of the material is still structured in the form of mere speculation, and most of the genuine narratives involved are adoptions of stories known from earlier texts.'[22]

Ulster cycle tales and sagas

The Ulster cycle is a large corpus of heroic tales, based on the deeds of the *Ulaid*, the Old Irish warrior-aristocracy in Ulster. The capital of this area in the tales is Emain Macha. The major tale of the Ulster cycle is entitled *Tain Bo Cuailnge* ('The Cattle Raid of Cooley'). It includes the well-known 'Boyhood Deeds of Cu Chulainn', for example. It is believed that *Tain Bo Cuailnge* was 'written down for the first time toward the middle of the seventh century by a *file* (poet) who may have had some of the Latin learning of the monasteries, and who also wished to record the native heroic tradition in a worthy form.'[23] The development of the epic has been analysed by many scholars, and the various stages of its development are thought to have occurred in three versions, to be discussed later. The basic material which the compiler used is believed to have derived from a version of the narrative which was committed to writing as early as the seventh century:

> This narrative is taken to encapsulate many aspects of the culture of the ancient Ulaid, portraying a warrior-aristocracy organised on the lines of a heroic society and providing an authentic picture from the inside of an Iron Age Celtic culture. The military-political situation described in the narrative was explained by a series of 'pre-tales' which were put together at a quite early date in support of the *Tain*. These 'pre-tales' also preserve fragments of myth and ritual from ancient tradition, and thus the general corpus evidences several details which can be compared with what Greek and Latin writers on the Continent attribute to the Celts known to them. The details include fighting from two-horse chariots, headhunting for prestige, single combat between warriors while opposing armies stand by, the awarding of the best portion of meat to the greatest champion at a feast, and the general custom of cattle-raiding as a test of martial prowess.[24]

Such subjects are also addressed in the other famous Ulster cycle tales, such as *Longes mac nUislenn* ('The Exile of the Sons of Uisliu'), *Mesca Ulad* ('The Intoxication of the Ulstermen'), *Fled Bricrend*

('The Feast of Bricriu'), *Tain Bo Froech* ('The Cattle-Raid of Froech'), and *Togail bruidne Da Derga* ('The Destruction of Da Derga's Hostel').

Cycles of the kings literature

These tales are not only about kings, but about kingship, the founding of dynasties, dynastic succession and the fortunes of the royal houses of Ireland and her provinces. Stories about several of the famous kings of Ireland, such as Conaire Mor, Conn of the Hundred Battles, Cormac mac Airt, Niall of the Nine Hostages and Domnall son of Aed, figure prominently. In such tales, the relation between the king and his realm is often portrayed as a marriage – the country is a woman, usually a goddess, the spouse of the king, and before her marriage to the destined king, she is often portrayed as an old hag or a deranged woman. The tales from this section also often tell of battles, perhaps most notably *Cath Maige Mucrama* ('The Battle of Mag Mucrama'), *Cath Almaine* ('The Battle of Allen'), *Orgain Denna Rig* ('The Destruction of Dind Rig'), and *Cath Maige Rath* ('The Battle of Moira'). Other of the cycles of the kings tales focus on adventures in the Otherworld, such as the well-known *Echtra Cormaic i Tir Tairngiri* ('The Adventures of Cormac in the Land of Promise'). Yet others tell of unusual ancedotes of a particular king, such as the story of King Eochaid having the deformity of horse's ears. Some tell of the death of a king, as with *Aided Muirchertach* ('The Death of Muirchertach'). These particular tales, which mention music in them, largely come from fifteenth-century manuscripts, but are believed to refer to a much earlier era.

Echtra/immrama literature

The *immrama* literature, often called 'vision/voyage' literature, is a genre that includes the motif of an individual, often a saint, travelling by sea to various island paradises. From *Betha Brennain* ('The Life of St. Brendan'), we have a good example of this literary genre, which developed out of the religious ideal and practice of pilgrimage overseas, the necessity of leaving family, friends and country for the love of God. This type of pilgrimage, the *peregrinatio*, is bound up with the ascetic tradition and practice of seeking out deserted places in order to lead a solitary life of prayer and contemplation dedicated to God. These vision/voyage accounts often portrayed how one could search all over the world, in many types of glamorous places in search of the ideal Christian life, only to end up preferring to return home, realising that the ideal Christian life can indeed be lived at or near one's own monastic community. Many of the Irish saints made such 'voyages' around the Continent and Britain, for which they became widely known as good teachers and examples of the ideal Christian life. The places portrayed in this vision/voyage genre may not be meant as literal portrayals of Heaven (or Hell) as in some other purely visionary literature; but they do represent some form of supernatural ideal, and are included here as many of these voyage tales have references to music in them.

Excerpts from the *Acallam na Senorach* ('Colloquy of the Ancients')

This work, from the Ossianic, or Fianna, literature, was written down in the late twelfth or early thirteenth century, and is a corpus of stories and tales about the Fianna that attempts to put them into a unified work called *Acallam na Senorach*. It portrays the last, noble, remaining Fianna warriors, who have survived their companions and live to a ripe old age, encountering St Patrick and his clergy on his travels throughout Ireland. St Patrick is portrayed as questioning them eagerly, as he is curious to learn about the customs and culture of early Ireland. Two of the old Fianna warriors in particular, Cailte and Oisin, respond eagerly to his questions, resurrecting the golden past in a spirit of noble melancholy. They then travel with St Patrick and his men throughout Ireland, and as they come to certain places connected with the names and deeds of the Fianna, they expound accordingly with tales of the heroes and events that took place, often with song or poetic verse. Music is referred to often, with particular focus on the supernatural music of Cascorach, a *sidhe* musician. At St Patrick's request, these stories and tales are written down by an assistant so that they might provide entertainment for lords and nobles until the end of time. Of course, many of the stories were in existence much earlier, and from the point of the writing down of the *Acallam*, the saga of the hero Finn mac Cumaill and his band of Fianna warriors has been a favourite subject of storytellers for generations.

Early Irish poetry

Here, we are concerned with the genre of Old Irish 'hermit poetry', as it is often called, as it pertains to various monks and hermits of the sixth to the eleventh centuries. The clerics who wrote these poems also wrote hymns, prayers, saint's lives and so on, both in Irish and Latin. Many of these Old Irish poems, up to and including the twelfth century, tell of life of solitude, often out in the wilderness, in dedication to God. Such poems portray the personal feelings of the hermit poet and of the joys and sorrows of Christian life. Many of these poems speak of the musical elements of nature and the earth around the hermit's hut (that is, the trees, the wind, and so on) and the 'music' of the river, for example. One can sense the personal feelings expressed by the hermit poet as to his life, with its characteristic heights and depths. Some of this poetry derives from the Old Irish glosses written on certain Latin manuscripts, and are today often preserved on the Continent.

Saints' lives, written in Old/Middle Irish

The Irish saints' lives written in Latin have not been chosen, as this study is largely confined to the literature written in the Irish language. Generally, the saints that are celebrated in Irish hagiography lived in the time period between the fifth and eighth centuries. The actual writing of the biographies began in the seventh century and continued until well after the end of the Middle Ages. Daithi O'hOgain states that the writers of Irish hagiography, like their counterparts abroad, drew on material from several different sources for their themes, plots and imagery. Such sources included not only the Old and New Testaments, the Apocrypha, and biographies of Continental saints, but also Irish and classical works of secular literature, as well as oral tradition from within the monasteries and from the populace in general.

> It is sometimes quite difficult to unravel the various strands of lore in the texts and to determine how much of the accounts have direct historical value, but it must always be born in mind that many of the biographies were written with the definite purpose of advancing the prestige of particular paruchiae or monasteries.[25]

So, the hagiographers often did not hesitate to borrow or greatly exaggerate material to enhance the profile of a particular saint.

Music references are prominent in the hagiography of Irish saints such as Adamnan, Brendan, Colman, Columcille, Declan of Ardmore, Fechin of Fore, Fursa, Kieran, Mochuda, Moling and Patrick.

Dating the excerpts

Many of the manuscripts in Old and Middle Irish were written down in the fourteenth or fifteenth centuries, from earlier manuscripts or oral tradition. Scholars have dated each manuscript according to its linguistic style and content. For example, a manuscript actually written down in the late twelfth century may be believed by scholars to refer to many tales and material from earlier times. In certain instances, scholars may differ as to a particular manuscript's age and/or origin, but for the most part there is a scholarly consensus. This book mainly uses material from written sources from the early medieval period; most oral narratives come from a much later time (mostly the late nineteenth and twentieth centuries) and would warrant a separate study.

Christian and 'pagan' material in the texts

All the texts come from Christianised Ireland and from Christian authors and scribes. I have no intention of entering the fierce debate about whether or how much of this material survives intact from the primal (that is, pre-Christian) period, or how much of the primal past can be accurately reconstructed from this Christianised material. This debate in the field of Irish Celtic studies is primarily stated in terms of 'nativist' and 'anti- nativist'.

Briefly, the 'nativist' position is that this early Irish literature retained barely adulterated respositories of pagan belief in the vernacular of Old or Middle Irish

> belief which had been handed on by lay scholars (though by now of course processed by very complacent clerics), handed on in a purely oral form (though by now of course more crudely reproduced in writing), in a ... largely superficially christianised Ireland. The end result: 'mere antiquarian assemblages' living on into a medieval Christian Ireland which somehow ... managed to exercise the most profound influence on cultural revival in continental Europe around the time of Charlemagne.[26]

The 'anti-nativist' view, in contrast, sees the existing corpus of early Irish literature as

> a coherent and flexible Christian *senchus*, constructed by monastic *literati*, both clerical and lay, primarily in Latin (though with some substantial use of the vernacular), in a cosmopolitan Ireland which boasted a typical medieval Western outlook, which was up-to-date in its learning and thoroughly influenced by the Bible and by prominent Patristic writings. The literature adapted, of course, and suitably modified a remnant of pre-Christian traditions which were oral up to the fifth century, but increasingly thereafter set down in writing by these same Christian monastic *literati*.[27]

As the focus of this book is in the area of the phenomenology of religion, with music as the focus, I will not attempt to defend one side or the other here. Instead, I make the distinction between overtly primal and overtly Christian *contexts* of each music reference. Similarities or continuities between these contexts may say something about a level of mutual accessibility of primal and Christian material; but *no* part of this book is to argue further issues about the inculturation of Christianity, much less to contribute to the nativist/anti-nativist debate.

Illustratory comparative material

Each chapter has *illustratory comparative* sections, designed to convey some sense of the commonality of features noted about music in the literature of other world cultures. Such examples are used here to illustrate that the early Irish were 'registering the realities' of music as it pertained to their culture, and were not alone in doing so. Other cultures, too, seem to regard music as an investigative and expressive medium, and it would clearly take another study to do a proper comparative study between any two cultures.

In particular, selected examples from Scotland and Wales are featured. But it is important to recognise that these cultures, although also termed 'Celtic', are not identical to the early Irish and would certainly warrant separate studies of their own in order to go into more detail about them and properly do them justice, so to speak. But they are certainly important to note here regarding references to music. We will now take a look, in turn, at each of the five major divisions of this material – *performers, instruments, effects, places* and *times* – as the references from the Celtic literature reveal. Let us begin our journey.

Notes

1. Jackson, K., *A Celtic Miscellany* (Harmondsworth: Penguin, 1971), p. 20.
2. Sullivan, L. (ed.), *Enchanting Powers*: Music in the *World's Religions* (Cambridge, MA: Harvard University for the Study of World Religions, 1997), pp. 5, 6.
3. Ibid., p. 7.
4. Mackey, J. P., *Power and Christian Ethics*, (Cambridge: Cambridge University Press, 1994), pp. 174–5.
5. Cooke, D., *The Language of Music* (London: Oxford University Press, 1959).
6. Ibid., p. 41.
7. Ibid., p. 44.
8. Ibid., p. 272.
9. Trevarthen, C., 'Sharing makes sense: intersubjectivity and the making of an infant's meaning', in R. Steele and T. Threadgold (eds), *Language Topics: Essays in Honour of Michael Halliday* (Amsterdam, 1987), pp. 189–191.
10. Ibid.
11. Cooke, *Language of Music*, p. 273.
12. Robertson, P., 'Music of the spheres', *Independent on Sunday*, 5 May 1996, p. 48.
13. Ibid., p. 49.
14. Le Mee, K., *Chant* (New York, 1994), pp. 123–5.
15. Ibid., p. 127.
16. Ibid.
17. Dossey, L., 'The body as music', in D. Campbell (ed.), *Music and Miracles*, (Wheaton, IL: Quest Books, 1992), p. 57.
18. O'Madagain, B., 'Functions of Irish song', *Bealoideas* (Dublin, 1985), p. 215.
19. O'hOgain, D., *Myth, Legend, and Romance: An Encyclopedia of the Irish Folk Tradition* (New York: Ryan Publishing, 1991).
20. Williams, J. E. C. and Ford, P., *The Irish Literary Tradition* (Cardiff, 1992), p. 35.
21. Ibid., p. 363.
22. Ibid.
23. Williams, *The Irish Literary Tradition*, p. 97.
24. O'hOgain, *Myth, Legend, and Romance*, p. 414.

25. Ibid., p. 379.
26. Mackey, J. P., *Christian Past and Primal Present* (Edinburgh, 1991).
27. Ibid.

2

Performers

M USICAL PERFORMERS IN THE early medieval Irish literature include a cast of characters of great variety. Chief among these are musical performers believed to inhabit another dimension of existence, that is what is often termed the Otherworld in discussions of Celtic literature. This Otherworld dimension was believed by the early Irish to be present in and around their everyday world, and to intersect with it in a dynamic way. Supernatural musical performers are often portrayed as special intermediaries between this world, the world of mortals, and the Otherworld, the world of the immortals.

Mortal performers in this literature occasionally embody traits of being 'sacred' or 'superhuman' in some way. Often they are given special skills and talents denied to ordinary mortal musical performers. In keeping with the ancient Irish tradition of the *aes dano*, that is those of the artistic elite who had special gifts and inspiration, many musicians, especially harpers, were considered to be of an elite class and more generally gifted than ordinary musicians.

First, we will take a look at the musical performers portrayed in a purely supernatural context, that is, those who live in another dimension of existence like Heaven or Fairyland, and who sometimes visit the ordinary, everyday world of humans. Then we will look at examples of those mortal performers who are portrayed as being more gifted than other human musicians, sometimes as a result of having been brought to an Otherworld dimension and then returned to earth from there. Such gifted mortal performers are specifically 'selected' or 'abducted' for an encounter by the

Otherworld beings. Such gifted performers were also members of the *aes dano*.

We will then look at those examples of mortal musical performers who, although they may not actually visit an otherworldly dimension or have any direct contact with supernatural beings, nonetheless have, or are deemed to have, special talent and musical gifts. They are also often considered to have a place in that privileged group in society, the *aes dano*. Such gifted mortal performers were considered to be somehow 'sacred', and therefore blessed with unique musical gifts from the Otherworld.

Finally, we will take note of those ordinary, everyday, mortal entertainers who, although not of the *aes dano*, were still highly appreciated in early Irish society.

But before a detailed analysis is attempted, it is important to say a few words about the privileged, somewhat sacred group called the *aes dano*, and about the Celtic Otherworld and its inhabitants.

The *aes dano*

According to one of the early Irish law tracts on rank and position in early Ireland, the *Uraicecht Becc* (eighth/ninth century), there were two major social distinctions in society. One was whether an individual was *nemed*, meaning 'privileged', or not; the other was whether someone was *soer*, 'free', or *doer*, 'not free'. The basic meaning of the Old Irish term *nemed* is 'sacred, holy', and most often applied to kings, the clergy, lords and members of what was called the *aes dano*, such as poets of the higher variety. The term 'dano' may have come from the Latin word 'donum', meaning a 'gift' of a special type, a charisma or inspiration, which may explain why these people were deemed *nemed*.

Kim McCone, in *Pagan Past and Christian Present*, states that the *aes cacha dana olchenae*, also called the *aes dano*, were 'the people of every art besides' and were part of the *doer-nemed* category.[1] Some law tracts include the harper as part of the *aes dano*, among those of the lower *nemed* class, along with physicians, judges, talented blacksmiths, especially gifted jewellers and other skilled craftsmen. It appears that harpers were singled out for special status that was not accorded to other musicians, and were thus considered privileged persons in society.

The *Uraicecht Becc* lists seven grades of *fili* (poet), each with its own privileges. Such higher grade *fili* not only recited poetry and genealogy, but were also credited with great supernatural powers and knowledge. Some, like certain musical performers, were seen as special intermediaries between the Otherworld and everyday, mundane reality. It *may* be that such gifted *fili* sang as well, in which case we could include them amongst musical performers. But scholars disagree as to what specifically constitutes a poetic song or a poetic incantation, and whether such practices can indeed be considered as musical performance(s). Lower grades of poets were called 'bards' as opposed to *fili*, and as Douglas Hyde states in *A Literary History of Ancient Ireland*, ' . . . the real name for a musician was *oirfideadh*, and the musicians, though a numerous and honourable class, were absolutely distinct from the bards . . .'[2] So it appears that bards were not considered to be musicians and, as there is still academic debate as to whether the *fili* sang or not, one cannot automatically assume that they were musicians *per se*.

In general, however, someone of the highest grade of *fili* was also considered to be a kind of poetic prophet, that is, an exceptional example of a supernaturally gifted individual of the artistic elite. This is not unlike one of the especially gifted master harpers, who was also considered to be a type of intermediary between the Otherworld and everyday, mundane reality.

A master harper was called a *sui cruitirechta*. McCone explains that 'low ranking wrights include chariot-makers, house-builders decorators, engravers and shield-coverers, but two of these crafts may be combined to obtain a modest increase to the same status as a master harpist.'[3] Obviously, the *sui cruitirechta*, a master harper, was held in high esteem, and the harp itself was placed above all other musical instruments in early Ireland. The *sui cruitirechta* also had the special privilege of entertaining kings and nobles on a regular basis.

McCone and other scholars believe that there was a type of elite artistic *aes dano* in the early monastic communities as well. There was a 'tribe of the church', with differing orders, grades, and functions; it was consciously modelled on the tribe of Levi, and it formed a network among the local kingdoms of early Ireland. As monastic communities were large, like cities, they naturally needed skilled musicians, poets, artisans, smiths and so on. McCone points out the great value of singers and musicians to the tribe of Israel. In Old Irish, a singer of psalms in the monastic community was called a *salmchetlaid*. McCone and other scholars believe that the Bible, particularly the legal sections of the Pentateuch, exercised a major influence upon both the theoretical framework and the actual contents of even the earliest Irish law tracts, whether canonical or secular, in Latin or the vernacular ... That said, it is indisputable that Old Irish law was consciously linked with that of the Old Testament.[4]

According to the *Uraicecht Becc* law tract on status, however, the only musical entertainer with independent legal status is the harper, the *crutiri*. He is expected to play music to bring on tears (*goltraige*), joy (*gentraige*) and sleep (*suantraige*). Other entertainers are described as belonging to subordinate professions. Fergus Kelly, in *A Guide to Early Irish Law*, clarifies this situation as follows:

> In addition to lower grades of musician (e.g. *cuislennach*, 'piper'), and *cornaire*, ('horn-player'), there are many other entertainers who perform at feasts and assemblies ... the juggler ... jester ... acrobat ... and others. [As a footnote:] The Irish esteemed the harp beyond all other instruments; thus, the proverbial saying 'every music is sweet until it is compared with the harp' ... Triad 89 (YBL version) gives the three excellences of Ireland as 'a wise quatrain, a tune from a harp, a shaving of the face'.[5]

The *sidhe* world and its inhabitants

Musical performers in this literature are often described as being part of the Otherworld; this other dimension of existence is their 'home'. This Otherworld, and the various supernatural personages in it, is often called the world of the fairies or the *sidhe*-folk, who are seen as special supernatural beings who intervene decisively from time to time in human affairs. Among them are other supernatural beings, the old gods and goddesses of pre-Christian Ireland now euphemerised in folklore. They are often called the 'little people' or the 'Good People'.

Daithi O'hOgain explains that this Otherworld community and its mythic beings was understood to be a kind of spiritual community whose nature was on a different plane to that of the human race. As such, they were called by the literati the Tuatha de Danann and were described as living in a timeless realm.'[6] Evans-Wentz states:

> The Tuatha de Danann, or *sidhe*-folk, the 'Gentry', the 'Good People', and the 'People of Peace', are described as a race of invisible divine beings eternally young and unfading. They inhabit fairy palaces ... and have their own music and minstrelsy ... and they are gods of light and good.[7]

Tomas O'Cathasaigh, in 'The Semantics of "Sid"', shows how the Old Irish term *sid* (pronounced 'shee') can mean both (1) an Otherworld hill or mound; and (2) peace/peaceful. He states that since

> the Irish conception of the Otherworld, as it is expressed in the literature, is extraordinarily complex . . . The character and nomenclature of the Otherworld show an admixture of native and ecclesiastical elements. A case in point is *tir tairngiri*, which came into Irish as a translation of 'terra repromissionis' (the Promised Land of the Old Testament), but which . . . is used in a thoroughly pagan context in other examples in the literature, with *tir tairngiri* generally thought of as the Land of Promise.[8]

O'Cathasaigh further clarifies the issue of the many various descriptive terms used for the Otherworld and of *sid/sidhe*:

> Amidst all the confusion, however, *sid* enjoys a special status as a term for the Otherworld; it is the normal generic term which can be used without further definition to denote the Otherworld. It differs in this important respect from *Mag Mell, Tir na mBeo*, etc. which are descriptive terms. It is true that, when used of a particular localization of the Otherworld, *sid* seems almost invariably to refer to a mound or tumulus.[9]

So, in this literature many descriptive terms of the Otherworld are used: *mag mell* ('the Pleasant Plain'), *eamhain abhlach* ('the Region of Apples'), *tir na nOg* ('the Land of Youth'), *tir innambeo* ('the Land of the Living') and so on, but the term *sid* or *sidhe* is considered the basic generic term.

The *sidhe* Otherworld is described as being inhabited by various supernatural personages, the *sidhe*-folk. Like angels in the Bible, such beings are believed to interact with our human world at times, although they are from an Otherworld realm. Many of these otherworldly personages are also described as musical performers, and are often portrayed as teaching a mortal musician special playing techniques. For a mortal musician to encounter such a personage is considered to be a most unusual event indeed, and one that is often described as dramatically life-altering.

Supernatural music performers

An example of such a supernatural musical performer is that of Cascorach, described as a musician of the *sidhe*-folk in this literature. He is a player of the *timpan*, a sweet-sounding stringed instrument.

This fairy musician, as one of the *sidhe*-folk or *Tuatha de Danann*, is described as walking, talking and interacting like a normal human being, yet we know he is not a mere mortal. From *Accalam na Senorach*, ('Colloquy of the Ancients'), Cascorach plays for the clergy:

> He took his timpan, tuned it, and on it played a volume of melody the equal of which for sweetness (saving only the dominical canon's harmony and laudation of Heaven's King and Earth's) the clergy had never heard. Upon them fell a fit of slumber and of sleep.'[10]

Cascorach is a famous *sidhe*-folk musical performer in the early Irish literature, and is a representative example of this type of performer. He is portrayed as a supernatural musician interacting with ordinary mortals, and his *timpan* playing consistently gets the very best reviews.

As an example of an elfin-sized *sidhe*-folk musician, Senbecc plays for the hero Cuchulainn while he is performing the feat of the nine heroes on the bank of the river Boyne. While catching salmon, Cuchulainn sees a tiny man in purple, in a small boat of bronze, and he asks him:

> 'What little thing is that ... ?' asked Cuchulainn. 'A small harp,' said Senbecc, 'and shall I play it to you?' 'I am pleased', said Cuchulainn. Then he ran his fingers over it, in such a way that Cuculainn kept shedding tears at the melancholy tune. Then he played the merry tune, and Cuchulainn kept laughing continually. He played the sleepy tune, and Cuchulainn was in sleep and continuous slumber from one hour to the other.'[11]

This literature has numerous other examples of such *sidhe*-folk musicians and their interactions with mortal humans. They are invariably described as coming from the various *sidhe*-folk realms, such as an earth mound, a cairn, an underwater world, or from the air. These musicians include Cnu Deroil, the famous elfin harper of the hero Finn mac Cumhaill, and other *sidhe*-folk such as the Dagda, Lugh, Midir, Manannan, Aillen mac Midhna, mermaids and the infamous 'nine pipers of the Sid Breg', who could slay but never be slain themselves.

We have already seen an example of a *sidhe*-folk musician, Cascorach, playing for the clergy. The implications of that encounter were then discussed by St Patrick and his colleague Brogan:

> 'A good cast of ... art was that ... ,' said Brogan. 'Good indeed it were,' said Patrick, 'but for a twang of the fairy spell that infests it; barring which nothing could more nearly than it resemble Heaven's harmony.'

Says Brogan: 'if music there be in Heaven, why should there not on earth?, wherefore it is not right to banish away minstrelsy.' Patrick made answer: 'neither say I any such thing, but merely inculcate that we must not be inordinately addicted to it.'[12]

As represented here, St Patrick is portrayed as believing that there was an alluring, seductive, or perhaps even downright dangerous quality to this enchanting fairy music. He describes it as having a 'twang of the fairy spell that infests it', indicating that this certain 'twang' is not of this world. Yet he seems to imply also that it may not be of a specifically Christian origin. However, he does not ban outright such music as evil; instead, he makes a warning 'not to be inordinately addicted to it'. He is portrayed as believing that there is a distinct possibility that one may indeed become addicted to this music's spell, as apparently even a clergyman is not immune!

St Patrick agrees that music has heavenly legitimation, but he is clearly worried about the question of *which* Otherworld dimension the music is associated with.

The supernatural performers which occur in Christian contexts include such musical performers as angels, trees, stones, insects, bells, mermaids and 'mysterious, unknown' music, that is music that is heard yet no performer is seen. Heaven or Paradise itself is also portrayed as a kind of musical performer all of its own (see Charts 1 and 2 in the Appendix at the end of the book).

One sterling example portrays the Christian Heaven (the 'Land of the Saints') filled with many musical performers:

> Everyone in the Land of the Saints is equally near to hear the songs and to contemplate the vessel in which are the Nine Orders of Heaven in accordance with their ranks and their station. Part of the time the Saints sing a marvellous song in praise of God, and the rest of the time they listen to the song of the Heavenly Host, for the Saints have need of nothing but to be listening to the music to which they listen and to behold the light to which they look at ... and the song of the birds of the Heavenly Host makes music for them. Glorious bands of the guardian angels are continually doing obeisance and service among these assemblies in the presence of the King ... They celebrate the eight canonical hours ... the choral song of the Archangels coming in in harmony. The birds and the Archangels lead the song, and all the Heavenly Host, both saints and holy virgins, answer them in antiphony ... there are three precious stones making soft sounds and sweet music between every two principal assemblies.[13]

31

This single example includes many supernatural musical performers in the Christian Land of the Saints – angels, archangels, the saints, birds and three precious stones. It is also clear that these various performers join in with the saints and holy virgins, all of whom sing praises to God.

In another instance, a special Tree of Life in Heaven is portrayed, with a singing flock of birds on it:

> the Tree of Life with its flowers, the space around which noble hosts were ranged, its crest and its showers on every side spread over the fields and plains of Heaven. On it sits a glorious flock of birds and sings perfect songs of purest grace; without withering, with choice bounty of fruit and leaves. Lovely is the flock of birds which keeps it, on every bright and goodly bird a hundred feathers; and without sin, with pure brilliance, they sing a hundred tunes for every feather.[14]

Here, both a special tree and birds are described, and it is clear that this music never ceases in Heaven.

From *Betha Brennain* ('The Life of St Brendan'), we have the Christian Heaven portrayed as inherently musical and as a unique performer of supernatural music itself. This is explained to St Brendan and his clergymen by a wise old hermit monk on an island paradise:

> 'Search ... and see,' says he, 'the plains of Paradise and the delightful fields of the land, radiant, famous, lovable, profitable, lofty, noble, beautiful, delightful. A land odorous, flower-smooth, blessed. A land many-melodied, musical, shouting for joy, unmournful.[15]

An example of the Christians recognising an insect as a supernatural musical performer occurs in a similar voyage by clergymen. In *Imram Curaig Ua Corra*, ('The Voyage of the ui Corra'), bees sing to flowers in Heaven:

> Another beautiful bright island was shown to them. Shining grass ... with a variety of purple-headed flowers. Abundance of birds and everlovely bees singing music to the heads of those flowers. A very aged, grey-haired old man playing a harp was in the isle. He was chanting a wonderful melody that was the sweetest of the melodies of the world.[16]

Another instance shows the Christian clergy encountering a mermaid as a supernatural musical performer while out at sea:

> As Beoan's people therefore navigated the sea, from under the currach they heard a chant as of angels and Beoan (the cleric) questioned: 'whence this song?' 'It is I that make it,' answered Liban, a mermaid.[17]

Mysterious music, which is clearly heard, yet no performer is seen, is portrayed in the following example from 'The Life of St Colman':

> the boy was brought up piously and humbly; and wherever he used to be they would hear psalms and choral song, and the sound of a bell at every canonical hour, and the singing of mass every Sunday, so that people would come to ask, 'what was the assembly that came here last night?'.[18]

In this instance, a bell is also considered to be part of the music of Heaven, in addition to the mysterious music constantly heard around the young Colman.

We will now look at the supernatural musical performers which are portrayed in the primal (that is pre-Christian) contexts. The same phenomena are described as being musical as in the Christian contexts above – birds, stones, trees, insects, a mermaid, mysterious music with no performer(s) present, and the realm of the primal Otherworld itself as a musical performer all of its own.

For example, from *Echtra Taidg maic Cein* ('Adventure of Teigue, son of Cian'), birds are featured as being musical in the primal Otherworld:

> Birds beautiful and brilliant feasted on these grapes ... as they fed, they warbled music and minstrelsy that was melodious and superlative, to which patients of every kind and the repeatedly wounded would have fallen asleep; with reference to which it was that Teigue chanted this lay following: 'Sweet to my fancy, as I consider them, the strains of this melody to which I listen.'.[19]

This is clearly reminiscent of the overtly Christian examples cited earlier where birds are portrayed as being a prominent part of the Christian Heaven.

A special musical stone is portrayed in an overtly primal context in the early twelfth-century tale *Immram Brain* ('The Voyage of Bran'):

> Then they row to the bright stone
> from which a hundred songs arise.
> Through the long ages it sings to the host
> a melody which is not sad,
> the music swells up in choruses of hundreds,
> They do not expect decay nor death.[20]

Trees also appear in the primal contexts, perhaps most notably in an example from *Serglige Con Culainn* ('The Wasting Sickness of Cuchulainn'):

> At the entrance to the enclosure is a tree
> From whose branches there comes beautiful
>   and harmonious music.
> It is a tree of silver, which the sun illumines,
> It glistens like gold.[21]

The fly, an insect, is portrayed as a musical performer in an overtly primal context in *Tochmarc Etain* ('The Wooing of Etain'). In this example Etain, a beautiful young maiden, is turned into a fly by the jealous sorceress Fuamnach. During this difficult time, she appears as a musical fly to her beloved Midir:

> Sweeter than pipes and harps and horns
> was the sound of her voice and the
> hum of her wings.[22]

A little bit later, Midir, in his lonely misery, has great comfort in Etain as a musical fly who still visits him:

> as long as he could watch the scarlet fly,
> Midir loved no women, and he did not enjoy
> food or drink or music, unless he could
> see it – (Etain, as a scarlet fly) – and
> listen to its music and its buzzing.[23]

Mermaids, too, appear in the primal contexts, especially in the place-lore, the *Metrical Dindshenchas*. In one such poem, the location of 'Port Lairge' near modern-day Waterford is described:

> And there he heard the sound,
> it was a lure of baleful might,
> the chant of the mermaids of the sea
> over the pure-sided waves ...
> The hosts of the world would fall asleep
> listening to their voice and their clear notes.[24]

Mysterious music, where no performer is seen, comes from the musical net at the door of a noble fairy woman's Otherworld home in a verse recension of the tale *Immram Curaig Maile Duin* ('The Voyage of Maile Duin'):

> She went from them and closed the noble pleasant
> fort: her net, manifesting mighty power,
> chanted good harmonious music.
>
> Her musical choir lulled them to sleep ... the
> noble woman's music used to play for them,
> but no banqueting hall was seen.[25]

As one can see, there are clearly a great variety of musical performers portrayed in the references from this literature, within both primal and Christian contexts.

Illustratory comparative material

Other cultures, too, have references to supernatural musical performers. Tales abound from Scottish sources regarding various types of supernatural musicians, as in the following example about a ghostly harper:

> A ghostly harper, said to have been murdered by the troops of the Duke of Montrose in pursuit of Campbell enemies, haunts the Castle of Inverary in Argyll. He appears most often to women visitors and has been seen, dressed in dark tartan, most frequently in the Blue Room of the Castle. His music, when it is heard, sometimes presages the death of one of the Dukes of Argyll, or sounds at the time of their funerals.[26]

Accounts of seeing an apparition of a musical performer occur in other Scottish tales, particularly those with the motif of the ghostly piper or drummer.

The fairy legend of the famous MacLeod family of Skye is a well-known one from Scottish sources, and features the songs of a woman of the *sidhe* who visits the heir of the MacLeod family:

> Soon after the heir of the MacLeods was born, a beautiful woman in wonderful raiment, who was a fairy woman or a banshee ... appeared at the castle, and went directly to the babe's cradle. She took up the babe and chanted over it a series of verses, and each verse had its own melody. The verses foretold the future manhood of the young child, and acted as a protective charm over its life. Then she put the babe back into its cradle, and, going out, disappeared across the moorlands. For many generations it was a custom of the MacLeod family that whoever was the nurse of the heir must sing those verses the fairy woman had sung them. After a time the song was forgotten, but at a later period it was partially recovered, ... it is one of the proud folklore heritages of the MacLeod family.[27]

The MacCrimmon family were pipers to the MacLeods of Skye, and have a number of tales as to how they acquired their piping fame from the Otherworld. J. G. Campbell quotes this version in his *Superstitions of the Highland and Islands of Scotland*:

> The MacCrimmons were ... the most celebrated musicians among the Scottish Gael ... 'The Blind Piper' (*am Piobaire dall*) was the first of

the MacCrimmons who acquired fame as a piper. Two banshis found him sleeping in the open air, and one of them blinded one of his eyes. The second Banshi asked that the other eye might be spared. It, however, was blinded also. The benevolent Fairy then suggested that some gift should be given that would enable the poor man to earn his living. On this the Fairy Carlin gave MacCrimmon a brindled chanter, which, placed in the bagpipes, enabled the player to outrival all pipers.[28]

In both of the above examples, it is also interesting to note the portrayal of female *sidhe* personages who are associated with the music of the Otherworld, a favoured theme in Celtic lore.

In Welsh folklore, although fairies are portrayed as being small in size, they are said to possess certain artifacts which belong to them and their supernatural race, the *Tylwyth Teg*. Among such tiny items as fairy ropes, fairy money and fairy clay pipes, diminutive magical fairy harps are sometimes described in folklore accounts. In many legends, one is reminded of a certain code of conduct which must be followed, on pain of punishment. In one tale, a harper who misused a fairy harp was forced to play it against his will until he was absolutely exhausted.[29]

In cultures other than the Celtic we also find Otherworld musical performers. For example, the Bible has angels and other supernatural beings who are portrayed as musicians. Probably the best-known is Lucifer, said to have been the best musician in Heaven before his rebellion. Other examples include: the four living creatures that 'never stop singing' in John's Revelation (Rev. 4: 8 and 5: 8); John's vision of many angels singing and chanting to God around the throne with the four living creatures (Rev. 5: 11); the seven angels with their seven trumpets to perform at the time of the Apocalypse (Rev. 8: 6); John's vision of Mt Zion, where he hears the sound of angelic harpists singing a new hymn around the throne (Rev.14: 2); later, these angelic beings also sing the hymn of Moses (Rev. 15: 3) at the time of God's Judgement.

In Jewish theology, specific angelic realms of the various Powers and Principalities have musical epithets. The Archangel Uriel is often described as 'the Angel of Music'.[30] The Seraphim, the highest order of God's angelic servants, are believed to 'ceaselessly chant in Hebrew the Trisagion – Kadosh, Kadosh, Kadosh–"Holy, holy, holy is the Lord of Hosts, the whole earth is full of His Glory", while they circle the Throne.'[31] These fiery supernatural beings of pure light are clearly portrayed as musical performers.

In Islamic theology, the Heavens are spoken of as being seven in number (sura 78: 12) as stated in the Qur'an.[32] 'Angels fill the "stairs" of Heaven (sura 70: 3f) and witness of themselves that they are ranked in progressive degrees (sura 37: 164–6). Those of highest standing sustain the throne of God, singing praise and glory to their Lord (sura 40: 7) and interceding on behalf of human beings.'[33]

The origins of Chinese music, according to the Chinese themselves, lies in the mysterious legendary period of the third millennium BC, where Chinese historians maintain that:

> the ancient texts of China associate the establishment of their music with five enigmatic, legendary personages, who, it is said, were China's first monarchs ... Divine in nature, these five rulers are credited with the entire genesis of the civilization ... The first of them, Emperor Fu Hsi, is said to have been the founder of the monarchy and the 'inventor' of music ... The following four divine rulers also placed great emphasis on music.[34]

We will now take a look at the mortal musical performers.

Mortal music performers – but with Otherworld influence

Another important category of musical performer exists in this literature. Here we have a very small but valued group of gifted mortals, who are described as having various special contacts with supernatural personages from the Otherworld. Often, these gifted mortals were also members of the *aes dano*, those of the privileged artistic elite in society. Members of this small group are often portrayed as having been selected or abducted at times by the *sidhe*-folk, to go with them to the Otherworld and play for them. These musical performers are usually described as coming back to the everyday, mundane world with the claim that they personally received music training and advice on special playing techniques and/or special melodies from these supernatural personages.

For example, the gifted harper and poet Corainn was offered a 'deal' by such supernatural beings, described as being of the Tuatha de Danann, in exchange for playing his exquisite harp music for them. Corainn, a gifted mortal musician, was blessed by the Tuatha de Danann, the implication being that he was either abducted or hired to play for them. As a result of the Tuatha de Danann being greatly pleased with his enchanting music, they offered him land in their world as payment – clearly an unusual opportunity for a mortal. The doctor of the Tuatha de Danann, Dian Cecht, is described in this example as Corainn's patron.

The *Metrical Dindshenchas* mention a specific location called 'Ceis Corainn' (literally, 'the harp of Corainn') to mark the very spot where Corainn was said to have had this experience. Corainn then returns to the everyday, mortal world, and this location remained in the memory of the people and is noted to this day:

> Here abode gentle Corainn
> playing on the harp – it was good riches;
> Corand white of skin was a poet
> in the service of Diancecht, giver of sound limbs.
>
> The Tuatha De (excellent name) bestowed
> land in fee, for his goodly music,
> on Corand of the soothing strains:
> for his knowledge he deserves high esteem.[35]

Another example involving Corainn is also from the *Metrical Dindshenchas*, this time referring to his supernatural patron and the consequent power of his music. Here, his beautiful harp music is portrayed as having a type of 'spell' or influence that can summon a pig from a distance. It appears that the animal was influenced by the music, although it was not anywhere near the vicinity of Corainn:

> Mag Corainn, whence the name? Not hard to say. Corainn, harper to Diancecht the Dagda's son, called with his harp, Caelcheis, one of Drebriu's swine.[36]

One instance from the Ulster cycle, from the tale *Tain Bo Froech* ('The Cattle Raid of Froech'), describes how a talented mortal harper summoned supernatural spirit-images around the strings of the harp while he played his music. Somewhat similar to Corainn's music summoning a pig from a distance, here we have a harper's music summoning spirit-images of snakes, birds and hounds while entertaining:

> 'Let the harpers play to us,' said Ailill to Froech. 'Indeed, let them,' said Froech. The harp bags were of otterskin and were decorated with Partian leather ornamented with gold and silver. The kidskin about the harps was white as snow . . . the coverings of linen about the strings were white as swans' down. The harps were of gold and silver and white gold, with the forms of snakes and birds and hounds in gold and silver on them; and as the strings moved, these forms would make circuits round the men.[37]

Such an incident seems to imply that an especially gifted mortal's music can summon ethereal spirit-images which are then seen to go around the musician as he plays. It also indirectly implies that this type of an experience is unusual, and that obviously not every harper has the power or ability to summon such spirit-images while playing.

Another way in which a selected mortal could have musical influence from the Otherworld is through a dream, as illustrated by the following example. A man goes up to a particular mountain (Cend Febrat), falls asleep and is then shown in a dream-like vision every fairy mound that was on the mountain. Then he wakes up, having 'received' the theme of his own song:

> As I slept (pleasant the manner)
> therein I met with the theme of my song:
> there was shown me truly and in full
> every fairy mound that is at Cend Febrat.[38]

So after the man woke up, he came back to the everyday, mundane world a musical performer with his own unique song with its special theme, obtained in this dream-like vision on the mountain, Cend Febrat.

A specifically Christian example of a selected mortal having interaction with the supernatural regarding music and then returning to everyday, mundane life occurs in the *Tripartite Life of Patrick*. Here, St Patrick, selected by God, goes up to Heaven and has a discussion with an angel about a particular special hymn which he then takes back to use in his often challenging missionary work. Before leaving Heaven, St Patrick asks the angel if there is anything else he can grant to him:

> 'There is,' says the angel: 'every one who shall sing this hymn, from one watch to the other, shall not have pain or torture.' 'The hymn is long and difficult,' says Patrick. 'Every one who shall sing it from 'Christus illum' to the end . . . and every one who shall perform penitence in Ireland, his soul shall not go to Hell' (said the angel).[39]

Another example of a selected Christian mortal encountering musical angels in God's Heaven and then returning to everyday, mundane life is that of St Fursa. In *Betha Fursa* ('The Life of St Fursa') he has an experience of going up to Heaven:

> a serious illness attacked him from one Saturday to another, as the Book of his own Life relates; and from evening to cockcrow he was taken out of his body, and he heard the chanting of angels of Heaven, and he beheld them before him. And this is what they were chanting: 'Ibunt sancti de

uirtute in uirtutem' (Psalm 83: 8) i.e., 'the Saints shall advance from virtue to virtue.' And this is also what they were chanting: 'Videbitur Deus deorum in Sion.' (Psalm 83: 8) i.e., 'the God of Gods will be seen on Mt Zion'.[40]

Not surprisingly, the selected Christian mortals are usually portrayed as clergy or saints. From *The Tripartite Life of Patrick*, at the very moment St Patrick was ordained in Rome, three choirs responded – the choir in Rome, the choir from the wood of Fochlad in Ireland and the choir of Heaven:

> Then, too, was the name 'Patricius' given to him, a name of power ... And when the orders were read out, the three choirs mutually responded, namely, the choir of the household of Heaven, and the choir of the Romans, and the choir of the children from the wood of Fochlad. This is what they all sang: 'All we Irish beseech thee, holy Patrick, to come and walk among us and to free us'.[41]

In this excerpt, two of the three choirs are portrayed as having some kind of a supernatural linkage, as one responded from far-away Ireland at the very moment of St Patrick's ordination, and the other responded from God's Heaven. The third choir, that of Rome, is portrayed as an ordinary mortal choir, present at the ordination, and singing as expected. The other two choirs represent supernatural musical performers singing simultaneously with this mortal choir, all celebrating the ordination of St Patrick.

In another example with a Christian context, St Brendan is portrayed as a selected mortal having a divine visitation from St Michael, in the form of a shining, singing bird. A student harper wishes to play again for St Brendan, and St Brendan resists his offer, putting wax in his ears, stating that he has heard better music, that of God's Heaven:

> I saw a shining bird at the window, and it sat on the altar. I was unable to look at it because of the rays which surrounded it, like those of the sun ... 'who are you?' said Brennain. 'The angel Michael,' it said, 'come to speak with you.' 'I give thanks to God for speaking with you,' said Brennain, 'and why have you come?' 'To bless you and to make music for you for your Lord,' said the bird ... [Says St Brennain to the student harper:] ... 'After *that* music, no music of the world seems any sweeter to me'.[42]

Again, in these examples with an overtly Christian context, we see a fascinating variety of musical performers portrayed.

Illustratory comparative material

One version of the tale of Thomas the Rhymer of Ercildoune from Scottish literature describes Thomas as a talented mortal lute player who has an abduction experience involving the Queen of Elfland. One day, as he is sitting in a small wooded area near Huntlie Bank in the Borders:

> [He] plucked idly at his lute strings, and heard above his own music a distant sound like the trickle of a hill-side stream. Then he started to his feet in amazement; for down one of those green pathways rode the fairest lady in the world . . . 'Play your lute to me, Thomas,' she said; 'fair music and green shade go well together.' So Thomas took up his instrument again, and it seemed as though he had never before been able to play such lilting tunes. When he had finished, the Elf Queen showed her pleasure.[43]

He then goes with the Elf Queen to her Otherworld abode, under the condition that he not speak one word while there for a period of seven years, a taboo. He does not speak, and returns rewarded with not only his musical skills, but the gift of prophecy as well. He then became known as a seer who always told the truth ('True Thomas') and as one who could foretell many events, in addition to his having outstanding musical skills. (For other versions of this well-known tale, and an important analysis of the Scottish ballads, see *Scottish Ballads* by Emily Lyle of the University of Edinburgh's School of Scottish Studies.)

Scottish legends and tales have many examples of situations where mysterious music is heard yet no performer is seen. Near Portree, in Skye, there is a hill called 'Sithean Beinne Bhoidhich', Scottish Gaelic meaning a fairy-dwelling of the pretty hill. Legend has it that those who pass by it at night hear the most beautiful music coming from under the ground, yet are never able to pinpoint exactly from where it emanates. Likewise, curious, alluring music, said to sound like a fairy organ, is said to be heard frequently from under the arches of Fraisgall Cave in Sutherland. This music is described as having strange singing qualities and unusual melodies, as if pleading with the listener to come away to the land Under the Waves.[44]

A mermaid as a supernatural musical performer is featured in the following tale from J. F. Campbell's *West Highland Tales*, where the king's daughter is desperately trying to find her lost husband. She took her harp to the shore and sat and played and the sea-maiden came up to listen, for sea-maidens are fonder of music than any other creatures, and when she saw the sea-maiden, she stopped. The sea-maiden said 'Play on,' but she said 'No, not till I see my man again'. So the sea-maiden put up his head. (Who do you mean? Out of her mouth, to be sure. She had swallowed him.) She played again, and stopped, and then the sea-maiden put him up to the waist Then she played again and stopped and the sea-maiden placed him on her palm. Then he thought of the falcon, and became one, and flew on shore. But the sea-maiden took the wife.[45]

Fortunately, the King's daughter was eventually rescued from the sea-maiden.

From Welsh folk tradition, we have the following account from an early twentieth-century informant to Evans-Wentz, recalling beliefs about fairies in the South Carnarvonshire district (now part of Gwynedd):

the *Tylwyth Teg* were a small, very pretty people always dressed in white, and much given to dancing and singing in rings where grass grew. As a rule, they were visible only at night ... At night, the *Tylwyth Teg* would entice travellers to join their dance and then play all sort of tricks on them.[46]

Ethnopsychologist Holger Kalweit in his research regarding the shaman found that ' ... in the Beyond, he is taught the songs he brings back to earth, the songs which express his shamanic power and by which he transports himself back'.[47]

In shamanic lore a visit to the Beyond can result in musical gifts. When an ordinary mortal musician has such an experience, he is usually portrayed as an especially gifted musician, and is so selected by supernatural beings for some kind of an encounter or experience. In a few instances, such a selected mortal can return from an Otherworld experience with new musical skills or knowledge.

An example from early this century of such a 'musician abduction' is described by an old piper of Co. Galway, who speaks of a brother piper he knew personally and of his experiences:

There used to be an old piper named Flannery who lived in Oranmore, County Galway. I imagine he was one of the old generation. And one time the Good People took him to Fairyland to learn his profession. He studied music with them a long time, and when he returned he was as great a piper as any in Ireland. But he died young, for the Good People wanted him to play for them.[48]

Another situation that often occurs in world folklore is that of an innocent, unsuspecting mortal (sometimes a musician, but not always) who is invited to attend a *sidhe* musical celebration. The mortal, if a musician, nearly always comes back to the everyday world with a new song and/or musical techniques. If not a musician, the mortal is still greatly transformed by such contact with these super-natural personages, for good or ill.

One example from Islamic folklore describes a young devout Muslim boy named Hussein who was 'tricked by the jinn' into join-ing their music and circle-dancing celebration while walking in a country valley at twilight:

> as he was walking in the valley, he gradually became aware of an evening celebration ... Robed figures were clapping and dancing as an old man played a fiddle. Laughter filled the air. As he drew closer, Hussein could tell from the clothes, and then the faces, that they were friends of his ... someone then welcomed him ... 'Hussein! We have been expecting you. Come and dance' ... The music was quite intoxicating, and the synco-pated clapping of his friends quickly spun the spell that drew Hussein into the center of the group. Soon he was lost in the haunting melody for hours ... Eyes blurry with dizziness, he happened to glance down ... and horror shot through him like lightening! ... [he then realized:] 'My friends – their feet are on backwards! They have hollow eyes! These are jinn! I've been tricked into joining a jinn celebration. Oh, God, save me ... oh, Ali, please save me'.[49]

The boy then was suddenly all alone and it was nearly daybreak; he had unknowingly been gone for hours. He was then ill for six months or so and nearly died, his family attributing this strange illness to the lure of the haunting music of the jinn.

As with the example of the *Tylwyth Teg* from Wales above, tales of fairies dancing, singing, and playing instruments in a circle or a ring to entice travellers to join them, sometimes for many years and against their will, is a common motif found in the folklore of many cultures.

Mortal musical performers: especially members of the *aes dano*

Gifted but ordinary mortal performers, even if they have not had the unique privilege of being selected by supernatural personages from the Otherworld, are still portrayed as having an important place in early Irish society. This literature consistently refers to various types of entertainers who play music at king's banquets, nobles' palaces, and the fairs and festivals of the people.

Irish harpers in particular were highly valued by the aristocracy and the monastic orders as well as by the people. The monk and scholar Giraldus Cambrensis (1146–1223), writing in his twelfth-century work, *Topography Hibernica*, describes them:

> They are incomparably more skillful than any other nation I have ever seen. For their manner of playing these instruments, unlike that of the Britons [or Welsh] to which I am accustomed, is not slow or harsh, but lively and rapid, while the melody is both sweet and sprightly. It is astonishing that in so complex rapid movement of the fingers the musical proportions [as to time] can be preserved; and that throughout the difficult modulations on their various instruments, the harmony is completed with such a sweet rapidity. They go into a movement and conclude it in so delicate a manner, and tinkle the little strings so sportively under the deeper tones of the bass strings – they delight so delicately and soothe with such gentleness, that the perfection of their art appears in the concealment of art.[50]

However, later in this same work, he continues:

> It is to be observed that Scotland and Wales ... strive in practice to imitate Ireland in their melodies ... In the opinion of many people, Scotland has not only equalled her mistress, Ireland, in music, but today excells and surpasses her by far. For that reason, people look upon her now as the fountain of the art.[51]

It is clear that both Irish and Scottish harpers were perceived as very gifted performers of international renown, in the late twelfth century.

Likewise, other mortal musical performers in early Ireland, particularly singers, are also described as very gifted. However, not all such gifted mortals were members of the *aes dano*. Usually, harpers were members, as were certain elite court singers; other musicians who usually were not members were the more common variety of singers, that is, travelling minstrels, horn-players, percussionists, and so on. As suggested at the beginning of this chapter, of those musicians who were considered to be members of the *aes dano*, there is an implication in the very name that they are 'gifted', not by special encounter, but by occupation of their profession; theirs is a permanent gift. And as they are 'nemed', the suggested source of the gift is the Otherworld. It is not easy to draw a clear distinction between *aes dano* musicians and others, only to give examples.

The later monastic communities in Ireland also regarded music highly, especially the singing of the psalms and hymns. The young boy who would later become St Mochuda is portrayed as explaining to the king why he had been gone so long:

> 'Sir, this is why I have stayed away – through the attraction of the holy chant of the bishop and the clergy; I have never heard anything so beautiful as this ... And I wish, O king, that I might learn' [their psalms and ritual].[52]

Mortal musical performers of the non-human variety frequently find mention in the early Irish sources. The hermit poetry of the early Irish Christian monastic communities in particular reflects an appreciation of a great variety of non-personal musical performers. Such highly valued performers of 'music' as blackbirds, ducks, bees, wrens, larks, swallows, wolves, stags, the sea, the wind and so on are all seen by the monks as having unique musical qualities of their own.

For example, from the famous tenth-century hermit poem entitled *King and Hermit:*

> swarms of bees and chafers, the little
> musicians of the world,
> A gentle chorus: Wild geese,
> and ducks, shortly before summer's end,
> the music of the dark torrent ...
>
> An active songster, a lively wren
> From the hazel-bough
> Beautiful hooded birds, woodpeckers,
> A vast multitude![53]

Another similar example is that of a ninth-century Christian hermit poem entitled 'The Scribe In the Woods':

> A hedge of trees overlooks me; a blackbird's
> lay sings to me (an announcement which I cannot
> conceal); above my lined book the birds'
> chanting sings to me.
>
> A clear-voiced cuckoo sings to me (goodly
> utterance) in a grey cloak from bush fortresses.
> The Lord is indeed good to me: well do I write
> beneath a forest of woodland.[54]

Such references show mortals, in this case monks, explaining how they perceive such musical performers as exemplifying God's glory in their environment. They clearly greatly appreciate such natural performers, and feel blessed to write about them.

Illustratory comparative material

The Bible certainly has a rich and varied tradition of valuing music and mortal musicians. Examples abound, such as: the music of tambourines and harps as joyful unto the Lord (Gen. 31: 27); the singing to Yahweh of the Song of Victory by Moses and the Israelites (Exod. 15); the mention of the sounding of the trumpet on the Day of Expiation (Lev. 25: 9); trumpets as a battle cry (Num. 10; John 8: 2 and 8: 6); the Psalms of David and so on. Such examples from the Judeo-Christian tradition seem to indicate a belief in the power of music in general, as well as an appreciation of the musicians themselves, whether clergy or lay persons.

According to the Sufi tradition, music expert Inayat Khan states that a musician or singer 'becomes an instrument of the whole cosmic system, open to all inspiration, at one with the audience . . .'[55] The famous performer from India, Ravi Shankar, when speaking of the great musical performers of the past, states that 'these great musicians were not just singers or performers, but also great yogis . . . they were pure, ascetic, saintly persons . . .'[56]

The power of certain singing is also referred to by Paramahansa Yogananda, who believed in something he aptly described as 'super-conscious singing'. Such singing by talented mortals had many different levels, for example 'singing aloud, whispered singing, mental singing, subconscious singing, superconscious singing . . .'[57]

Conclusion

In these references to music from the early Irish sources there is a continuity of line of musical performers, starting with the purely supernatural musicians, like angels or fairy harpers, who are portrayed as living in an Otherworld dimension. Below them, there is a small group of gifted mortals who are occasionally 'selected' or 'abducted' by supernatural personages, taken to the Otherworld and taught or given special musical gifts, and then returned to earth. These experiences can be either postive or negative.

Next, there are other mortal musicians who, although talented and gifted, are not specifically 'selected' by supernatural beings for an encounter involving music. We then have the other more ordinary musical entertainers, like travelling minstrels, horn-players and so on, who were still highly appreciated in early Irish society. We then saw a further continuity to birds, animals and natural elements, portrayed in this literature as being musical performers in some way.

The overall impression is that of an unbroken line of musical performers ranging from the purely supernatural to the most mundane, with the originating and most powerful influences coming from the Otherworld, and the most mundane music also being capable at times of revealing links with the supernatural Otherworld realm. This is true whether the context of the example is overtly Christian or primal. All musical performers, simply by being performers, are linked by music to its ultimate Otherworld source, even if they are only ordinary, everyday musicians, birds, animals or the natural elements.

One example of this continuity in an overtly Christian context is that of ordinary choirs of monks singing their psalms in praise of God; they are thus seen as connecting to a divine source through their music. St Basil in his teaching on prayer comments on vocal prayer, or divine psalmody, and directs his monks to be diligent regarding it:

> Psalmody, he says, is divine both in its measures and in its words ... it is the continuation of the harmonies of Heaven ... [it is] the sweet song of the Holy Spirit Himself ... St Basil directs his monks to devote themselves with alacrity, diligence, and fervor ... at their disposal of rendering honor and glory to God.[58]

In the examples we have seen from the early Irish literature, it is the *music itself* that clearly binds all members of this unbroken line of musical performers together. It is also the connection to the supernatural Otherworld source of the ultimate perfect music and harmony.

Just as there is this continuity regarding music in the Christian and the primal sources, there is also a certain parallelism in the personnel of performers at each level in these two sets of contexts. In the primal Otherworld examples, there are *sidhe*-folk musicians, birds and the natural elements portrayed as musical performers. In the Christian contexts, too, there are angels as musicians, birds and the natural elements, all of which are portrayed as being an integral part of the glory of God's Creation.

This parallelism would seem to indicate a continuity of line of various musical performers and, as a consequence, of some supernatural influence, in *both* primal and Christian terms. Take, for example, Patrick's encounter with the fairy harper Cascorach.

In the earlier example where St Patrick and his clergymen encounter the *sidhe* musician Cascorach, St Patrick refers to a 'twang of the fairy spell' to the music. He later cautions his fellow clergymen not to become 'inordinately addicted' to the fairy music, implying that it has great power. He also refused to ban his clerics from listening to the fairy music.

By not banning the music outright, St Patrick seems to be acknowledging a qualified acceptance of the *sidhe*-music as special and valuable in some way. However, if he feels that such bewitching *sidhe*-music is acceptable as part of worldly goodness, he is cautious about it.

It is as if he is concerned as to *which* 'Otherworld' or 'Heaven' such bewitching *sidhe*-music might come from or lead to, and thus warns his fellow clergy that 'we must not become inordinately addicted to it', as it has a suspicious 'twang of the fairy spell' to it.

Here, the Christian spokesman, St Patrick, is portrayed as recognising the power of the *sidhe*-music as very real. There seems to be a continuous line of various musical performers portrayed in this literature and a recognition of the supernatural source(s) of the music. This recognition seems common to both the Christian and the primal contexts; it is the background for a certain degree of recognition, at least from the Christian side, of the power of music which we see in this particular example.

Such *sidhe*-music is acknowledged by the clergy to come from an Otherworld realm, but St Patrick is portrayed as warning his fellow clergymen about the possible dangers of such music and of the possibility of being lead into an unknown and/or non-Christian Otherworld. In his view, nothing can compare with the harmony of the Christian Heaven, a realm from which he implies that the bewitching *sidhe*-music of Cascorach does not originate. Therefore, he seems to imply, good Christian listeners should be careful not to be lead astray by such enticing musical temptations.

Performers are conceptualised in this literature as often being influenced by the Otherworld, whether the context of the particular example is Christian or primal, and, it is also implied, so is the listener of the music.

We will now turn our attention to the musical instruments referred to in the references about music from this literature.

Notes

1. McCone, K., *Pagan Past and Christian Present in Early Irish Literature*, (An Sagart, Ireland: Maynooth, 1990), p. 86.
2. Hyde, D., *A Literary History of Ireland* (London: T. Fisher Unwin, 1967) p. 496.
3. McCone, *PPCP*, p. 86.
4. McCone, *PPCP*, p. 31.
5. Kelly, F., *A Guide to Early Irish Law* (Dublin: DIAS, 1988), p. 64.
6. O'hOgain, D., *Myth, Legend, and Romance: An Encyclopedia of the Irish Folk Tradition* (New York: Ryan Publishing, 1991), pp. 185–7.
7. Evans-Wentz, W. Y., *The Fairy-Faith in Celtic Countries* (New York: University Books, 1966; 1911 orig.), p. 307.
8. O'Cathasaigh, T., 'The semantics of sid', *Eigse* vol. 17 (Dublin, 1977–9), p. 149.
9. Ibid.
10. O'Grady, S. (ed.), '*Accalam na Senorach*/Colloquy with the Ancient Men', *SG* II (London, 1892), p. 191.
11. Meyer, K., 'Comracc ConCulainn re Senbecc', *RC* 6 (Paris, 1884), p. 183.
12. O'Grady, *SG* II, p. 191.
13. Jackson, K., *A Celtic Miscellany* (Harmondsworth: Penguin, 1971), pp. 288–95.
14. Ibid., pp. 295–6.
15. Stokes, W., *Lives of the Saints from the Book of Lismore* (Oxford, 1890), p. 114.
16. Stokes, W., 'The Voyage of the Ui Corra', *RC*, 14, (Paris, 1893), p. 50.
17. O'Grady, *SG*, II, p. 267.
18. Meyer, K., *Life of Colman, son of Luachan*, RIA Todd Lecture Series, Vol 17, (Dublin, 1911), p. 15.
19. O'Grady, *SG*, II, p. 390.
20. Jackson, *CM*, p. 174.
21. Cross, T. and Slover, C., *Ancient Irish Tales* (New York: Barnes & Noble, 1969), p. 189.
22. Bergin, O. and Best, R., 'Tochmarc Etaine', *Eriu*, 12 (Dublin, 1938), p. 153.
23. Gantz, J., *EIMS* (London, 1981), p. 46.
24. Gwynn, E., *Metrical Dindshenchas* III (Dublin, 1913), p. 191.
25. Cross, T. and Slover, C., (eds), *AIT*, p. 189.

26. Sanger, K. and Kinnaird, A., *Tree of Strings: crann nan teud* (Temple, Midlothian: Kinmor Music, 1992), p. 7.
27. Evans-Wentz, *Fairy Faith*, p. 27.
28. Campbell, J. G., *Superstitions of the Highland and Islands of Scotland* (Glasgow, 1900), pp. 139ff.
29. Gwyndaf, R., 'Fairylore: memorates and legends from Welsh oral tradition', in P. Narvaez (ed.), *The Good People* (New York: Garland, 1991), p. 170.
30. Godwin, M., *Angels: An Endangered Species* (New York: Simon & Shuster, 1990), p. 74.
31. Ibid., p. 25.
32. Bell, R., *The Qur'an, translated with a critical arrangement of the Suras* 2 vols (Edinburgh: T & T. Clark, 1967).
33. Musk, B., *The Unseen Face of Islam* (Eastbourne, E. Sussex: MARC Publishers, 1989), p. 226.
34. Tame, David, *The Secret Power of Music* (New York: Destiny Books, 1984), pp. 63–4.
35. Gwynn, *MD* III (Dublin, 1913), p. 439.
36. Gwynn, *MD* IV (Dublin, 1924), p. 293.
37. Gantz, *EIMS*, pp. 117–18.
38. Gwynn, *MD* III, p. 227.
39. Stokes, W., *Tripartite Life of Patrick* (London, 1887), pp. 114–15.
40. Stokes, W., 'Betha Fursa', *RC* 25 (Paris, 1901), p. 390.
41. Stokes, *TLP*, pp. 32–3.
42. Jackson, *CM*, p. 283.
43. Wilson, B., *Scottish Folktales and Legends*, (Oxford: Oxford University Press, 1954), pp. 8–9. (This work is a retelling of tales based on Campbell's *Waifs and Strays of Celtic Tradition*.)
44. Robertson, R., *Selected Highland Folktales* (Colonsay, Argyll, 1995; 1961 orig.), p. 3.
45. Campbell, J. F., *West Highland Tales*, vol. 3, (London, 1890), p. 98. (The Gaelic title of this tale is 'A Mhaighdean Mhara'.)
46. Evans-Wentz, *Fairy Faith*, p. 143.
47. Kalweit, Holger, *Dreamtime and Inner Space: The World of the Shaman* (Boston: Shambhala, 1988), p. 228.
48. Evans-Wentz, *Fairy Faith*, p. 40.
49. Musk, *Unseen Face*, p. 37.
50. Joyce, P. W., *A Social History of Ancient Ireland* (London: Longmans Green & Co., 1903), pp. 573–4.
51. Sanger and Kinnaird, *Tree of Strings*, p. 31.
52. Power, P., *Life of St. Mochuda of Lismore*, Irish Texts Society (London, 1914), p. 80.
53. Meyer, K., *Selections from Ancient Irish Poetry*, (London: Constable, 1911), p. 51.

54. Murphy, G., *Early Irish Lyrics* (Oxford: Clarendon Press, 1956), pp. 4–5.
55. Khan, I., *On Music* (Claremont, CA: Hunter House, 1988), p. 33. (reprint of 'The Sufi Message of Hazrat Inayat Khan', Geneva, 1959).
56. Shankar, R., *My Music, My Life* (London: Jonathon Cape, 1969), p. 29.
57. Hamel, M., *Through Music to the Self* (Shaftesbury: Element, 1978), p. 64.
58. Murphy, Sr M., *St. Basil and Monasticism* (New York, 1971; 1930 orig.), p. 90

3

Instruments

MUSIC IN EARLY MEDIEVAL Irish society was played on many types of instruments. Chief among these were the harp, timpan, fiddle, bagpipe, horn, trumpet, pipe or recorder, and the bell. In this chapter we will first look in some detail at the various instruments involved and later explore the references to them.

These instruments are consistently mentioned in the early manuscripts and law tracts which form the chief sources for analysis. These major instruments in Old Irish are: the *crott* or *cruitt* (harp), *fidli* (fiddle), *timpan* (timpan), *tinne* (a set of bagpipes), *cuisle* (a single pipe in the *tinne*), *pipai* and *buinne* (other pipe instruments), *stoc* or *sturgan* (trumpet), *corn* (horn) and *cloc* (bell).

The *crott* or *cruitt* (harp)

The Old Irish terms for the harp include the *crut*, *crott*, and *cruitt*; *crott* or *cruitt* is translated as harp or lute in the Royal Irish Academy dictionary.[1] A later Irish term for a harp is the *clairseach*. Several harps, and harpers, are sculptured on the high crosses of early Ireland, from which we can attempt to form a picture of their shape and size, and possibly try to determine more clearly what the instrument might have been like in the early medieval, pre-Norman time period. Mr. Keith Sanger and Ms. Alison Kinnaird in *Tree of Strings: crann nan teud*, state the following regarding the history of the harp in Ireland and Scotland:

By the 8th or 9th century, the time of the earliest iconographical representations, there seem to have been several different stringed instruments being played in Scotland and Ireland. There is academic debate whether these should be described as 'lyres' or 'harps'. The two names seem to have been used indiscriminately by early writers and this, added to the fact that the sources of our information have sometimes been translated from Gaelic into Latin and subsequently into English, compounds the confusion … many of the writers were also foreigners and were ignorant of musical terminology, particularly that of the alien culture that they were attempting to describe.[2]

Thus, we need to clarify what terms are used to describe what instruments. For our purposes here, the Old Irish term of *crott* or *cruitt* has been correctly translated as 'harp', while the Old Irish term *timpan* refers to a similar, but not identical, stringed instrument, to be discussed later. According to musicologist Curt Sachs, the harp has the strings running away from the soundboard, exposed on both sides, and the lyre has strings which run across the board, often over a bridge.[3]

The carved stone high crosses of Ireland show instruments which appear to be four-sided, rather than the three-sided harp more familiar to us today. Joan Rimmer, in her classic work on *The Irish Harp*, has done a study of the images of harps on the high crosses of early Ireland. The carving on the South Cross at Castledermot shows a musician with a quadrangular harp on his knee; this carving is believed to be ninth-century. This harp, with its six strings, seems to be quite similar in structure and size to the remains of the six-stringed harp found in the Saxon ship burial at Sutton Hoo in England.[4] The tenth-century cross at Clonmacnoise shows a round-topped four-sided lyre in its depiction of the Scriptures, and is also portrayed as being played on the knee of the musician. The tenth-century cross of Muireadach at Monasterboice includes a depiction of what Rimmer describes as 'an oblique topped lyre'.[5] It also shows a bird perched on top of the instrument and a player of triple pipes. There are many other such crosses of the pre-Norman time period in Ireland, but what is striking is that 'there are few which can be regarded as harps and no triangular-framed harps at all. There are no representations on the Irish crosses of the triangular-framed harp as we know it.'[6]

It seems that, regarding the harp in the period before the twelfth-century in Ireland, what is generally referred to as a harp is a quadrangular instrument, that is four-sided. Some of the early texts make reference to *coir-cethar-chuir*, 'four-angled music', which some experts believe may refer to a four-sided instrument. The first undisputed example of a three-sided harp in Ireland appears on the Shrine of St Mogue, which probably dates from the eleventh-century. So the theory that the early Irish harp was most probably a four-sided instrument seems to be confirmed both by the early texts and by evidence from the early medieval stone crosses of Ireland.

It appears that the *cruitt* (harp) of the eighth, ninth, tenth and eleventh centuries in Ireland was of a medium or smaller size than the harps of today, the average height being about thirty inches, and some appear to have had up to twenty-five strings. They were often made of willow with brass strings. Smaller harps, usually eight-stringed and around sixteen inches, were used to accompany singers or poets. This harp was often called a *ceis*, and was used to accompany the larger harps as well as by the *fili* (poets) to accompany their verse. The tuning key for the harps, called *crann-glesa* ('tuning wood') was considered so important that provision was made in the Brehon Law, with penalties, for its prompt return should a harper lend it out.[7]

Some scholars believe that the early Irish clergy sometimes played the harp, and carried a small, portable harp with them on their missionary journeys to Gaul. The clergy used the harps in conjunction with the singing and chanting of the psalms, in the tradition of King David, and it is believed that the type of harp they used may have been an eight-stringed psalterium, similar to the early Assyro-Hebrew psalterium used in Jewish services. The number of strings, eight, seems to indicate the use of the diatonic scale in church music.

The history of the harp as an instrument and how it may have arrived in Ireland is a point of great debate and conjecture. The sources begin with the first-century BC Roman writer Diodorus Siculus, who described the instrument used by the Celtic bards as similar to the Roman lyre. Nearly 500 years later, another Roman historian, Ammianus Marcellinus, who lived around AD 360, stated that the Celtic bards sang to a sweet-sounding lyre. Unfortunately he did not elaborate on exactly what the perceived differences were between this Celtic lyre and the Roman lyre he was referring to, and one must remember that the Romans did not invade Ireland. The learned Giraldus Cambrensis, in his *Topographia Hibernia iii*, describes the musical instruments in use in early Ireland, Scotland and Wales in the twelfth-century. He heard the Irish harpers in AD 1185, and in a famous passage quoted earlier he exalts their great talent as well as that of the Scottish harpers, and attempts to describe their playing techniques.[8]

From his comments, it appears that Giraldus was clearly referring to an instrument that was plucked with the fingers, and not bowed. He then later states that the Irish had two major instruments, notably a type of harp and the timpan. From the first example, it would seem that Giraldus was clearly referring to a harp, while the second seems to imply that this instrument was *not* identical to the timpan and that he was familiar with both.

For comparison and further analysis, we may look to the early Welsh material, written down in the twelfth and thirteenth centuries, from which the History of Wales by Caradoc of Lhancarvan was extracted. The Welsh term here for harp is *telyn*, which was also used in the Welsh Laws for the instrument meaning a harp. It is clear from the early Welsh Laws that a harp with a 'horse-hair' bow was in use in Wales in the twelfth-century, but was considered the type of harp used by inferior harpers. The chief harper was entitled to a fine from each minstrel who exchanged this 'hair-strung harp' for a 'better' one, most likely of brass strings, on becoming a fully qualified harper.[9] Early Welsh harpers often went to Ireland to learn their craft, but a hair-strung harp is not mentioned in early medieval Ireland as the *crott* and *cruitt* are believed to have had metal strings.

In Scotland, it is known that the earliest triangular harps on the Pictish stones occur from the eighth century. All of the early stones in Scotland show triangular harps, except for two which are quadrangular. These two date from the eighth century, and occur in the context of an Irish immigrant community on the west coast of Scotland. Also, the first Irish portrayals of triangular harps do not occur until the late eleventh century on a reliquary, and the twelfth century on stone. So it would appear that the triangular harp was present in Scotland before it arrived in Ireland, and that the earliest harps in use in Ireland were quadrangular.

The four-sided psalterium seems to have been the preferred instrument of ecclesiastics, while the *crott* or *cruitt* was primarily for lay purposes and was an earlier instrument in Ireland. The psalterium is mentioned as being part of Irish monastic life and may be similar to the *kinnor* (harp) of the Hebrews, a likely candidate for the instrument that David played for King Saul in I Samuel 16: 23. The Old Testament instrument called the *Hhasor*, which most likely had ten strings, is mentioned along with the *kinnor* and the *nebel* in Psalm 92: 3.

The harp is the national symbol of Ireland, and was long portrayed as such by continental writers. Likewise, many European writers through the centuries extolled the harp as an Irish phenomenon, often giving the highest compliments to the Irish and Scottish harpers and their legendary skills, as did Giraldus. The references from this literature also seem to glorify the harp as an instrument and extol the effects of its music. The term 'lyre' was, unfortunately, also used interchangeably with the term 'harp' by the various English translators of this material from the Old and Middle Irish sources. Because of this situation, it is not possible to decide for sure from the collection references whether the so-called 'lyre' they mention is in any way different from what they call the 'harp', and, if so, in what manner.

The *Timpan*

The *timpan* is believed to have been a stringed instrument similar to a harp with metal strings. Some musicologists believe that it might also have been bowed, unlike any references to the *crott* or *cruitt*. According to Cormac's *Glossary*, the *timpan* (or, properly, what is referred to as a timpan) had a frame of willow wood with brass strings; it is also described in the *Acallam na Senorach* as having treble strings of silver, bass strings of white bronze and tuning pins of gold.[10] In Ireland, the *timpan* is often described as hand-held and rather small, and seems to have had few strings, perhaps up to eight. In other instances, it appears to be a small harp plucked with the fingers. It is often described as being a 'sweet-sounding' stringed instrument.

Musicologists are divided on the issue of exactly what the timpan was. But most believe that the Irish *timpan* was an instrument with metal strings, and was most likely plucked with the fingers, like a wire-strung harp, or perhaps it was bowed as some scholars maintain. Anne Buckley in her comprehensive study believes the *timpan* to have been a lyre type of instrument and not a harp.[11] John Bannerman points out that in medieval Latin *tympanum* meant 'drum', 'tambourine' or occasionally 'psaltery', a stringed instrument, but that in Gaelic *timpan* clearly described a stringed instrument, and believes it to have probably meant the quadrangular lyre-shaped instrument, not a triangular one.[12] So it appears that all we can really conclude, albeit cautiously, is that in this particular literature of early medieval Ireland, the *timpan* was most probably a type of quadrangular-shaped stringed instrument that had metal strings.

The fiddle

Fiddles are referred to in the literature of early Ireland and Scotland, although the references are quite scanty. The only example we have from this collection is the Old Irish term *fidil* (fiddle) which is referred to along with other musical instruments in a description of the Fair of Carmun in the *Dindschenchas*.

In Scotland, as in England, the fiddle was often called the *fethill*, after the Latin *vidula*. Francis Collinson, in *The Bagpipe, Fiddle, and Harp*, states that the Scottish terms for fiddle were *fedyl* and *rybid*. He also mentions the *croud*, which was also a bowed instrument, that is portrayed on Scottish stone carvings in Rosslyn Chapel and Melrose Abbey. The fiddle is obviously of the same class of instrument as the viola and violin.[13] However, many of the earliest medieval references in Europe to a 'fiddle' may not have necessarily been bowed instruments as we think of them today. One example, the early Norse *fidlu*, did not mean a bowed instrument, as referred to in the Old Norse epics before AD 1200. In early Ireland, unfortunately, we do not have specific enough detailed descriptions of what is termed a *fidli* to know for sure exactly what the precise nature of the instrument was.

The bagpipes

The Old Irish term for bagpipe is *tinne*, meaning the whole set of pipes. The pipers themselves are called *cuslennach*; a *cusle* or *cuisle* means one of the pipes in the *tinne*. Musicologists acknowledge that the bagpipes are of very ancient origin, as they were known in the ancient Middle East and in oriental countries, and they have the design of a double pipe.

The first medieval mention of bagpipes comes from the ninth-century Epistle of Dardanus of St Jerome, where the term 'chorus' meant a type of bagpipe which has a bag or skin with two brass tubes, one of which formed the mouth-piece of the bagpipe, and the other the chanter.[14] Roderick Cannon states that:

> The earliest evidence of bagpipes in the British Isles relates to England: an Anglo-Saxon riddle of the eleventh century, for which 'a bagpipe' seems to be the answer, and a rather crude carving on a gravestone in Northumberland, thought to date from 1200 A.D. Definite historical records begin with payments to bagpipers who played at the king's court. The word 'bagpipe' itself first occurs in such records in 1334, and in literature, in Chaucer's Canterbury Tales, c. 1386. The oldest existing fragments of a bagpipe are also English ... from Weoley Castle in Warwickshire and have been dated to the late thirteenth, or fourteenth, century.[15]

The situation in early medieval Ireland is rather difficult to ascertain exactly, as it appears that the early *fili* and scribes might have continued for some time to apply old names to new instruments, so that where they write *cuisle* (which strictly means a flute or single pipe), they were likely referring to a bagpipe, according to Sean Donnelly in his work on the pipes in Ireland.[16] In one example from this collection, an Irish scholar does translate the term *cuislennaig* for 'bagpipers', for example.

The Welsh name of the bagpipe, as it is written in the Welsh Laws, is *pybeu*, which is similar to the early Irish instrument referred to as *pipai* meaning 'pipes'. This is also similar to the Old Norse term for the bagpipe *pipa*. The early Irish bagpipe seems to be similar to the modern Highland type of bagpipe, which is inflated by the mouth.

Pipes/whistles

Other than the bagpipes, single-pipe wind instruments were also in use in early Ireland. It appears that a simple pipe was popular, and was referred to in Old Irish as a *buinne* or *bunne*, perhaps resembling what we think of today as a recorder. This was similar to the *cuisle* or *cuislenn*, meaning a single pipe in the *tinne*, the entire bagpipe complex. It has also been used to mean a type of flute. In the Old Irish Glosses, the Latin term 'tibia', a type of pipe or flute, is explained by the Old Irish term *buinne*. A player of the *buinne* was called a *buinnire*.

There is another Old Irish term for a musical pipe called a *cuisech* or *cuisig*. This pipe apparently differed in some slight manner from the *binne*, although one cannot now be sure as to exactly how. These wind instruments, we can surmise, were probably early versions of the flute and recorder. A whistle in Old Irish was called a *fedan*, and a whistle-player a *fedanach*. The tin whistle still maintains an important role in Celtic folk music today.

Trumpets and horns

The Old Irish terms for trumpets include *stoc* and *sturgan*. It is possible that the Sanskrit 'Stu', to 'praise or glorify', shows a close relationship between Sanskrit words and the early Irish terminology. This type of trumpet resembled a long cylindrical bore that emitted a loud, shrill blast. Other Old Irish terms for early Irish trumpets were: *corn, buabaill, adharc, dudag, galltrompa* and *barra-buad*. The *corn*, a horn-like instrument, was the longer one, it appears, while the *stoc* was of the shorter variety. A trumpet player was often called a *stocaire*, while a horn-blower was referred to as a *cornaire*. We cannot be certain what each type of trumpet or horn looked like; however, we do know that among the household of every king and chieftain there was a band of trumpeters, some of which were fortunate enough to get a coveted seat at the yearly Assembly of Tara, a great honour.

In Scotland, the oldest musical artefact is nearly three thousand years old, and is a fragment of a side-blown horn cast in bronze. It was found in Kirkcudbrightshire (now part of the region of Dumfries & Galloway), and dates from some time before the eighth-century BC The carnyx, a large sheet bronze horn, was an early Scottish horn, and a large fragment was unearthed in 1816 near Dexford in Banffshire (now part of the Grampian region), with Pictish designs on it.

Trumpets and horns were primarily used for warfare, as their shrill blasts served the purposes of signalling to troops, frightening enemies and motivating men to fight. Trumpets as a 'battle cry' occur in the Bible, as in Revelation 8: 2, the seven trumpets of the seven angels of the Apocalypse are sounded at Doomsday, and in the Old Testament the city of Jericho was destroyed by the sound of trumpets in Joshua 6: 4. Trumpets are mostly referred to as war instruments in early Celtic society, and only sometimes as instruments of mere entertainment.

The early Irish trumpets and horns are of various shapes and sizes and many can be viewed in museums today. Some are of the straight metal variety, others are curved. Trumpets were common in early Ireland, and many have been well preserved in bogs in Co. Cork and Co. Limerick, for example. They were often made of thin hammered bronze; some appear to have had the blowing aperture on the side, while others were blown from the end, like our modern-day trumpets and cornets. The first proper study of the playing potential of these remaining horns in Ireland was made by Siomon O'Duibhir, and 'the original horns and rattles were first recorded in 1989 and 1991, when it became clear that the sound world that can be produced from them is extensive and immensely impressive'.[17] Similar work is being done in Scotland with the carnyx.

Bells

Bells in early Irish society appear to have been used primarily by the clergy. The Old Irish term for bell is generally *cloc*, which is believed to be a loan-word from the lower Latin word 'clocca'. The origin of the word itself is obscure. The *cloc* or *clocc* was an open bell with a clapper, four-sided or round, often made of metal, and was usually used in the service of the church.

The *cloc* or *clocc* was a hand-held bell made of metal, and was in general use by the clergy in the late eighth century. These bells were used on the altar or as part of Mass. They were also used in monasteries to summon the monks to the refectory for meals, or to assist in the singing and chanting of the Psalms. Gradually, it seems that the *cloc* later became the exclusive name of large bells placed in the steeples of churches, that is the belfry. The distance around a church that the bell was heard was believed to represent the scope of its legal boundaries, so that early Irish law states that a church was entitled to a share in the property of strangers dying within the sound of its bell, for example. The original bell of a *tuath*, ('tribe' or 'people') around which it had placed its protection, often determined the rights of a church, and it was often one of the chief objects in the entire building. The 'bell house' was called a *cloictech*.

For our purposes here regarding early medieval Ireland, most of the references to the music of the bell, the *cloc* or *clocc*, are referring to the smaller hand-held variety. These bells were often sounded by striking them, and many can be seen in museums today. The other type of bell referred to is the small, closed type, spherical in shape, with a loose ball or pea of metal inside, that is 'jingle bells' in popular jargon. These bells are portrayed as being heard on on Froech's horses in *Tain Bo Froech*, an early Old Irish tale. The term for these bells was *cluicine*.

Cnamfir

The Old Irish term *cnamfir*, used in the Carmun Fair example, is translated to mean a 'bone-player'. This seems to indicate a type of percussion instrument, perhaps using the 'clapping' sound of bones. Musicologist Curt Sachs indicates that the 'bones' were a type of medieval 'clapper' percussion instrument. However, no one knows for sure what the early Irish term specifically means, as we have only this one example of it. Rudolf Thurneysen, in *A Grammar of Old Irish*, translates the Old Irish term *cnami* as 'bones', and the term *cnaim* means 'bone' in Old Irish.[18] So the *cnamfir*, in its singular form, would mean a 'man of (the) bones'.

Fer-cengail

This term is translated as 'gleemen', as by Ed Gwynn in the *Metrical Dindshenchas*. It is believed by other scholars that this Old Irish term did not really refer to a musician *per se*, but rather to a jester-like figure who 'danced about' in a peculiar kind of hopping or springing dance, known in the twelfth-century as the 'Espringale'. It seems as if they were perceived as some sort of 'dancing gleemen'. Perhaps, like dancing jesters, the *fer-cengail* were entertainers often seen with musicians, especially at fairs. Some Continental medieval descriptions of dancing jesters, and 'dancing men', are similar to what may be referred to here by *fer-cengail*.

The musical branch

The musical branch occurs primarily in *Immram Brain* ('The Voyage of Bran') an eighth-century tale. It is preserved in several manuscripts, the earliest being the *Lebor na hUidre*, an early twelfth-century manuscript. The Old Irish term used for the musical branch in *Immram Brain* is *croib n-arggait*, meaning 'a branch of silver'. In other references, it is also called *craebh ciuil*, 'a musical branch', or *crann ciuil*, a 'musical tree'. It is often described as having golden apples on it, or fruit in general. It was also recognised as a sacred object of the poet's (*fili*) craft in early Ireland. In Celtic references in general, the silver branch is given to the mortal by a *sidhe* woman, or an unknown Queen of the Otherworld or one of her female accomplices. The Golden Bough of classical tradition was often associated with the cult of Nemea, a goddess. The Irish silver branch also serves the function of being a kind of passport to the Otherworld. The musical branch is portrayed as a source of poetic inspiration and of Otherworld connections, and as a special link to the Muses or goddesses.

In summary, the major musical instruments of early medieval Ireland as found in the references from this collection consist primarily of: the *crott* or *cruitt* (harp), *timpan* (timpan), *fidil* (fiddle), *tinne* (a set of bagpipes), *cuisle* (a single pipe or flute), *buinne* (a single pipe), *stoc* (trumpet), *corn* (horn) and *clocc* (bell). We also encounter a percussion-like instrument played by *cnamfir* (the 'men of the bones') and the silver branch.

We will now examine the references to these instruments, dividing them into three main categories: (1) instruments in a purely Otherworld context; (2) instruments in everyday life, yet with some otherworldly influence(s); and (3) instruments in everyday life with no otherworldly influences.

Supernatural instruments: in a purely Otherworld context

From this literature we have several examples of what appear to be purely supernatural instruments, such as those that play by themselves, have the power to 'hear' or 'listen' of their own accord, or have the power to take commands from their owner. Not surprisingly, such supernatural instruments are often the same ones played by supernatural *sidhe* personages or angels in a purely Otherworld context. Because of the inherent Otherworld quality to these references, the instruments themselves are portrayed as also taking on supernatural qualities. We will now examine the references which refer to supernatural musical instruments that occur only in a purely Otherworld context.

One reference is from the early Irish mythological cycle. In it, a harp itself has the ability to 'hear', and listens to the specific chants from its owner, the Dagda, a *sidhe* god. The Dagda had previously 'bound' melodies into this particular harp with a certain charm or spell, so it could then only respond to his call, and to no other. From *Catha Maige Tuired II* ('The Second Battle of Mag Tured'):

> Now Lug and the Dagda and Ogma pursued the Fomorians, for they had carried off the Dagda's harper whose name was Uaitne. Then they reached the banqueting house in which were Bres, son of Elatha and Elatha, son of Delbaeth. There hung the harp on the wall. That is the harp in which the Dagda had bound the melodies so that they sounded not until by his call he summoned them forth; when he said this below:
>
> > Come Daurdabla!
> > Come Coir-cethar-chuir!
> > Come summer, come winter!
> > Mouths of harps and bags and pipes!
>
> Now that harp had two names, Daur-da-bla, 'Oak of two greens', and Coir-cethar-chuir, 'Four angled music'. Then the harp went forth from the wall, killed nine men, and came to the Dagda.[19]

The Dagda then plays his special harp; this aspect of the reference is further discussed in chapter 4. The above example also illustrates the Dagda making reference to the seasons and the concept of a 'four-angled music'.

The supernatural music of a silver musical branch is also featured, namely from *Immram Brain* ('The Voyage of Bran'). Here, Bran hears mysterious music and soon afterwards a musical branch materialises in his environs:

> At last he fell asleep at the music, such was its sweetness. When he awoke from his sleep, he saw close by him a branch of silver with white blossoms, nor was it easy to distinguish its bloom from that branch. Then Bran took the branch in his hand to his royal house . . . [then they all] saw a woman in strange raiment.[20]

In this situation, the musical branch appears to manifest itself from nowhere. We later discover that this silver branch is an Otherworld gift from a *sidhe* woman, who then sings fifty poetic verses to him and invites him to her Otherworld paradise.

King Cormac also has an encounter with a musical branch in his journey to the Otherworld of *tir tairngiri* ('the Land of Promise'). Cormac receives an unusual Otherworld visitor to his court one day, a *sidhe* man named Manannan:

> A branch of silver with three golden apples was on his shoulder. Delight and amusement enough it was to listen to the music made by the branch.[21]

The instrumentality of the branch is portrayed here, as the branch plays music on its own, reflecting the Otherworld status of Manannan. Cormac later follows Manannan to the Otherworld.

From *Serglige Con Chulainn* ('The Wasting Sickness of Cuchulainn'), a late-eleventh century tale, we have what appears to be a tree with an inherent musicality of its own, in the purely Otherworld dimension of *mag mell*. Loeg, Cuchulainn's charioteer, reports back as to what he has seen there:

> A tree at the doorway to the court
> Fair its harmony
> A tree of silver before the setting sun
> Its brightness like that of gold.[22]

From the *Dindshenchas*, the poem entitled 'Loch Garman' further illustrates the concept of a tree having an inherent musicality. Cathair, a regional king of Erin from Alenn, has an unusual dream, and asks the high king's druid to interpret it for him:

> This is the stately music
> that was in the crown of the enduring tree –
> thy noble eloquence, lovelier thereby,
> when appeasing a multitude.[23]

The druid interprets this vision of a musical tree in the dream as symbolising Cathair's future destiny, which was to be king of Ireland one day, and have great eloquence of speech.

The inherent instrumentality of water in a purely Otherworld dimension is also portrayed in certain instances, where it is implied that the water itself is to be seen as an 'instrument' with its own music. With such a viewpoint, the unknown, mysterious supernatural performer from the Otherworld is using the water as its 'instrument'. An example would be the fountains with their musical streams in the primal Otherworld.

The human voice is probably the very oldest musical instrument known to humanity. Vocal music is portrayed in some of the references as part of an Otherworld context. This singing is often from supernatural personages like angels or *sidhe*-folk, as one might expect, or it simply occurs out of nowhere, from a mysterious, unknown source.

Illustratory comparative material

Instruments that involve the supernatural Otherworld dimension also occur in Scottish and Welsh sources. Sanger and Kinnaird, in *Tree of Strings*, relate two versions of the Scottish tale 'How Music First Came to the Western Isles' which features a harp:

> It tells how a boy found a strange musical instrument floating in the sea. When he pulled it out and held it so that the wind caught the strings, it made a wonderful sound. The boy sat fingering the strings, day after day, but could not find the way to make the magical music again. His poor mother, in desperation, went to a 'dubd-sgoiler'– a practitioner of the Black Arts – to beg him either to give her son the skill of harping, or to quell his desire for it. 'Give me your soul', said the 'dubdsgoiler', 'and I will put the skill of music into your boy; or, give me your body and I will quench his longing for it.' 'My soul is to you here and now,' said the woman, 'and the skill of music for my boy.' When she went home she found her son, his face lit up with joy, making wonderful music on the harp. But when he found what his mother had sacrificed in order that he should receive the gift, he was torn with horror and remorse.[24]

The Eigg version of the story says that from then on, during the daytime, the happiness of his music would draw the eagle from the dove, but when night fell the boy's harping would sob with the agony of his mother's lost soul. The Skye version of the tale says that when he discovered his mother's pact with the powers of darkness, from that moment he played only music so sad that the birds in the air and fish in the sea stopped to listen, and that this is the reason why it can be so difficult at times for anyone to draw joyful music from a harp.[25]

From Wales, the following account was given to Evans-Wentz earlier this century by the Rev. John Davis of the Gower Peninsula in Glamorganshire. It features the sweet music and dancing of the 'Verry Volk' while they have a fairy feast:

I heard the following story many years ago ... The tenant on the Eynonsford Farm here in Gower had a dream one night, and in it thought he heard soft, sweet music and the patter of dancing feet. Waking up, he beheld his cow shed ... filled with a multitude of little beings, about one foot high, swarming all over his fat ox, and they were preparing to slaughter the ox. He was so surprised that he could not move.[26]

The voice is also a musical instrument and often in fairylore accounts, the unsuspecting mortal who encounters the fairies will describe a group of beings dancing in a circle, usually singing and playing musical instruments. In the above example, the sleeping mortal was made aware of the fairies' presence through a dream, and then awoke to discover them.[27]

The German mystic monk Blessed Henry Suso (*c.* 1295–1366), a contemporary of Yorkshire mystic Richard Rolle of Hampole, 'not only heard and saw angels playing rebecs, fiddles, and harps ... he joined with them in round-dances, such as Dante had recently described in his *Paradiso*. Suso, a follower of Meister Eckhart, lived as a monk and wandering preacher ... '[28] One of his mystic visions involves vocal music in Heaven, with the voices as musical instruments:

> Now, on the night before the feast of All Angels, it seemed to him in a vision that he heard angelic strains and sweet heavenly melody ... [He heard] a portion of the song which the dear elect saints will sing joyously at the last day, when they shall see themselves confirmed in the everlasting bliss of eternity. At another time, on the same festival, after he had spent many hours in contemplating the joys of the angels ... there came to him a youth who bore himself as though he were a heavenly musician sent to him by God.[29]

Suso then joined the young heavenly musician and the other angels, singing and taking part with them in circle dances.

The story of how bamboo harps were to become the basis of all music on Bali comes from the following Balinese legend, as told by Swiss ethnomusicologists Theo Meier and Ernst Schlager in *Nada Brahma: The World is Sound*, by Joachim-Ernst Berendt:

> Lord Shiva once sat on Mt. Meru ... Out of the distance, he heard soft tones of a kind he had never heard before. He summoned Narada, the wise man, sending him to the Himalayan hermitages to find out where the tones were coming from. Narada went on his way and finally reached the hermitage of the sage Dereda. There the tones sounded stronger. He entered the hermitage The hermit told him that the wondrous tones

66

were, indeed, coming from his land. The hermitage was surrounded by a bamboo grove. Dereda had made holes in the bamboo canes to tie them together. Now, when the wind blew through the holes, the most diverse tones would be sounded. Dereda said he had been so delighted by this discovery that he had tied a bunch of bamboo canes with holes together and hung them up in a tree [creating a sound box like an aeolian harp], for no other reason than to produce a continual, pleasant sound. Narada returned to Lord Shiva to report to him what he had learned. Shiva decided that these bamboo harps were to form the basis of all music on Bali.[30]

Instruments from everyday life but with Otherworld influence

The following references do not occur in a purely supernatural Otherworld *per se*, like those above. However, in the context of normal everyday life, musical instruments are sometimes portrayed as having supernatural characteristics. This situation often occurs as the result of an intervention from the Otherworld in some manner.

The following reference, from the tenth-century tale entitled *Inni diata cuslinn Brighde ocus Aidhed mic Dhichoime* ('Whence is St Brigit's Pipe, and the Death of Dichoim's Son'), is part of the cycle of the kings literature. Also entitled 'King Eochaid Has Horse's Ears', the focus here is on King Eochaid, and a short synopsis will now be given. In this tale, King Eochaid had an unusual disability, that of being born with horse's ears. In a desperate attempt to hide this condition from his kingdom, he would kill every man who would shave him. One day, one of the shavers tried to kill him first, and the two of them then made a pact – the young shaver, Mac Dichoime, could remain, as long as he did not reveal the secret. The shaver eventually got very ill, but was then cured of the burden of having to keep the situation a secret by the spilling of his blood near a grove of tree saplings which 'overheard' him. Soon afterwards, a harper with his fellow musicians from Munster stopped at the site for a rest on their journey. The harper's harp 'heard' from the tree saplings the secret of the king. Ironically, the musicians were on their way to play for King Eochaid's court anyway, and the harper's harp revealed the secret that the king had horse's ears which it had overheard from the saplings. Furious, King Eochaid tied up the musicians who insisted on their innocence. Eventually realising that the tree saplings had revealed the secret and not the young shaver Mac Dichoime, the king freed the musicians and rewarded the harper. Then, the young shaver Mac Dichoime went back to the site of the grove of trees and made himself a double pipe from them, and later became king himself.[31] Mac Dichoime so greatly valued the special pipe made from the same grove that he never lost sight of it throughout his kingship.

In this story, the harp of the Munster harper overheard the secret from the tree saplings and then revealed it at the king's court. The harp is portrayed here as having some supernatural characteristics, although the context occurs as part of everyday life. The grove of tree saplings is also portrayed as being unusual. The reader is left with the clear impression that the double pipe of Mac Dichoime had much to do with his eventually becoming king himself.

Bells are sometimes portrayed as having unusual qualities as part of everyday life, especially in the saint's Lives. Here we often see examples of a tongueless bell sounding on its own, again, this miracle of God again reflecting the otherworldly status of the Christian Heaven. From *Betha Colmain* ('The Life of Colman'), we have a situation in everyday Christian life where a tongueless bell sounds of its own accord at a particular location. This is taken as a signal from God that a monastery is to be built there. In a similar instance, thirty monks were sent by an angel from St Mochuda to go and find St Colman's community at Lann. They set out with the tongueless bell of St Mochuda, and the bell suddenly sounds after a period of seven years, when they arrive at Lann.[32]

In another instance, a bell also sounds of its own accord, yet it *does* have a clapper. This occurrence is not considered to be a usual one in the course of everyday Christian life, as some kind of divine intervention is needed to create such an event. In *Betha Kieran* ('The Life of St Kieran'), St Patrick gives St Kieran a bell, and tells him it will sound at the site of the special well of Uaran, which it does.[33]

Another unusual situation involving a bell in everyday life, yet with Otherworld influence, is from *Betha Colmain* ('The Life of St Colman'). Here, the Finnfaidech ('sweet-sounding bell') from Heaven miraculously materialises out of thin air.[34]

The *Tripartite Life of Patrick* also presents the reader with examples of the power of a saint's bell. Here, a birch tree grows through the handle of the bell of St Patrick, called the Bethachan:

Patrick flings his handbell under a thick brake there. A birch [bethe] grows through its handle. It is this that Dicuill found, the Bethechan, Patrick's bell, a little bell of iron, which is now in the Oratory of Dicuill.[35]

The power of the Bethechan after St Patrick's death is also mentioned, where it is portrayed as still having significant power at Doomsday to summon those to be saved.[36]

Occasionally, a saint's bell is portrayed as causing supernatural events to occur as part of a curse upon those who would not convert to Christianity, or as having a central role in banishing demons. From *Betha Fechin Febair* ('The Life of St Fechin of Febair') we have an example of a king's horses and herds which were killed by the power of St Fechin's bell:

Of a time when Fechin was learning with Presbyter Naithi in Achad Conairi, he is set one day to keep the meadow lest it should be stripped bare by strangers' cattle. Thereafter the king's horses and herds are put into it in spite of Fechin. Fechin cursed them, and struck his bell at them, so that they found death therewith. When the king heard that, he comes before Fechin, and flung himself on his knees, and sought forgiveness of his sins. Fechin gives him absolution, and brought his horses and his herds back to life; and God's name and Fechin's were magnified by that miracle.[37]

Occasionally, the human voice is portrayed in everyday life with some kind of Otherworld influence(s). Usually this is portrayed as being part of a chant or incantation of some kind, such as when Cu Roi chants a protective spell over his home from abroad, or when St Columcille chants a hymn to protect a grove of trees from fire.

Illustratory comparative material

The English and Scottish Popular Ballads by F. J. Child has a ballad entitled 'The Twa Sisters', in which we encounter a harp that 'accuses' someone of a crime, as it was made out of the bones of the victim. In this ballad, a young maiden, wooed by a knight, is drowned by her jealous elder sister. Her body is found by a harper, who, to quote Sanger and Kinnaird:

in some versions makes a harp from her bones; in others he uses her finger bones for tuning-pins; and, in some, strings his harp with locks of her golden hair. At a feast, which is sometimes the wedding feast of the elder sister and the knight, the harp then magically accuses the murderess:

> He leant his harp against a stane,
> And straught it began to play its lane.
>
> O yonder sits my faither the king
> And yonder sits my mither the queen.
>
> And yonder sits by brother Hugh
> And by him my William, sweet and true.
>
> And the lasten tune that the harp did play
> Was 'Wae tae my sister, wha drooned me.'[38]

So, the harp announced that her elder sister had drowned her, at a most embarrassing moment. This motif of the supernatural power of a harp to reveal a secret is reminiscent of the early Irish example where a harp revealed, at the most inopportune time, that King Eochaid had horse's ears.

The Welsh tale *Culhwch and Olwen* also addresses the issue of a supernatural harp. In it, the Chief Giant Ysbaddaden asks who has come to seek his daughter. Culhwch, son of Cilydd, responds that it is he. Then, Ysbaddaden proceeds to give Culhwch a very long list of demands, one of which is to locate the magic harp of Teirtu, an extremely difficult task. Yet, Culhwch claims that, for him, it would be easy:

> [Ysbaddaden]: ... 'There is that [which] thou will not get. The harp of Teirtu to entertain me ... When a man pleases, it will play of itself; when one would have it so, it will be silent. He [Teirtu] will not give it of his own free will, nor can thou compel him.' [Culhwch]: 'It is easy for me to get that, though [you say] it is not easy.'[39]

Next, Ysbaddaden requests that Cuhlwen find 'the birds of Rhiannon, they that wake the dead and lull the living to sleep, must I have to entertain me on that night.'[40]

The characteristics of the harp of Teirtu, an instrument that plays by itself when it suits its owner, is somewhat similar to the early Irish reference to the Dagda summoning his special harp from the wall, an instrument that only responds to his specific call. These tales also seem to imply that such instruments are not ordinary ones in the normal course of everyday life.

Instruments in everyday life

We will now examine those references which specifically mention certain musical instruments as part of everyday life. In the early Irish sources, everyday life presents us with many examples of instruments and their use, often as a key part of fairs or festivals. From the place-lore poem entitled 'Carmun', part of the *Dindshenchas*, several instruments are noted at the Carmun fair:

> Pipes, [*pipai*], fiddles, [*fidli*], gleemen, [*fir cengail*],
> bones-players [*cnamfir*], and bag-pipers, [*cuslennaig*],
> a crowd hideous, noisy, profane,
> shriekers and shouters ...
> ... Tales of death and slaughter,
> strains of music ...[41]

> These are the Fair's great privileges: trumpets, [*stuic*],
> harps, [*cruitti*], [*cuirn chroes-tholla*] hollow-throated horns,
> pipers, [*cuisig*], timpanists [*timpaig*] unwearied,
> poets and meek musicians ...[42]

The harp is frequently mentioned in many situations in everyday life, as one might expect in early Ireland. The court of a king was a popular context in which harpers might play. It was said that the three kinds of music that kings enjoyed most were the music of harps, the melody of timpans and the humming of Trogan's son Fer-tuinne.[43]

Vocal music, as either singing or chanting, also occurs fairly frequently as part of everyday life experience.

The natural elements as 'instruments' are mentioned frequently in the monastic hermit poetry, as a celebration of all of God's creation. These references speak of the 'music of the pines' or the 'music' of the birds' singing, for example.

The music of chariots is mentioned in the context of the Taltiu fair in the *Dindshenchas*:

> A fair with gold, with silver, with games, with music of chariots.[44]

The 'music' of the swords in battle is illustrated in the following example from *Cath Maige Rath* ('The Battle of Moira'):

> 'Hateful to me now,' said the spy, 'is the varied music I hear throughout the battle, the swish of the swords in the hands of heroes.[45]

A unique category regarding music in an everyday context is the comparison of one instrument to another; most frequently the human voice is being compared to the sweet music of harps, for example. Another instance of such a comparison is in *Togail bruidne Da Derga* ('The Destruction of Da Derga's Hostel'):

Sweeter the music of that sword than the sweet sound of the golden pipes that drone in the royal house.[46]

The term a 'hero of a hundred songs' is made in reference to the great deeds of the warrior Conall, in the following example from the poem entitled 'Mag Luirg' from the *Dindshenchas*:

> From this deed at Cuan Cairn
> the plain received its great name:
> the Cherishing of Conall, hero of a hundred songs,
> is well-known to me without obscurity.[47]

Such comparisons seem to indicate something about how the early Irish might have perceived or valued music; in such instances a mainly positive perception of music tends to predominate.

Illustratory comparative material

Musical instruments are mentioned in many texts in world literature regarding their use in everyday life. From Japanese tradition we have the following tale involving two instruments, the *koto*, a stringed instrument like a dulcimer, and a flute. Here, a young lady is puzzled by a mysterious flute accompaniment to her music on the koto. Eventually, she finds out it is a young nobleman and they fall in love:

> Fujiwara Toyomitsu was the governor of the province of Uzen about 1,200 years ago, during the reign of Emperor Mommu. He had a daughter named Akoya who was endowed with talent and beauty. One autumn evening as she was playing a koto the faint sound of a flute was heard outside, accompanying the tune of her koto. Its tone was sweet and charming and it blended in harmony with the tune of the lady's koto in the serenity of the late autumn night. The player of the flute was a noble young man in a green dress. His name was Natori Taro, and he lived at the foot of Mt. Chitose. The two young people fell in love with each other.[48]

Probably some of the best known references to the lyre in everyday life in early western culture are those from the *Iliad* and the *Odyssey* of Homer. In the *Odyssey* the lyre is mentioned frequently; the following example illustrates a bard playing music for guests at a banquet:

> The steward returned with a very splendid lyre for Phemius, whose hap it was to play the bard for them, under compulsion. He ran his hands over the strings, plucking out an exquisite air.[49]

72

Even in Celtic societies today, many of the same instruments referred to in the early Irish sources are still in use, such as the harp, fiddle, bagpipes, whistle and so on. Storytelling and music competitions like the Gaelic Mod, the Welsh Eisteddfod and so on are important modern-day events that keep the spirit of the earlier traditions alive.

Conclusion

The instruments discussed in this chapter have been presented in three major categories: (1) those shown to be in a purely Otherworld context; (2) those presented in everyday life, yet with some Otherworld influence(s); and (3) those in everyday life, with no Otherworld influence(s) at all.

Many of the instruments listed are those which we, today, would consider a musical instrument, such as a harp, a fiddle, a bagpipe and so on. However, in this literature, we also have references where it seems that certain inanimate objects, such as swords in battle or chariot wheels, are also perceived as having musical qualities all their own.

The essential question here of course is whether the early Irish viewed swords and chariot wheels, for example, as musical instruments in some way. As an instrument is something that is played upon by a performer, the vexing question their worldview seems to challenge us in modern times with is this: what precisely *is*, or can be, a 'musical instrument'? What are the criteria that determine whether or not something is an instrument? What are the parameters? Who determines them? And how?

The viewpoint of the early Irish of what constitutes a musical instrument was clearly much broader than our view of instruments today, as we do not generally think of swords as musical, for example.

From the hermit poetry references, we seem to encounter a viewpoint of the natural elements themselves being 'instruments' of God as part of everyday life experience. Chief among these are water and trees, such as 'the music of the pines' or the 'music' of a woodland.

In the references that pertain to a purely supernatural Otherworld, whether in a primal or Christian context, we also have the imagery of a tree as having a kind of music of its own, an instrument

73

of a supernatural, unknown performer. Examples are: Bran who sees a silver musical branch materialise out of nowhere; King Cormac who sees a musical silver branch in *tir tairngiri*; Loeg who reports back to Cuchulainn about a musical tree in *mag mell*; a king's son who sees a shining musical tree in a dream.

Also from the poetry references, we have what appears to be a perspective that water, especially the waterfall, has an inherent musicality of its own. The descriptions comment on the 'psalm-pure psalms' of where a river meets the sea or of the musical waterfalls of a river, all as part of everyday life experience. In the purely Other-world examples, water is portrayed as having an inherent instrumentality all its own, of being used as a musical instrument by a supernatural, unknown performer. Examples are: the waters of Assaroe in Munster, where the music of *tir tairngiri* can be heard; the seven musical streams of the underwater Well of Connla; the five melodious streams from a shining fountain in *tir tairngiri* as heard by King Cormac; and so on.

Certain instruments have references in all three categories, and probably the most prominent in this aspect is the human *voice* itself. In category 2 – instruments with some Otherworld influence(s) – we have a rather unique situation where the voice is usually portrayed as a vocal instrument to chant a particular incantation or spell, or to bless or curse.

In category 1 – supernatural instruments – we have a range of situations, such as the singing of the leech-doctors of the *Tuatha de Danann*, the singing of angelic choirs in Heaven, or the singing of a severed head. Although certainly unusual singers, they are listed here as the *voice* itself is also a musical instrument. The following references from the collection all pertain to singing: the leech-doctors around the Well of Slane, *sidhe* singers in the fairy mounds, mermaids singing while out at sea, a singing severed head, beautiful singing of angels and archangels in the Christian Heaven, sirens on an island paradise with their alluring voices, *sidhe* beings singing on island paradise out at sea and *sidhe* birds in the primal Otherworld, and of course there are numerous instances of birds singing beautiful hymns in the Christian Heaven.

Bells as an instrument occur in all three categories. In examples from everyday life, for example, we have a portrayal of a 'sweet little bell' on a warrior's uniform in *Mesca Ulad* ('The Intoxication of the Ulstermen'). There is also mention of the bells of hermits in daily monastic life. Occasionally in everyday life experience, something unusual occurs regarding the bell; it sounds of its own accord, or assists a saint in an exorcism. In a purely supernatural context, we have one example where St Columba tells a man that in Heaven there are bells that ring of themselves every canonical hour. Other references also portray a bell as being an integral part of the Christian Heaven.

It appears that the early Irish viewpoint about the power of the bell to help exorcise demons is echoed in the writings from the first and second centuries, where it was believed that:

> demons could not endure noise ... or, above all, the sound of gongs and bells. This superstition was so deeply rooted that Christian mothers also hung little bells around their children's necks and on their wrists to keep away the harmful influence of the demons. Chrysostom (a Church Father) had to point out with great severity that only the protection which came from the Cross could keep the children from harm.[50]

It seems that Chrysostom may have felt that this widespread belief in the power of bells to ward off evil was rooted in earlier pagan practices, and warned the Christian mothers about them, implying that they did not really need the bells to ward off evil, only the Cross. Ironically, it seems as though the early Irish church may have disagreed with Chrysostom, judging from the frequent use of the bell in monastic life, and especially the many portrayals of the primacy of the power of the bell in the descriptions of saints exorcising demons in the saints' lives. This may indicate that the early Irish church acknowledged the power of the bell to assist in the banishing of evil. It seems as though they did not necessarily view the Cross and bells as opposing each other, as from these references it appears that they used the bells *on behalf of* the power of the Cross.

Harps are mentioned as being part of everyday life experience, and usually with a positive connotation. One unusual example is where a harp reveals a secret. Another example involving a harp fits the purely supernatural category, where the Dagda chants to a harp on the wall; it immediately responds to his special chant only, and then comes to him on its own.

Once more, as in Chapter 2, we see a continuity across what would otherwise seem the distinct areas of the otherworldly and the mundane and the supernatural and the natural. This is true whether the context of the reference is overtly Christian or primal. By appearing in all three categories, a single instrument, like a harp for example, can convey through this complex of literary references a sense of the unbroken line that joins the supernatural Otherworld and the everyday, mundane world.

Notes

1. *RIA, A Dictionary of the Irish Language*, (Dublin, 1913–57) C, pp. 552, 562.
2. Sanger, K., and Kinnaird, A., *Tree of Strings: crann nan teud*, (Temple, Midlothian: Kinmor Music, 1992), pp. 12–13.
3. Sachs, C., *The History of Musical Instruments* (London: Oxford University Press, 1942), p. 268.
4. Rimmer, J., *The Irish Harp* (Cork, 1977), p. 20.
5. Ibid.
6. Ibid., p. 17.
7. Joyce, P. W., *A Social History of Ancient Ireland*, vol. I (London: Longmans, Green & Co., 1903), p. 579.
8. Ibid., p. 573.
9. *Ancient Laws* and *Institutes* of Wales, *Anomalous Laws*, c.ii, s. 29, p. 396 (fol. edn).
10. Farmer, H. G., *A History of Music in Scotland* (London, 1947), p. 26.
11. Buckley, A., 'What is the Tiompan?', *Jahrbuch für Musikalische Volks und Volkerkunde*, 9 (Berlin, 1978), pp. 53–88.
12. Bannerman, J., 'The Clarsach and the Clarsair', *Scottish Studies*, 30 (Edinburgh, 1991), p. 9.
13. Collinson, F., *The Bagpipe, Fiddle and Harp* (Blanefield, Stirlingshire, 1983) no page given (facsimile of chapters from his earlier book *The Traditional and National Music of Scotland*, London: Routledge & Kegan Paul, 1966).
14. St Jerome, 'Epistle to Dardanus', *S. Eusebii Hieronymi Stridonensis Presbyteri opera omnia*, ed. Abbé Migne t. xi., p. 213.
15. Cannon, R., *The Highland Bagpipe and its Music* (Edinburgh, 1988), p. 7.
16. Donnelly, S., 'The Warpipes in Ireland', *Ceol*, V (1) (Dublin, 1981), pp. 19–24.
17. Purser, J., *Scotland's Music* (Edinburgh: Mainstream, 1992), p. 21.
18. Thurneysen, R., *A Grammar of Old Irish* (Dublin, 1980), pp. 62, 103.
19. Stokes, W., 'Cath Maige Tured II', *RC* 12 (Paris, 1891), p. 109.
20. Nutt, A. and Meyer, K., *The Voyage of Bran, son of Febal* (London, 1895), p. 2.
21. Stokes, W., 'Cormac's Adventure in the Land of Promise', *Irische Texte*, Series 3 (Leipzig, 1891), p. 193.

22. Gantz, J., *EIMS* (London, 1981), pp. 155–78.
23. Gwynn, E., *MD* III (Dublin, 1913), p. 183.
24. Sanger, and Kinnaird, *Tree of Strings*, p. 3.
25. Ibid.
26. Evans-Wentz, W., *The Fairy-Faith in Celtic Countries* (New York: University Books, 1966; orig. 1911), p. 159.
27. Ibid.
28. Godwin, Jocelyn, *Harmonies of Heaven and Earth* (Rochester, VT: Inner Traditions International, 1987), p. 72.
29. Ibid.
30. Berendt, J., *Nada Brahma: The World is Sound* (London, 1988), p. 176. [*Note*: For futher information regarding the Balinese legend about the origin of the bamboo harp, see Schlager, Ernst, 'Rituelle Siebenton-Musik auf Bali', *Forum Musicologicum*,Hans Oesch ed., (Bern, 1976).
31. Meyer, K., 'Stories and Songs from Irish manuscripts IV', *Otia Merseiana*, III (Liverpool, 1903), pp. 46–54.
32. Meyer, K., *Life of Colman* (Dublin, 1911), p. 27.
33. O'Grady, S., 'Life of St. Kieran', *SG* (London, 1892), pp. 2–3.
34. Meyer, *Life of Colman*, p. 65.
35. Stokes, W., *Tripartite Life of Patrick* (London, 1887), pp. 248–9.
36. Ibid., p. 120.
37. Stokes, W., 'Life of St Fechin of Fore', *RC* 12 (Paris, 1891), pp. 324–5.
38. Sanger and Kinnaird, *Tree of Strings*, p. 8.
39. Jones, G. and Jones, T., *The Mabinogion*, Engl. trans. (London: J. M. Dent; 1993 edn; orig. 1949), p. 97.
40. Ibid.
41. Gwynn, E., *MD*, III (Dublin, 1913), p. 21.
42. Ibid., p. 19.
43. O'Grady, S. (ed.), *'Accalam na Senorach'*, *SG*, II (London, 1892), p. 112.
44. Gwynn, E., *MD*, IV (Dublin, 1923), p. 151.
45. Marstrander, C., 'Cath Muigi Rath Anso', *Eriu*, V (London, 1911), p. 243.
46. Gantz, J., *EIMS* (London, 1981), p. 89.
47. Gwynn, E., *MD*, III (Dublin, 1913), p. 399.
48. Dorson, Richard, *Folk Legends of Japan* (Rutland, VT, 1962), p. 146.
49. Homer, *The Odyssey*, Book I, trans. T. E. Shaw, Penguin Classics reprint (London, 1992), p. 5.
50. Quasten, Johannes, *Music and Worship in Pagan and Christian Antiquity* (Washington, DC: National Association of Pastoral Musicians, 1983; English trans. of 1973 German orig.), p. 16.

4

Effects

T HE EFFECTS OF MUSIC as described in this literature range from great appreciation of it in everyday life to quite dramatic portrayals of its effects on the listener. These effects may be joyful or ecstatic, healing, peaceful or relaxing, or they may be melancholic, destructive or even deadly. Similar effects of music are described, whether the context is primal or Christian, or whether it is in the mundane, everyday world or the Otherworld.

On the evidence of this literature, the early Irish were deeply concerned with the various effects of music. It seems that the effects of music were noticeable and important to them, so much so that they consistently included such descriptions in their tales, saint's lives, Christian hermit poetry and so on.

In this chapter, these descriptions are divided into two main categories: (1) The supernatural or Otherworld effects of music, and (2) the effects of music in everyday, mundane life. If these two categories are placed side by side, many of the same types of effects listed in each of the two categories are noticeable, such as joy or ecstasy, melancholy, healing and so on.

However, it is also noticeable that the more extreme or dramatic the effect of the music on the listener(s), the more likely it is to be portrayed in an otherworldly context, whether it is primal or Christian. It seems that the degree of supernatural influence tends to determine how dramatic the effect on the listener is. So, in those references where the music is portrayed as being heard directly in an Otherworld dimension, the effects are often shown to be rather extreme, as compared to those in everyday life.

Introduction

But first it is appropriate to add a few words about how a society such as early Ireland might have viewed music and its effects. Many of the references in this literature seem to reflect a different worldview than that of our modern-day, western society where materialism and rationalism are key components of the predominating philosophy. Regarding these early Irish sources, when the effects of music are portrayed, one will rarely see them described as merely 'beautiful' or 'haunting', for instance, as a modern-day concert-goer might reflect after hearing a certain piece of music. Often in these references, the effects of music are portrayed as affecting individuals in the audience in quite a dramatic manner, as beyond mere 'commentary' on the performance itself. So one must try to consider *their* worldview and the possible role of music in it in order to do this material justice.

As far as we can tell, music has always been important to humanity, and musicologist A. P. Merriam in *The Anthropology of Music* states that 'there is probably no other human cultural activity which is so all-pervasive and which reaches into, shapes, and often controls so much of human behavior.'[1] Of particular interest to the early Irish period is the question of how they might have perceived the role of music and its effects in their culture. Merriam addresses this issue for a 'primal society', taking into account that much important knowledge in primal cultures is commonly stored in heroic tales, sagas, poetry, place-lore or songs,[2] precisely the sort of literature from which many of the references in this book are drawn. Ethnomusicologist Nettl believes that, in contrast to modern Western viewpoints, such primal societies did not necessarily view music as an abstract entity:

> The concept of music as 'beautiful' seems to be generally undeveloped ... Informants speak of songs as being 'good'. No doubt the prevailing functionality of music is responsible for this designation, for beauty is an end in itself, while 'good' implies usefulness for a specific purpose: a song may be good for curing, good for dancing, etc. ... some informants describe songs as 'powerful', probably because the songs have some sort of supernatural function.[3]

Breandan O'Madagain also comments on how the early Irish may have possibly viewed music and its effects in their society:

And so music was a supernatural instrument of power, as well as being universally the medium for communication with the supernatural. The Irish and Scottish Gaelic tradition has clear echoes of such ideas. The gods, later the *Sí*, were closely associated with music and its origin, and the hallmark of their music was its transcendant beauty. They sometimes favoured mortals with the gift of music, usually instrumental, but sometimes vocal.[4]

So it appears that the early Irish worldview considered that music was – or could be – a vehicle for a divine or supernatural influence, and could therefore affect the listener accordingly.

This seems to be borne out in the example cited earlier, in which St Patrick and the clergy, after hearing fairy music from a *sidhe* harper, all fell into a trance-like sleep state to the music in spite of themselves. Upon awakening, they admit to the music's great effect on them and begin a lively debate, with St Patrick implicitly acknowledging the supernatural power(s) of the effects of the music by cautioning the clergy about the danger of becoming 'inordinately addicted to it'.[5]

Bearing in mind how a primal society like that of early Ireland might have viewed music and its perceived effects on them, let us look at the examples that illustrate the first of our two catgories, the supernatural effects of music.

Supernatural effects: primal contexts

We have quite a number of references in primal contexts that include supernatural effects of the music on the listener in some way. These effects include joy, melancholy, a trance-like sleep state, protection, prosperity, healing, danger and so on.

The Three Strains: *suantraigi, genntraigi, golltraigi*

So important are the three strains and the corresponding categories of effects that a story of their origin is told in the *Tain bo Froech* ('The Cattle Raid of Froech'), where musicians play for the court of King Ailill:

'Let the harpers play for us,' said Ailill to Froech. 'Indeed, let them,' said Froech ... The harpers played, then, and twelve men died of weeping and sorrow. The three harpers were fair and melodious, for they were

80

the fair ones of Uaithne, three brothers, Goltraide and Gentraide and Suantraide, and Boand of the Side was their mother. They were named after the music that Uaithne, the Dagda's harper, played. At first, the music was sad and mournful because of the sharpness of the pains; then it was joyful and happy because of the two sons; finally, it was quiet and peaceful because of the heaviness of the birth of the last son, and he was named for the last third of the music. After that, Boand woke from her sleep. 'Receive your three sons, O passionate Uaithne,' she said, 'for the music of sleep and laughter and sorrow will reach the cattle and women of Ailill and Medb that bring forth young. Men will die from hearing their music.' The harpers ceased to play, then.[6]

In this general account the music of the three strains and their effects have supernatural origins attributed by the story itself: *gentraide*, for a joyful strain, *goltraide*, for a melancholy strain, and *suantraide* for a sleep strain. This three-strain motif and its supernatural origin has become a theme of its own in Irish folklore.

The following example from *Cath Maige Tuired II* ('The Second Battle of Mag Tured') illustrates Lugh, a legendary god of early Ireland, playing the three strains:

'Let a harp be played for us,' said the hosts. So the warrior Lugh played a sleep-strain for the hosts and for the king the first night. He cast them into sleep from that hour to the same time on the following day. He played a wail-strain, so that they were crying and lamenting. He played a laugh-strain, so that they were in merriment and joyance.[7]

A further example, cited in full earlier, includes the three-strain motif; it is from *Comracc Con Culainn re Senbecc* ('Combat of Cuchulainn with Senbecc'). As you may recall, the hero Cuchulainn encounters a tiny man in a bronze boat with a harp on the river Boyne, who then plays the three strains for him.[8]

One may note that in each of these accounts of the three strains, a supernatural origin for the music is implied by the stories themselves, and that the effects are rather dramatic.

The following subsections give more specific accounts of the effects of music on the listener.

Trance-like sleep effect(s): *suantraigi*

Music is often said to cause the listener(s) to 'fall asleep', that is to enter an altered state of consciousness, often for a period of days. The literature of early medieval Ireland includes numerous references to the power of music to put the listener into a trance-like sleep state, which is portrayed as a supernatural effect. There is a distinct impression that the listener cannot help himself, in spite of his efforts to remain in the state of normal, waking consciousness.

The following ninth-century tale *Aislinge Oenguso* ('The Dream of Oengus') shows such an effect on King Oengus, who had a dream one night in which an unknown spirit woman came to him and played music to him on her timpan, after which he fell asleep:

> and then he saw a timpan in her hand, the sweetest ever, and she played for him until he fell asleep.[9]

Far from this being a simple lullaby or a merely relaxing tune, King Oengus later becomes obsessively 'haunted' by this dream. It keeps repeating itself, with its powerful musical effects, again putting him into a trance-like sleep state.

From the *Metrical Dindshenchas* we have a description of two fairy birds from the Otherworld singing to the host, putting them all to sleep:

> Bruide son of Derg from Cruachan Dubthire ... and his foster-brother Luan ... used to visit Estiu in the shape of two birds, and sing a plaintive song to the host till it put them to sleep ... Then they chanted to the host a song, shrill, wistful, unceasing, till all the host fell asleep at the song of the fairy folk.[10]

The effects of the music to induce this special trance-like sleep state were often seen to be quite dramatic. Descriptions of it often include mention of how the very sick, the wounded, the depressed, the dying, women in childbirth and so on would be quickly soothed and put into a powerful trance-like sleep state by the music.

One such example, quoted earlier, is from *Accalam na Senorach* ('Colloquy of the Ancients'), from the fifteenth-century Book of Lismore. Here, one may note that the legendary *sidhe* musician Cascorach puts St Patrick and his clergy to sleep, with his exquisitely beautiful music.[11]

Also from the *Accalam na Senorach*, we have the story of a talented *sidhe* musician himself being given as a special gift by Bodb Derg, the King of the Fairies of Munster, to the three sons of King Lugaid:

> 'A gift from me to them,' said Bodb Derg: 'a good minstrel that I have (Fer-tuinne mac Trogain is his name) and though saws were being plied where there were women in sharpest pains of childbirth, and brave men that were wounded early in the day, nevertheless would such [people] sleep to the fitful melody that he makes.[12]

Clearly, the powerful effects of his music were very highly valued by King Bodb Derg and the musician was deemed worthy of special status.

From *Immram Brain* ('The Voyage of Bran') the phenomenon of what I call 'mysterious or unknown music' is portrayed as having the power to put the listener into a trance-like sleep state. Here, no musician is present at all, and no instrument is seen, only the sound of sweet music emanating from a mysterious source. You may recall the reference quoted earlier where Bran is portrayed as being in his royal courtyard one day, and hears mysterious music. He then falls asleep to it despite himself; upon awakening, he finds a musical branch.[13]

Another example of mysterious, unknown music and its sleep-inducing effects is from the tale *Immram Curaig Maile Duin* ('The Voyage of Mael Duin'). Mael Duin and his fellow clergymen encounter an island while travelling out at sea. It is the site of a noble *sidhe* woman's fort and the musical net at its entrance:

> She went from them and closed the noble pleasant fort:
> her net, manifesting mighty power, chanted good
> harmonious music.

> Her musical choir lulled them to sleep, as had been
> enjoined. Next day she came to them – a woman unshamed.

> Thus they were, in the same condition, till the third
> day; the noble woman's music used to play for them,
> but no banqueting hall was seen.[14]

Like Bran, such music emanating from a mysterious source seems to transport Mael Duin and his clergymen into another dimension, causing sleep to come upon them, a trance-like state of consciousness that is different from everyday awareness.

Some of the examples include certain emergency preventative measures taken to *avoid* falling into a trance-like sleep state as a result of hearing the music. Desperate to stay awake, mortals and immortals alike in this literature resort to such measures as putting melted wax in their ears, putting a sharp tip of a sword to the forehead to stay awake, putting fingers in the ears and simply running away as fast as possible from the music.

Sometimes such measures are taken as part of warfare, for example to enable one's own side to escape unharmed while the enemy falls into a deceptive sleep induced by a harper's enticing melodies.

Harp music is even used to aid a seduction. In the following reference, the gifted harper Craiphtine is portrayed in such a role. It is from the tale *Orgain Denna Rig* ('The Destruction of Dind Rig') from the cycle of King Labraid:

> Scoriath had a daughter, whose name was Moriath. They were guarding her carefully, for no husband fit for her had been found ... Her mother was keeping her. The mother's two eyes never slept at the same time, for one of the two was watching her daughter ... (however) the damsel loved Labraid. There was a plan between her and him. Scoriath held a great feast ... This is the plan they made – after the drinking, Craiphtine should play the slumber-strain, so that her mother should fall asleep and Labraid should reach the chamber. Now that came to pass. Craiphtine hid not his harp that night, and the loving couple came together.[15]

Here, the beautiful strains of Craiphtine's harp put the mother to sleep, so that the lovers Labraid and Moriath came together.

Joyful or ecstatic effects: *genntraigi*

Probably the best known example of the effect of music causing such ecstasy that certain members of the audience 'died of yearning' is from *Tain bo Froech* ('The Cattle Raid of Froech'). Froech's horn-players are here described entertaining King Ailill of Connacht with quite alarming effects:

> Froech's hornplayers preceded him into the court, then, and such was their playing that thirty of Ailill's dearest ones died of yearning.[16]

Another clear example of music causing great joy is from *Cath Maige Mucrama* ('The Battle of Mag Mucrama') where Eogan and King Lugaid go to visit Art, son of Conn:

> as they came along the flat land by the river, in a clump of yew that overhung a certain rapid water they heard music. Back to king Oilioll then they convey a wee man whom they had plucked out of the clump, in order that the king ... should arbitrate between them: a man it was with three strings to his timpan. 'What is your name?' they had asked, and 'Fer fi, son of Eogabal', he had answered. 'What has turned you back?' said Oilioll. 'Quarreling we are about this man.' 'And what manner of man is this?' asked king Oilioll. 'A good timpanist.' 'Let him play his music for us,' Oilioll said; and the musician said, 'it shall be done.' ... he played the *gentraighe*, or laughter-strain, so forcing them all into a cachination such that it was barely but their very lungs became visible.[17]

Another example portraying the joyful effects of music comes from *Immram Brain* ('The Voyage of Bran') where the effects of the music create an overall atmosphere of ecstatic joy for the listener, as described by a mysterious *sidhe* woman to Bran:

> Colours of every hue gleam
> throughout the soft familiar fields;
> ranked around the music, they are
> ever joyful in the plain south of Argadnel ...
>
> Riches, treasure of every colour
> are in Ciuin, have they not been found?
> Listening to sweet music,
> drinking choicest wine.
>
> Then they row to the bright stone
> from which a hundred songs arise.
> Through the long ages it sings to the host
>
> a melody which is not sad,
> the music swells up in choruses of hundreds,
> They do not expect decay or death.[18]

Melancholy or sad effects: *golltraighi*

From the tale *Cath Maige Mucrama* we have a classic example of the tragic effects of the *golltraighi* strain. Here, King Ailill and his men listen to wee elfin harper Fer fi:

> Then he played them the *golltraighe*, or weeping-strain, reducing them to weep, wail, and bitterly to lament, until it was besought of him that he would desist.[19]

Lament was seen by the early Irish as very powerful, and involved special chanting as well as a unique type of wailing song called 'keening', which was performed, generally by women, at funerals. This custom has continued down into the present day in certain areas of western Ireland, although it is dying out. In the early Irish period, however, the 'Lament of the Fairy Women' is portrayed as having especially powerful melancholic effects upon the listener:

> they gave forth their cry, so that the people who were in the court were thrown prostrate. Hence it is that the musicians of Ireland have got the tune 'The Wail of the Fairy Women'.[20]

Another powerful example of the melancholic effects of music upon the listener occurs after a battle between the men of Leinster and the men of Munster, where the severed head of the minstrel Donn Bo is discovered by a warrior of the Munstermen. The head mourns the loss of King Fergal:

> The warrior heard a voice from a head in the wisp of rushes, and sweeter was that tune than the tunes of the world! . . . the warrior went towards it. 'Do not come to me,' says the head to him. 'What? How are you?' asks the warrior. 'I am Donn Bo,' says the head, 'and I have been pledged to make music tonight for my lord, that is, for Fergal, not by any means for Murchad. So do not annoy me.' 'Where is Fergal himself?' says the warrior. 'That is his body, the shining one . . .,' says the head. [The warrior then takes the severed head of Donn Bo to where the Leinstermen were.] 'I have brought Donn Bo's head,' the warrior answered. 'Put it on the pillar yonder,' says Murchad . . . 'make minstrelsy for us, O Donn Bo, for the sake of God's Son . . . Then Donn Bo turned his face to the wall of the house so that it might be dark to him . . . it was sweeter than any melody . . . and all the host were weeping and sad at the piteousness and misery of the music that he sang.[21]

Truly tragic effects, resulting in the suicide of a *sidhe* maiden by drowning in a river, occurred as a result of hearing the 'doleful' music of the *sidhe* mounds:

> Among the streams of the eddying bays, she perished lamentably in her boat of fair bronze. The maiden with the white hands, bright and gold, never reached the hero her lover: she leapt overboard, not mastered by a spell, but at the doleful music from the fairy mounds![22]

The effects of music to inspire or teach other musicians

In certain instances, *sidhe* musicians inspire or teach other musicians with their enchanting music. One example of this is from *Accalam na Senorach* ('Colloquy of the Ancients'), where Finn mac Cumaill and his five Fianna musicians claim to have learned 'a fairy music' from a wee harper named Cnu Deroil, who says he comes from the mountain Slievenaman:

> We were, along with Finn, between the crota and Slievenaman; when on the green bank beside us there we heard a perfect music. To him we listened then . . . the swelling music, well sustained, had lulled us all to sleep. Cumaill's son Finn . . . spoke out . . . and said: 'from where do you come, small man, that with a touch so smooth and deft play the harp?' 'Out of Slievenaman come I' . . . Four fists were the stature of the man, three in his harp so mild and dear: full-volumed was the sound of the soft delicate instrument, sweet the outpourings of his little harp. The

five musicians of the Fianna were in a body brought to him; so that in those yonder parts from Cnu ... we learned a fairy music.[23]

This is one of the few physical sightings of Cnu, as it were, as when his beautiful, ethereal music is heard, he is very rarely if ever seen in portrayals of him in this literature.

Another example is that of famed *sidhe* timpanist Cascorach, who inspires the Birds of Paradise to sing along with him in accompaniment. Initially, there is no musician present at all, only the sound of the waters of Assaroe in south-western Ireland. Inspired by the mysterious music of these waters, Cascorach then feels compelled to pick up his timpan and play for the Fianna, *in accompaniment and harmony with* the Birds of Paradise, who then join him in a chorus. So it appears that not only are mortals affected by hearing the music, but here a *sidhe* musician is also so inspired by the music of *tir tairngiri* ('The Land of Promise') that it prompts him to take specific action himself. As Caeilte, an aged Fianna warrior relates, recalling the days of old:

> they heard a sound, a gush of music, draw near from the water of Assaroe: melody for sake of which one would have abandoned the whole world's various strains ... 'it was Uainebhuidhe out of the sidh of Dorn buidhe from Cleena's Wave in the south, and with her the birds of the Land of Promise, she being minstrel of that entire country. Now is her turn to visit this sidh, and every year she takes some other one.' [said the sidh people to Fianna warrior Caeilte] ... [Then] ... Cascorach handled his timpan, and to every piece that he played the birds sang him an accompaniment. 'Many's the music we have heard,' Caeilte said, 'but music so good as that, never.'.[24]

Cleena, the minstrel of the Land of Promise, is said to visit a new *sidhe* home every year. In other Irish folklore accounts, it is said that the fairies change dwellings at every quarter festival, like Beltaine or Samhain, and often music may be involved.

Healing or therapeutic effects

Both physical and emotional healing effects are described as the direct result of hearing music. Cures from serious battle wounds, depression, pains of childbirth and so on are often described as occurring while, or shortly after, music is played. For example, in the tale *Cath Maige Tuired II* ('The Second Battle of Mag Tured'), the leech-doctors of the mythical Tuatha de Danann are portrayed as not only healing wounded men in battle, but also as restoring the dead back to life through the power of their chanting around the well of Slane:

> Diancecht and his two sons ... Octriuil and Miach, and his daughter Airmed, were singing spells over the well named Slane. Now their mortally wounded men were cast into it as soon as they would be slain. They were alive when they would come out. Their mortally wounded became whole through the might of the chant of the four leeches who were about the well.[25]

Chanting to assist what appears to be healing by an image of the cauldron of rebirth, the leech-doctors succeed in reviving those wounded and killed in battle.

Emotional healing from depression and low morale is portrayed in the following reference from *Echtra Taidg maic Cein* ('The Adventure of Teigue Son of Cian'). Teigue and his men have been out at sea on a particularily long and exhausting voyage and are very tired, depressed and demoralised. Then birds from *tir tairngiri* ('The Land of Promise') are sent to them by Cleena, minstrel of *tir tairngiri*, to sing for them:

> And they saw enter to them ... three birds ... They eat an apple apiece, and warble melody sweet and harmonize, such that the sick would sleep to it. 'Those birds,' Cleena said, 'will go with you; they will give you guidance, will make you symphony and minstrelsy and until again you reach Ireland, neither by land nor by sea shall sadness or grief afflict you.' Then the birds struck up their chorus for them ... for ... they were so grieved and sad at renouncing that fruitful country out of which they had come, these modulations gladdened and soothed them that they became merry and of good courage all.[26]

In some of the references, music is used in a comparative manner to portray a general sense of overall well-being in the community. For example, the peaceful reign of King Conaire is described as having such an abundance of good will that no one killed each other in the entire country during his reign, and that one's neighbour's voice seemed as sweet as the strings of lutes.

Relaxing effects

Music is frequently referred to as especially 'sweet' or 'lovely' in this literature, usually in descriptions of the music of the *sidhe* musicians, or music with some type of supernatural influence attached to it. For example, the music of the Otherworld is portrayed as being calm, sweet, peaceful and relaxing; hearing it in turn calms and relaxes the listener. From *Immram Brain* ('The Voyage of Bran'), the Otherworld is described as a comforting place, beneficial to the mortal individual:

> There is nothing rough or harsh, But sweet music striking the ear.[27]

From *Tochmarc Etaine* ('The Wooing of Etaine'), Midir, a man from the *sidhe* mounds, is separated from his love Etain, who was turned into a scarlet fly by the evil sorceress Fuamnach. He is lonely and feels great comfort and relaxation, however, from the 'music' of the buzzing of Etain as a fly:

> Sweeter than pipes and harps and horns was the sound of her voice and the hum of her wings.[28]

Prosperity effects

In one particular example music is portrayed as contributing directly to the overall wealth and prosperity of the community. The following reference describes the effects of the singing of the mythological singer Noisiu, of the legendary Sons of Uisliu:

> It happened one day that Noisiu was standing alone on the rampart of the stronghold of Emuin, and he was singing. The singing of the sons of Uisliu was very melodious: every cow that heard it gave two thirds more milk, and every man who heard it grew peaceful and sated with music.[29]

As cattle were one of early Irish society's greatest resources, the fact that upon hearing such music a two-thirds increase in milk production would occur seems to indicate a positive belief about the effects of music and its relationship to increasing prosperity.

Dangerous or deadly effects

At times music is portrayed as being very dangerous, if not deadly, to the listener. Aillen mac Midhna, the infamous *sidhe* musician who annually destroyed Tara (the centre of kingship in early Ireland), is portrayed as causing great destruction by first lulling everyone to sleep with his music then emitting a deadly blast of fire:

> For it was Aillen mac Midhna of the Tuatha de Danann ... used to come to Tara: the manner of his coming being with a musical timpan in his

hand ... which whenever any heard it, he would at once fall asleep.
Then, all being lulled, out of his mouth Aillen would emit a blast of fire.
It was on the solemn samhain-day he came every year, played his
timpan, and at the fairy music that he made, all would fall asleep. With
his breath he used to blow up the flame and so, during a three-and-
twenty years' spell, yearly burnt up Tara.[30]

Hero Finn mac Cumaill later took it upon himself to defend Tara,
avoiding the inevitable effects of falling asleep to the music by
putting the point of the magic spear of Fiacha mac Congha to his
forehead, thus bringing Aillen's destructions to an end.

Another example is that of the legendary *sidhe* pipers of Sid Breg,
who 'will slay, but ... cannot be slain'. From a description reported
by a spy of the 'Room of the Pipers' from the tale *Togail bruidne Da
Derga* ('Destruction of Da Derga's Hostel'), we have the following
report:

[The Room of the Pipers]: I saw an apartment with nine men in it: all
had fair, yellow hair ... overhead there were nine pipes, all four-toned
and ornamented; and the light from the ornamentation was sufficient
for the royal house. Explain that, Fer Rogain. 'Not difficult that,' said
Fer Rogain. 'They are the nine pipers that came to Conare from Sid
Breg because of the famous tales about him; their names are Bind,
Robind, Rianbind, Nibe, Dibe, Dechrind, Umal, Cumal, and Cialgrind.
They are the best pipers in the world. Nine tens will fall by them at the
first onslaught, and a man for each weapon, and a man for each man.
They will match the performance of anyone in the hostel; each of them
will boast of victories over kings and royal heirs and plundering chief-
tains, and they will escape afterwards, for combat with them is combat
with a shadow. They will slay and will not be slain, for they are of the
Side'.[31]

In one other reference, from the *Metrical Dindshenchas*, a *sidhe*
harper named Cliach played and sang 'sweet melody'. However, his
alluring music attracted a deadly dragon to that very spot, where he
was then killed:

> Here a man of the fairies made music,
> Cliach of the harp sweet sounding,
> he met a horror, amid the charm of his noble chant ...
>
> At the spot where he died of terror,
> Cliach sang sweet melody;
> there seized him there suddenly, not unprotected,
> the loathly dragon that dwells in this place.[32]

Music as having the power to 'summon'
something or someone

Here we have a category of references in which the power of music itself is enough to 'summon' a person, an animal or a group of people to the source of the music. Unlike Cliach being mauled by a dragon, that is, an involuntary summoning, here we have instances where the musician is deliberately trying to attract something, or someone, to him. In one instance, a *sidhe* harper's music summoned a magic pig. In another example, taken from *Immram Brain* ('The Voyage of Bran'), a group of *sidhe* women is summoned to the plain where the birds from the Otherworld dimension sing:

> If one has heard the sound of music, the song of the little birds from Imchiuin, a troop of women comes from the hill to the playing-field where it is.[33]

Cascorach's harp music is portrayed as having the power to summon and subdue troublesome wild wolves in the following example from *Accalam na Senorach* ('Colloquy of the Ancients'):

> He got up early next day and went to the top of the cairn, and was playing and continually thrumming his lute till the clouds of evening came down. And ... he saw three wolves coming towards him, and they lay down before him and listened to the music ... (and they went away from him at the end of the day) ... Cascorach came next day to the same cairn, and posted his followers around ... and the wolves arrived at the cairn, and lay down on their forelegs listening to the music.[34]

Other cases of music summoning someone occur when a mortal individual, often a king, hears music and then is transported or lured to another dimension. Not unlike the *suantraigi* sleep/trance category, this section focuses on the *luring to* or *transporting to* the Otherworld via music, though sleep or trance may or may not be involved. For example, King Cormac visits *tir tairngiri*, the Land of Promise, and is lured there by the enchanting music of the musical branch of Manannan, a branch of silver with three golden apples on it, as quoted in full earlier in the Chapter 3.[35]

Later on, Cormac encounters a shining fountain with five melodious streams in *tir tairngiri*:

> Then he sees in the garth a shining fountain, with five streams flowing out of it, and the hosts in turn drinking its water. Nine hazels of Buan grow over the well. The purple hazels drop their nuts into the fountain, and the five salmon which are in the fountain sever them and send their

husks floating down the streams. Now the sound of the falling of those streams was more melodious than any music that men sing.[36]

The legendary King Bran was also lured or transported to the Otherworld dimension by hearing mysterious music and then falling asleep to it:

> when he awoke from his sleep, he saw close by him a branch of silver with white blossoms ... then Bran took the branch in his hand to his royal house ... they saw a woman in strange raiment.[37]

It is interesting to note that in this instance, the *sidhe* woman comes after he has received the musical branch and heard the music. She then sings fifty poetic quatrains to Bran about the wonders of the Land of Promise, to which Bran then decides to accompany her to see for himself. Music here is again portrayed as being an important part of the Otherworld dimension.

Protective effects

In one noteworthy instance a worried landowner, King Cu Roi, chants a musical song over his home every night from wherever in the world he might be to obtain protection for his home:

> In whatever part of the world Cu Roi might be in, he sang a spell over his stronghold each night; it would then revolve as swiftly as a mill wheel turns, so that its entrance was never found after sunset.[38]

Here, the chant or spell apparently 'activates' the stronghold to revolve swiftly, so that no possible intruder might see the entrance. The motif of the revolving mill wheel also comes up in other areas of world folklore, and is generally believed to be symbolic of an image of the World Tree or world axis, *axis mundi*.

Blessings and gifts bestowed

Hearing music often motivates the listener to reward the talented musician with gifts and rewards, as portrayed in this literature. An example of this is shown in this excerpt from *Accalam na Senorach* ('The Colloquy of the Ancient Men'):

> Cascorach played his timpan, inspiring it with a certain fairy cadence; whence it is reported that to the marvellous magic music which he made for them, wounded men would have slept. Which done, jewels and things of price were given to the minstrel.[39]

Effects of music to prophesy a future king's realm

From the place-lore, we have several examples of episodes in which Cathair, regional ruler of Erin from Alenn, has a dream and asks the king's druid to interpret it for him. In one of his prophetic dreams, the music heard from the crown of a tree signifies to the king's druid that Cathair himself will one day be king of all Erin himself, and that he will have great eloquence in governing.(40) This example was quoted in full earlier.

Illustratory comparative material

In the ballads of Scotland, numerous descriptions of the effects of hearing the music of fairy harpers are illustrated. For example, the following excerpt is from Buchan's *Ballad of the North of Scotland* as told by Keith Sanger and Alison Kinnaird in their informative book *Tree of Strings: crann nan teud*:

> Mortal men or maidens were likely to succomb to the charms of faery harp-music. The evil Knight in some versions of 'Lady Isobel and the Elf Knight' begins his seduction of the earthly princess by playing his harp to bind the rest of the household in sleep.

> > 'He's taen a harp into his hand
> > He's harped tyhem all asleep
> > Except it was the King's daughter
> > Who one wink couldna get.'[41]

The idea of using music to enchant and seduce a potential lover and to put rivals to sleep, is also one that is found in the folklore of other cultures.

Also from Scotland, we have the following reference from J. G. Campbell's *More West Highland Tales*. In the tale entitled 'Bramble Berries in February', a hero's mother's sister puts the Humming Harp of Harmony (*Chruit Chananaich Chiuil*) at the hero's bedside so that he may sleep better:

> Then she gave him food and drink ... she put him to bed, and at his head she placed the Humming Harp of Harmony, that he might the better slumber.[42]

The idea of music, especially harp music, having the effect of putting one to sleep quickly and effectively is a rather popular motif in Irish and Gaelic tales.

This motif also occurs in the well-known Welsh tale of Branwen in the Second Branch of the *Mabinogion*. Here, only seven men return as survivors from the Island of the Mighty during the tragic war in Ireland. The men are grieving, having buried their beloved Branwen. They carry with them the severed head of Branwen's brother. To rescue them from their despair, three special birds appear–the Birds of Rhiannon–at Harlech, and sing to them a most enchanting song for seven years.[43]

In Welsh tradition the fairies are called the *Tylwyth Teg*, and are described here as having a powerful effect on the listener who might come across them dancing and singing on a hill:

> It was a common idea that many of the *Tylwyth Teg*, forming in a ring, would dance and sing out on the mountain sides, or on the plain, and that if children should meet with them at such a time they would lose their way and never get out of the ring.[44]

Tales of the enchanting music and circle dancing of the fairies luring humans to the Otherworld are quite common in world folklore in general, and exemplify the power of music to entice.

Hearing mysterious, ghostly music is also documented in cases of the training of Zulu shamans. When a young shaman receives his calling from the Otherworld, sometimes against his or her own will, the individual is often very ill for weeks, having many unusual dreams and visions. The moment of initiation by the spirits of the Otherworld occurs when the individual in question 'receives his song'–previously completely unknown to him. This moment of receiving his own individual song from the Otherworld is greatly celebrated by the elders of the tribe. Here, a young man speaks of his new shamanic status:

> now there are things which I see when I lie down. When I left home I had composed three songs, without knowing whence they came; I heard the song, and then just sang it, and sang the whole of it without ever having learnt it.[45]

Mircea Eliade in his classic work *Shamanism* states that many shamans often describe their initiation in terms of receiving songs in a dream state: 'In the Apapocuva Guarani tribe, the prerequisite for becoming a shaman is learning magical songs, which are taught by a dead relative in dreams.'[46] In such cases, the phenomenon of mysterious music, with no musician present, serves a function as part of a spiritual initiation from the Otherworld.

Probably one of the best known examples of the joyful effects of music in early world literature is that of Krishna, from the *Puranas* of Hindu tradition. Portrayed as a flute-playing god, Krishna's beautiful music is depicted as being especially seductive and women come to the sound of his ecstatic and joyful music: 'None is able to resist Krishna's beauty and charm. He is described as retiring to the woods, where he plays his flute on autumn nights when the moon is full. Hearing the music, the women are driven mad with passion.'[47] Again, here is an acknowledgement of the power of music to entice and inspire.

Also well-known, from Homer's *Odyssey*, are the dangerous and deadly effects of the singing of the Sirens. In a passage from Book V, Lady Circe warns Odysseus what he will next encounter on his journey:

> your next landfall will be upon the Sirens: and these craze the wits of every mortal who gets so far. If a man comes on them unwittingly and lend their ear to the Siren-voices, he will never again behold wife and little ones ... The thrilling song of the Sirens will steal his life away, as they sit singing ... amongst skeletons which flutter with the rags of skin rotting upon the bones.[48]

Supernatural effects: Christian contexts

A similar range of supernatural effects of music is also found in the more overtly Christian examples.

Joyful or ecstatic effects of music in Heaven

The music in the Christian Heaven is clearly portrayed as very joyful. Often such joy borders on the ecstatic, as the music of God's Heaven is often viewed as indescribable in our mortal, earthly terms. In many of these references, a saint goes up to Heaven in a vision and then returns to earth or, after death, his departing soul is greeted in Heaven by the joyful music of the heavenly hosts. Visions of both Heaven and Hell are portrayed here, and descriptions of music abound.

The music references in this collection, although often written in the same time period, in the same monasteries and referring to the same saints, are from a tradition clearly distinct from the early Irish

Apocrypha visions of Heaven and Hell, as so aptly clarified by Professor Maire Herbert, University College Cork, when discussing the Irish Apocrypha tradition:

> Although visits to Heaven and Hell seem to be an integral part of this tradition, it should not be confused with the theme, popular from the time of Plato throughout the Middle Ages, of visions of Heaven and Hell with detailed descriptions of the Otherworld. In this case, [with the Apocrypha] there are no descriptions and the 'tour' is described as part of the natural progress of every soul.[49]

A good number of the examples here, then, do tend to come with more detailed descriptions of the Otherworld and often specifically portray the music in it as having especially joyful or ecstatic effects.

In one of the clearest instances of the pure joy of the plains of Paradise, this example is taken from *Betha Brennain* ('The Life of St Brendan'), in which St Brendan and his men encounter an old hermit monk on an island Paradise:

> 'Search ... and see,' says he, 'the plains of Paradise and the delightful fields of the land, radiant, famous, lovable, profitable, lofty, noble, beautiful, delightful. A land odorous, flower-smooth, blessed. A land many-melodied, musical, shouting for joy, unmournful.'.[50]

Another example that illustrates the joyful Christian Land of the Saints is from *Fis Adamnan* ('The Vision of St Adamnan'):

> For the Saints have need of nothing but to be listening to the music to which they listen and to behold the light which they look at ... and the song of the birds of the Heavenly Host makes music for them. Glorious bands of the guardian angels are continually cooing obeisance and service among these assemblies in the presence of the King ... They celebrate the eight canonical hours ... the choral song of the Archangels coming in in harmony. The birds and the Archangels lead the song, and all the Heavenly Host, both saints and holy virgins, answer them in antiphony ... there are three precious stones making soft sounds and sweet music between every two principal assemblies.[51]

The Land of the Saints is portrayed as very musical, with utterly joyful effects, including the various harmonious interactions among the angelic hosts, three precious stones, birds, and saints who are all portrayed as singing praises to God in an atmosphere of ecstatic joy in God's Heaven.

Complete absence of any effects of music in Hell

Hell itself is portrayed as being completely devoid of any music at all, as the only sounds heard are the pathetic howls of the damned in this example from *Fis Adamnan* ('The Vision of St Adamnan'):

> Then, the angel shows Adamnan Hell, and explains: Now while the saintly companies of the Heavenly Host sing joyfully and gladly the harmonious chorus of the eight canonical hours, praising the Lord, the souls give forth pitiful and grievous howls as they are beaten without respite by throngs of demons.[52]

Clergy put into a trance-like sleep state by music

In this category, clergymen are portrayed as falling into a trance-like sleep state after listening to music, especially that of the *sidhe* musicians. As cited earlier, St Patrick and his fellow clergy fell into a trance-like sleep state to the fairy music of the harper Cascorach. Some of the saints, too, while out at sea, are portrayed as encountering the music of the Otherworld and falling asleep to it in spite of themselves.

In the following example, from *Betha Kieran* ('The Life of St. Kieran'), St Kieran of Saighir has performed the miracle of reviving eight harpers from the dead after they had been dead in a loch for a month:

> They took to them (the harpers) their harps, and in presence of the king, (St) Kieran, and of all the rest in general, played delicious melody: in which music was delightfulness such that a great number of the multitude fell asleep to it; and glory was given to God and to Kieran.[53]

It may be noted that after hearing the music, 'a great number of the multitude' are portrayed as having fallen asleep to it.

'Mysterious' music heard in a Christian context

This category includes such phenomena as mysterious music heard around a church at the time of the birth of a saint, or the ethereal music constantly heard around a young boy who was later to become St Colman. Such mysterious music is heard in these examples, yet no musician is ever seen:

> On the night, however, when Colman son of Luachain was born ... That night bishop Etchen stayed in Tech Lomain, and when matins had come

and the clerics rose up for it ... they heard many marvellous kinds of music around the church on every side; and nothing more marvellous and more melodious had ever been heard by them before ... angels of Heaven making welcome to Colman son of Luachain, as on the night of the birth of Christ angels made many marvellous kinds of music around Bethlehem on every side.[54]

Also, regarding the young St Colman:

the boy was brought up piously and humbly; and wherever he used to be they would hear psalms and choral song, and the sound of a bell at every canonical hour, and the singing of mass every Sunday, so that people would come to ask, 'what was the assembly that came here last night?'.[55]

Other examples of unseen performers and mysterious music include those situations where a saint's personal bell suddenly rings of its own accord, as referred to in Chapter 3. The following example illustrates this, and that of the mysterious 'Keepers of St Patrick' who are said to be still alive but hidden according to the *Tripartite Life of Patrick*:

There are, moreover, keepers belonging to Patrick's household alive in Ireland still. There is a man from him in Cruachan Aigle – they hear the voice of his bell, and he is not found.[56]

Effects of saint's music with beneficial, protective effects

This category includes references that pertain to a particular saint using his bell to aid or bless others, to assist the clergy in some manner or to automatically 'ring' when the proper site for a monastery is found. The following example, from *Betha Colmain* ('The Life of St Colman'), illustrates the beneficial effects of the sweet-sounding bell of St Colman called the *Finnfaidech*:

And he [the priest] had no bell with him to sound the summons for hearing his Mass, so that then the Finnfaidech [sweet-sounding bell] of Colman mac Luachan was sent down to him from Heaven, and the mark of its rim is still there in the stone. So the bell was struck by them.[57]

A saint's musical chanting was also cited as having a beneficial or protective effect. Often, when blessing someone or something, a saint will be described as chanting the psalms or hymns of God. In this example, St Patrick has a conversation with an angel, and is then given a special protective hymn:

'Is there anything else He grants to me?' says Patrick. 'There is,' says the angel: 'every one who shall sing the hymn … shall not have pain or torture.' 'The hymn is long and difficult,' says Patrick. 'Every one who shall sing it from 'Christus illum' to the end, and every one who shall … perform penitence in Ireland, his soul shall not go to Hell …' [said the angel to Patrick.][58]

Healing or therapeutic effects of music

The music of Heaven is often 'sent' to a saint here on earth during especially difficult times in their missionary work. This is often illustrated by the birds of Heaven or the saint's bell, as discussed earlier. In the following example, from the *Metrical Dindshenchas*, the location of the 'White Lake of Carra' was named after St Patrick was visited by beautiful white birds from God, who sing to him during a time of great duress:

> God sent to comfort him at that season, a flock of birds, angelic, purely bright, over the clear loch unremittingly, they sang a chorus, a gentle proclamation.[59]

Saint's music with destructive, cursing effects

Sometimes the power of a saint's bell and its music was to be greatly feared, as it was used against pagan kings or as an exorcism measure. In many instances it is used in a deliberately destructive way by a saint to punish those who would not convert to Christianity, as the following example from *Betha Fechin Fabair* ('The Life of St Fechin of Fore') illustrates:

> Of a time when Fechin was learning with Presbyter Naithi in Achad Conairi, he is set one day to keep the meadow lest it should be stripped bare by strangers' cattle. Thereafter the king's horses and herds are put into it in spite of Fechin. Fechin cursed them, and struck his bell at them, so that they found death therewith. When the king heard that, he comes before Fechin, and flung himself on his knees, and sought forgiveness of his sins. Fechin gives him absolution, and brought his horses and herds back to life; and God's name and Fechin's were magnified by that miracle.[60]

Saints are also sometimes portrayed in this literature as chanting maledictive psalms and hymns 'at' someone or something as a curse, often to drive out demons as an exorcism measure, or against someone who refuses to convert to Christianity or help the Christian community. Such verbal curses by a saint may seem remarkably similar to the cursing 'satires' by the *fili*, as noted by scholar Tomas O'Cathasaigh: 'To call one of them a curse and the other a satire is a matter of nomenclature only; we tend to use *curse* for the malediction of a saint, and *satire* for that of a *fili* . . . the extent of the overlap between the two categories remains to be determined.'[61] Regarding such musical maledictions, however, both have the same destructive effects through the chanting.

From *The Tripartite Life of Patrick*, the following example shows St Patrick, like Moses, on a retreat of prayer on top of a mountain for forty days and forty nights. He encounters demonic black birds, sings maledictive psalms and flings his bell at them, and God later sends lovely, musical white birds to bless him:

> Now at the end of those forty days and forty nights the mountain was filled with black birds, so that he knew not Heaven nor earth. He sang maledictive psalms at them. They did not leave him because of this. Then his anger grew against them. He strikes his bell at them, so that the men of Ireland heard its voice, and he flung it at them, so that its gap broke out of it, and that bell is 'Brigit's Gapling' . . . No demon came to the land of Erin after that till the end of seven years and seven months and seven days and seven nights. Then the angel went to console Patrick, and . . . brought white birds around the Cruachan, and they used to sing sweet melodies for him.[62]

The date of *The Tripartite Life of Patrick* has been a matter of Celtic scholarly debate, with Kenneth Jackson commenting that it does have much material that is quite old and stating that he believes that 'there is a very large tenth century element, in some cases earlier.'[63]

Music used to 'summon' saints

Similar to the earlier examples in a primal context where music is used to summon people, we have a Christian example where music is used to summon individuals to a holy site. In one instance, St Columcille is portrayed explaining to his fellow cleric Baithin how St Patrick will come for the men and women of Ireland on the Day of Doom, after everyone is summoned to the holy mountain Cruachan Aigle by the bell of St Patrick.

This summoning category also includes those instances where a particular saint is transported *to* an Otherworldly dimension, here, the Christian Heaven. In the following example, St Fursa is transported to Heaven and hears the musical chanting of angels:

> When he had built the church we have mentioned, a serious illness attacked him from one Saturday to another, as the Book of his own Life relates; and from evening to cockcrow he was taken out of his body, and he heard the chanting of angels of Heaven, and he beheld them before him. And this is what they were chanting: 'Ibunt sancti de uirtute in uirtutem' [Psalm 83: 8] i.e., 'the saints shall advance from virtue to virtue.' And this is also what they were chanting: 'Videbitur Deus deorum in Sion' [Psalm 83: 8] i.e., 'the God of gods will be seen on Mount Zion'.[64]

On occasion, God sends otherworldly messengers *from* the Christian Heaven down to earth, to visit a saint or chosen individual. In the following example, referred to in part earlier, a student harper wishes to play again for St Brendan, but St Brendan resists, putting balls of wax in his ears, as he claims the best music he has ever heard came in the form of a shining bird, St Michael in disguise:

> 'After *that* music, no music of the world seems any sweeter to me ... and to hear it, I take to be but little profit. Take a blessing, student, and you shall have Heaven for that playing,' said Brennain.[65]

The student harper, then, at least received a blessing from St Brendan for his good intentions!

Upon death, a saint's holy spirit is summoned to Heaven, often portrayed as being accompanied by the beautiful music of choirs of angels. From the *Amra of Choluimb Cille*, a late eleventh-century manuscript, we have a description of the departing soul of St Columba of Iona being summoned to the Christian Heaven:

> The whole world, it was his:
> It is a harp without a key,
> It is a church without an abbot ...
>
> he reached the plain where they know the custom of music,
> where sages do not die ...
>
> He went with two songs to Heaven after his cross.[66]

The motif of a saint's spirit going to Heaven accompanied by the beautiful music of angels is a theme found in many saint's lives worldwide.

Illustratory comparative material

Perhaps one of the best-known examples of the effects of music from the Judeo-Christian tradition is that of David playing his harp to comfort King Saul. From I Samuel 16: 14, the servants of King Saul are quite worried about his condition of great depression, due to an evil spirit, and recommend music to him as a beneficial remedy:

> 'Look for a skilled harpist; when the evil spirit from God comes over you, he will play and it will do you good.' Saul said to his attendants: 'Find me, please, a man who plays well, and bring him to me.' ... David went to Saul and entered his service ... And whenever the spirit from God came over Saul, David would take a harp and play; Saul would then be soothed; it would do him good, and the evil spirit would leave him.

Ethnomusicologist Gilbert Rouget interprets the above episode as David's harp and its music serving the function of reconciling Saul with God. He does not accept the theory that its effect is merely therapeutic or healing, as the text does specifically mention the influence of an 'evil spirit', and Saul was apparently obsessed with this aspect of his problem. However, Rouget does not believe the theory that the music served the function of only a mere exorcism either, mainly because the ultimate effect of David's soothing music on Saul was that Saul was reconciled with the good spirit of Yahweh:

> By playing his lyre David reestablishes God's presence, which means that he restores in Saul, in an attenuated form, the state of inspired prophet that he had momentarily lost. Granted, this is a rather complicated interpretation, but it does have the advantage of taking into account all the textual data. It also remains within the general system of relations between music and prophetic inspiration among the Hebrews.[67]

Perhaps, then, the main reason why Saul was so concerned and depressed was that he felt he had 'lost' the prophetic inspiration of Yahweh and he wanted to regain it, assisted by the use of music.

From *Revelation* in the New Testament, we have John's vision of Heaven and the music of the angels in it. Their joyful hymns to God, along with the consistent chanting of the four living creatures, exemplify the songs of the Heavenly Host and the joyful effects on John, the listener:

> In my vision, I heard the sound of an immense number of angels gathered around the throne and the living creatures and the elders;

there were ten thousand times ten thousand of them and thousands upon thousands, loudly chanting ... [Rev. 5: 11]. [Later in text:] And I saw in Heaven another sign, great and wonderful: seven angels ... all had harps from God, and they were singing the hymn of Moses, the servant of God, and the hymn of the Lamb. [Rev. 15: 3].

Mundane, everyday effects: primal contexts

We will now take a look at the effects of music that are portrayed in the primal sources.

Effects of music in warfare

Music is often portrayed as being present on the battlefield, usually described as the 'music' of the swords. For example, from *Catha Maige Tuired I* ('The First Battle of Mag Tured') the Dagda is portrayed as rushing to a battle scene after hearing the music of the swords.[68]

The 'music' of the sword of the famed warrior Conall is portrayed in the following instance from *Cath Ruis na Rig for Boinn* ('The Battle of Ross Na Rig on the Boyne'):

It is then that Conall drew the sharp long sword out of its sheath of war, and played the music of his sword on the armies. The ring of Conall's sword was heard throughout the battalions on both sides ... However, as soon as they heard the music of Conall's sword, their hearts quaked. [Later in text:] Conall came along the armies and played the music of his sword on them, till ten hundred armed men fell by him.[69]

Joyful effects of music in everyday life

In *Esnada Tige Buchet* ('The Songs of Buchet's House'), the clearly joyful effects of the music at a nobleman's celebration are described:

The song of Buchet's house to the companies: his laughing cry to the companies: 'Welcome to you!' ... The song of the fifty warriors with their purple garments ... to make music ... the song of the fifty maidens ... their song delighting the host. The song of the fifty harps afterwards till morning, soothing the host with music. Hence is the name 'The Songs of Buchet's House.'[70]

Music as being beneficial for a king's realm

The effects of music are often portrayed as being good for a king and the overall success of his reign. From the *Metrical Dindshenchas*, the poem entitled 'Taltiu' describes the music of Taltiu, a goddess in early Ireland, and it also relates to the important annual Fair of Taltiu and its music:

> White-sided Taltiu uttered in her land a true prophecy, that so long as every prince should accept her, Erin should not be without perfect song.[71]

Likewise, in the following example, St Patrick is told by Caeilte, a legendary very old survivor of the Fianna:

> Three sorts of music, and O music of three kinds, that comely kings enjoyed! Music of harps, melody of timpans, [and the] humming of Trogan's son Fer-tuinne.[72]

One other example from a ninth-century poem comments on the early Irish kingship site of the Hill of Alenn and music in everyday life there:

> The music of its bent hard anvils, the sound of its songs from the tongues of poets, the fire of its men at the great contest, the beauty of its women at the high assembly ...
>
> Its lovely melodies at every hour, its wineship on the blue wave, its shower of silver of great brilliance, its gold neckbands from the lands of Gaul.[73]

Music and its disturbing or jarring effects

Some of the musicians present at the fairs are portrayed as being quite obnoxious, and the effect of their music disturbing. For example, consider the effects of the bawdy musicians at the annual Fair of Carmun:

> Pipes, fiddles, gleemen,
> bones-players and bag-pipers,
> a crowd hideous, noisy, profane,
> shriekers and shouters.[74]

Pleasant or calming effects of music in everyday life

From the same Fair of Carmun, other musicians present are portrayed in much better terms – as the fair's 'great privileges':

These are the Fair's great privileges: trumpets, fiddles, hollow-throated horns, pipers, timpanists unwearied, poets and meek musicians.[75]

It seems that the effects of such mild-mannered 'meek musicians' are seen as preferable to the loud, boisterous type of musicians depicted earlier. The musicians portrayed here are appreciated in the everyday life of the community and as an integral part of the fair.

Poetry and the effects of the music of nature

Great appreciation of the effects of the 'music' of the natural elements is often noted in the poetry of the early Irish period. While much of this imagery is in an overtly Christian context, some has a primal context, as exemplified by the following ninth-century poem entitled 'May Day', which is attributed to hero Finn mac Cumaill of the Fianna:

Woodland music plays; melody provides perfect peace; dust is blown from dwelling-place, and haze from lake full of water ...
　　Swallows dart aloft; vigour of music surrounds the hill soft rich fruit flourishes ... the hardy cuckoo sings; the trout leaps.[76]

This description is similar in tone to the following reference from *Echtra Airt meic Cuind* ('The Adventures of Art Son of Conn'), which also describes the effects of the music of the natural elements, 'the harmony of the wind over sea', in everyday life in a primal context:

As for the maiden, she found a coracle which had no need of rowing, but leaving it to the harmony of the wind over sea she came to Ben Edair meic Etgaith.[77]

A similar range of effects of music at a more mundane, everyday level is also found in the overtly Christian contexts. The major category here is the description by the Christian hermit monks of their tremendous appreciation of the effects of the 'music' of the natural elements in and around them in their everyday lives.

Joyful effects of music in hermit's everyday life

The great joy of the 'music' of the natural elements is portrayed by the hermits as being a celebration of God's wonderful Creation in everyday life. They often show a great appreciation for the creatures of the wild and of the birds, seeing them as God's little musicians.

Such prayerful gratitude is seen in the following example, quoted in full earlier:

> A clear-voiced cuckoo sings to me (goodly utterance) in a grey cloak from bush fortresses. The Lord is indeed good to me: well do I write beneath a forest of woodland.[78]

Melancholy effects of an absence of music in winter

One reference clearly shows a hermit's distress at the complete lack of any music or the sound of bells at all in the bitter cold of winter. From the Old Irish tenth-century poem entitled 'Uath Beinne Etair', we have the following commentary on the dreary silence of winter:

> The fishes of Innis Fail are a-roaming,
> There is no marge nor well of waves,
> In the lands there is no land,
> Not a bell is heard, no crane talks.[79]

Peaceful, calming effects of music in hermit's everyday life

The generally calming and peaceful effects of the music of wildlife is described here in the poem 'Summer Has Gone':

> The cuckoo sings sweet music
> and there is smooth soft sleep ...[80]

Music causes a trance-like sleep state in hermit

The spokesman in the following poem 'The Cry of the Garb' (attributed to both St Mo Ling and/or Suibne Geilt) falls asleep to the melodies of the birds by the river Garb:

> Musical birds of the shore, music-sweet their
> constant cryings! Lonely longing has seized me
> to hear their chanting as they sing the hours ...
> I sleep to those melodies on mountain tops and
> tree tops; the tunes which I hear are music to
> my soul.[81]

Far-reaching effects of saints' singing

An example of the far-reaching effects of a saint singing the psalms in everyday life is described in *Betha Coluimb Cille* ('The Life of

St Columcille'). In this account, the young boy Columcille is described as having a singing voice that could be heard up to a mile and a half away by a convent of nuns. He is portrayed as diligently memorising the psalms and having very powerful effects with his singing while still a boy.

Music as inspiring the search for a vocation

St Mochuda, while still a young boy, when asked by the king why he had been gone so long and worried everyone, had the following to say:

> Mochuda replied, 'Sir, this is why I have stayed away – through attraction of the holy chant of the bishop and clergy; I have never heard anything so beautiful as this ... And I wish, O king, that I might learn their psalms and ritual'.[82]

The young Mochuda was so inspired by the music, that he decided to become a monk.

Conclusion

We have now seen the major categories of the effects of music from this literature. When analysing the effects of music in the material in these categories, one cannot help but note the following: *the more extreme or dramatic a given effect of music is, the more likely it is to also be portrayed in a supernatural context.* In the early Irish worldview it seems as though the degree of supernatural influence tends to determine the degree of dramatic effect on the listener. This seems to apply in both the overtly primal and the overtly Christian contexts.

For example, consider the effect of joy, happiness or ecstasy on the listener as a result of hearing music. In the examples from everyday life, whether in an overtly Christian context or not, such an effect is described as delighting the hosts at a celebration, a lovely moment at a party is described as 'no mournful music', a 'pleasant sound' or as 'lively the tune' and so on.

However, in a supernatural context, whether primal or Christian, this same joyful or ecstatic effect is generally portrayed in a far more dramatic manner. For example, the supernatural joy of the *gen-ntraigi* ('laughter-strain') of the harp is described in the primal contexts as '... forcing them all into a cachination such as their very lungs became visible ...', or as causing thirty of King Ailill's men to 'die' of rapture. Clearly these are situations that are uncommon in everyday life experience.

From the supernatural Christian examples we also find dramatic descriptions of the music of Heaven. Here, not only all of the saints, archangels and birds of Heaven sing in harmony with the Heavenly Hosts, but three precious stones also make soft sounds and sweet music.

Also, one may note that while Heaven and the primal Otherworld are almost always described as having sweet, joyful music, the dimension of Hell and the season of winter are shown in sharp contrast to have a complete absence of any music at all. For example, only the howls of the damned are heard in Hell, and the howls of wolves at night in the winter.

A similar pattern emerges in references to the trance-like sleep state in everyday life experience. Here, the sleep state is described in more ordinary terms such as '... musical birds ... I sleep to those melodies on mountain tops ...'[83], or 'I hear melodious music in the river Garb'[84], and '... the cuckoo sings ... there is smooth, soft sleep ...'[85] The listener in such examples tends to experience an overall feeling of being relaxed or calmed by the music, and then falling to sleep to it.

However, when this same effect is portrayed in the supernatural contexts, we often have a situation where the listener falls asleep for an extended period of time, even for days on end, or where those in great pain would very quickly fall asleep to the music – again, unusual situations in terms of ordinary everyday life experience.

Consider this description of the music of the prized fairy harper Fer-tuinne mac Trogain: '... though saws were being plied where there were women in sharpest pains of childbirth, and brave men that were wounded early in the day, nevertheless would such people sleep to the fitful melody that he makes ...'[86] In the normal experience of reality, those in great pain might be calmed by the music, but would very rarely, if ever, quickly fall asleep to it.

Also, consider these examples: the '... musical choir lulled them to sleep ... they were in the same condition, till the third day ...'[87]; when the clergy heard the music, they fell '... asleep till the end of three days and three nights. Thereafter they awake.'[88] While not all of the supernatural examples are quite so extreme, they often speak of the music as being so beautiful that many would sleep to it. The overall impression is that the early Irish are trying to distinguish the effects of this supernatural type of music from those of the ordinary music of everyday life by dramatising them.

Chanting in everyday monastic life is often portrayed in quite prosaic terms, as the clerics sing at periodic intervals throughout the day and night, chanting the hours, and go about their business in their monastic environment. But when chanting is described as part of God's Heaven, it takes on more unusual characteristics, as one might expect: 'The birds and the Archangels lead the song, and all the Heavenly Host, both saints and holy virgins, answer them in antiphony.'[89] When a particular saint or poet deliberately chants for certain specific effects, be they good (healing) or ill (cursing), the powerful results seem to indicate some kind of intervention from another dimension into everyday life in order to create such an effect.

Melancholic effects are noted in all of the categories, as are calming, pleasant or peaceful effects. The 'three strains' motif occurs only in the examples from the primal contexts, however, and not from the Christian. Joyful effects are portrayed across the board, and the trance-like sleep state is portrayed in some way in all of the categories.

The correlation of dramatic effects with supernatural intervention is perhaps most graphic when the results are tragic or destructive. Some examples are the most memorable, such as the drowning of a fairy maiden on the river Boyne, who fell overboard from her boat through listening to the sad, 'doleful music' of the fairy mounds;[90] Aillen mac Midhna's notorious annual destructions of Tara each Samhain;[91] the nine deadly pipers of Sid Breg 'who will slay, but they cannot be slain';[92] and fairy harper Cliach, killed by a dragon, who was attracted to him by his sweet music[93].

The Christian supernatural contexts, too, show music as potentially deadly. For example, the curse of St Columba befell anyone who disturbed a certain sacred bell sanctuary: a sign of malediction was put upon the intruder that he should die within a year. In other instances, St Columba is portrayed cursing a man who would not give him an island for his ministry, while St Patrick sings particularily effective maledictive psalms at menacing black birds on a mountain.[94]

But the examples of beneficial effects are just as powerful. In the overtly primal everyday examples, one reference states that for as long as every prince accepts Taltiu and its fair, Ireland 'should not be without perfect song'.[95] It would appear that certain music can bring prosperity, such that 'each cow and each animal that heard it, two thirds surplus milk always was milked from them.'[96] In everyday Christian monastic life, music is also portrayed as having largely positive effects, such as a calming influence for the monks, or inspiring a young boy to become a monk, and later a famous saint.[97]

When portrayed in supernatural contexts, the positive effects of music are also more dramatic. Examples include instances where St Patrick's famous bell, the Bernan of Patrick, banishes away demons, St Columba's protective musical chants save a grove of trees from fire and a protective hymn is given to St Patrick by an angel.

Music is shown to have a direct healing effect in the supernatural contexts. For example, God sends angelic white birds to make music for St Patrick during a time of duress;[98] the leech-doctors of the Tuatha de Danann sing spells around the well of Slane, rejuvenating the wounded and dead;[99] the singing of the birds of *tir tairngiri* ('The Land of Promise') emotionally heals the depression and low morale of Teigue and his men on their journey out at sea.[100] And the healing effects of music could also extend to an entire kingdom, as when during the reign of King Conaire, 'no one slew the other'.[101]

It appears that such beneficial effects of music have been known for centuries. The temple priests and physicians of Rome 'used music therapy up until the point when the empire was completely Christianised. The Arabs of the 13th-c. had music rooms in their hospitals. Paracelsus practiced what he called a "musical medicine"'.[102]

Down through the ages, the healing effects of music have been valued very highly. The monastery of Cluny was founded in 909 AD, and devoted to a mission of compassion and peace leading directly to the Pax Dei. They developed a series of infirmary practices concerning the care of the dying based on the Gregorian chants.

The pioneering Chalice of Repose Project in the USA, which uses music to aid the terminally ill and dying in the present day, bases its successful medical effort on the Cluny approach. Its pioneering work is called 'music thanatology'. Founder Terese Schroeder-Sheker explains that 'specific music is played for conscious patients, other music for those who are comatose, those in physical pain, mental agony, etc.'[103] She remarks that the hospital where the project is based 'is the only hospital in the world with twenty-seven harps and resident singing-harpists in training.'[104] The project and its aims are similar to examples described in the literature of early

Ireland about healing, where harp music and singing are used to assist those in extreme pain or near death.

Also prevalent in this literature are portrayals of the beautiful music of the Christian Heaven or Paradise. For a sterling example of this, recall the 'Land of the Saints' and its sacred music as described in the Vision of Adamnan, referred to earlier.[105] Integral to this concept is the idea of constant, everpresent music in God's Heaven. For example, the departing soul of St Columba upon its arrival in Heaven is greeted by supernatural music: '... he reached the plain where they know the custom of music.'[106] This is somewhat similar to Dante's description of the last two Heavens in his cosmology, where 'in these last heavens light and music are everywhere ... he stands numb before the singing of those that continuously sing the music of the eternal spheres'.[107]

Cyril Scott, in commenting on the effects of music, states:

> music operates on the mind and emotions of man through the medium of suggestion. To paraphrase Aristotle's statement, if we repeatedly hear melancholy music, we tend to become melancholy; if we hear gay music, we tend to become gay, and so forth. Thus the particular emotion which a given piece of music depicts is reproduced in ourselves ... we may with justification formulate the following axiom – as in music, so in life.[108]

In this literature we can also detect a similar belief in the power of music and its effects in everyday life, as when a listener hears melancholy music, he is shown to become more melancholy himself. Upon hearing joyful music, especially that of the Otherworld, he, too, becomes more joyful. It is exactly *how* joyful that is of interest; it seems that it is largely the degree of supernatural influence that determines how joyful the effect will be. So, the joy of music and its effects in the everyday monastic life of a Christian hermit is portrayed as much less dramatic than the harmony of God's angelic choirs in Heaven, perhaps reminiscent of Cyril Scott's famous phrase, 'Whereas Melody is the cry of Man to God, Harmony is the answer of God to Man.'[109]

In the next chapter, we will now shift our focus from the effects of the music to the places and locations where it is heard.

Notes

1. Merriam, A. P., *The Anthropology of Music* (Evanston, IL: Northwestern University Press, 1964), p. 218.

2. Ibid., pp. 280–1.

3. Nettl, B., *Music in Primitive Cultures* (Cambridge: Cambridge University Press, 1956), p. 20.

4. O'Madagain, B., 'Gaelic Lullaby: a Charm to Protect the Baby?', *Scottish Studies*, 29 (1989), p. 31.

5. O'Grady, S. (ed.), 'Accalam na Senorach', *SG*, II (London, 1892), p. 191.

6. Gantz, J., *EIMS* (London, 1981), pp. 117–18.

7. Stokes, W., 'The Second Battle of Mag Tured/Cath Maige Tured II', *RC*, 12 (1891), p. 80.

8. Meyer, K., 'Combat of CuCulainn with Senbecc', *RC*, 6 (Paris, 1884), p. 184.

9. Gantz, *EIMS*, p. 108.

10. Gwynn, E. (ed.) *MD*, IV, RIA Todd Lecture Series 2, (Dublin, 1924), pp. 351–3.

11. O'Grady, *SG*, II, p. 191.

12. Ibid.

13. Nutt, A. and Meyer, K. (eds), *The Voyage of Bran, son of Febal* (London, 1897), p. 2.

14. Murphy, G. (ed.), *EIL* (Dublin, 1961), pp. 102–3.

15. Stokes, W., 'The Destruction of Dind Rig/Orgain Dind Rig', *ZCP*, 3 (London, 1901), p. 11.

16. Gantz, *EIMS*, p. 121. (The English translation of the Old Irish word *sirechtai* by Bryne, M. and Dillon, M., in *EC*, 2 (1937) is 'rapture', where as Gantz translates it as 'yearning'. In modern Irish, the word *sireachtach* means 'ecstatic' or 'longing'.]

17. O'Grady, *SG*, II, p. 349.

18. Jackson, K. (ed.), *CM*, (New York, 1971), pp. 173–4.

19. O'Grady, *SG*, II, pp. 348–9.

20. Jackson, *CM*, p. 172.

21. Stokes, W., 'The Battle of Allen/Cath Almaine', RC, 24 (Paris, 1903), pp. 59–63.

22. Gwynn, E. (ed.) *MD*, IV (Dublin, 1924), p. 4.

23. O'Grady, *SG*, II, p. 116.

24. Ibid., p. 253.

25. Stokes, 'Second Battle of Mag Tured/Cath Maige Tuired II', pp. 12, 95.

26. O'Grady, *SG* II, p. 396.

27. Meyer, K., *Selections from Ancient Irish Poetry* (London: Constable, 1911), pp. 3–4.

28. Bergin, O. and Best, R., *Eriu*, 12 (Dublin, 1938), p. 153.

29. Gantz, *EIMS*, p. 260.

30. O'Grady, *SG*, II, p. 142.

31. Gantz, *EIMS*, pp. 82–3.

32. Gwynn, *MD*, III, p. 225.
33. Jackson, *CM*, p. 174.
34. Ibid., p. 163.
35. Stokes, W., *Cormac's Adventure in the Land of Promise*, in *Irische Texte*, 3, [ed.] Windisch and Stokes, W. (eds) (Leipzig, 1891), p. 212.
36. Ibid., p. 213.
37. Nutt, and Meyer, *The Voyage of Bran*, p. 2.
38. Gantz, *EIMS*,, p. 247.
39. O'Grady, *SG*, II, p. 213.
40. Gwynn, *MD*, III, p. 183.
41. Sanger, K. and Kinnaird, A., *Tree of Strings: crann nan teud* (Temple, Midlothian: Kinmor Music, 1992), p. 4.
42. Watson, W., MacLean, D., and Rose, H., (eds), *More West Highland Tales*, I (Edinburgh, 1994 edn; orig. 1940), p. 415. Tales collected by J.F. Campbell.
43. Gwyndaf, R., 'Fairylore: Memorates and Legends from Welsh Oral Tradition', in Navarez, P. (ed.), *The Good People: New Fairylore Essays*, (New York: Garland, 1991), p. 161.
44. Evans-Wentz, W., *The Fairy Faith in Celtic Countries* (New York: University Books, 1966), pp. 207–8.
45. Kalweit, Holger, *Dreamtime and Inner Space: The World of the Shaman* (Boston: Shambhala, 1988), p. 83.
46. Eliade, M., *Shamanism: Archaic Techniques of Ecstasy* (Princeton, NJ: Princeton University Press, 1964), p. 83.
47. Kinsley, D., *Hindu Goddesses* (Berkeley, CA, 1986), p. 84.
48. Homer, *Odyssey*, Book V, trans. T. E. Shaw (Hertfordshire: Wordsworth Editions, 1992), p. 70.
49. Herbert, M., 'The Seven Journeys of the Soul', *Eigse*, 17 (Dublin, 1977–9), p. 3.
50. Stokes, W. (ed.), *LSBL* (Oxford, 1890), p. 259.
51. Jackson, *CM*, pp. 288–95.
52. Ibid.
53. O'Grady, *SG* II, p. 8.
54. Meyer, K., *Betha Colmain/Life of Colman, son of Luachan*, RIA Todd Lecture Series, Vol. 17 (Dublin, 1911), p. 11.
55. Ibid., p. 15.
56. Stokes, W. (ed.), *The Tripartite Life of Patrick/Bethu Phatraic* (London, 1887), pp. 102–3.
57. Meyer, *Betha Colmain*, p. 65.
58. Stokes, *TLP*, pp. 118–19.
59. Gwynn, *MD*, III, p. 379.
60. Stokes, W., 'The Life of St. Fechin of Fore', RC, 12 (Paris, 1891), pp. 324–5.
61. O'Cathasaigh, T., 'Curse and Satire', *Eigse*, 21 (Dublin, 1986), p. 15.

62. Stokes, *TLP*, pp. 114–15.
63. Jackson, K., 'The Date of the Tripartite Life of St. Patrick', *ZCP* (Tübingen, 1986), p. 15.
64. Stokes, W., 'Betha Fursa', RC, 25 (Paris, 1901), p. 391.
65. Jackson, *CM*, pp. 282–3.
66. Clancy, T., and Markus, G., *Iona: The Earliest Poetry of a Celtic Monastery* (Edinburgh: Edinburgh University Press, 1995), pp. 105–11.
67. Rouget, G., *Music and Trance* (Chicago: University of Chicago Press, 1985), p. 158.
68. Gray, E., *The Battle of Mag Tuired/Cath Maige Tuired*, Irish Text Society, No. 52 (London, 1982), p. 31.
69. Hogan, E., *Cath Ruis na Rig for Boinn*, RIA Todd Lecture Series, IV (Dublin, 1892), pp. 47–9.
70. Stokes, W., 'Esnada Tige Buchet', *RC*, 25 (Paris, 1904), pp. 30–2.
71. Gwynn, *MD*, IV, p. 151.
72. O'Grady, *SG*, II, p. 112.
73. Greene, D. and O'Connor, F., *A Golden Treasury of Irish Poetry* (London: Macmillan, 1967), pp. 68–70.
74. Gwynn, *MD*, III, p. 21.
75. Ibid., p. 19.
76. Murphy, *EIL*, pp. 158–9.
77. Best, R., 'The Adventures of Art, son of Conn', *Eriu*, 3 (Dublin, 1907), p. 153.
78. Murphy, *EIL*, pp. 4–5.
79. Jackson, K., *CM*, 65.
80. Greene, and O'Connor, *GTIP*, pp. 137–8.
81. Murphy, *EIL*, pp. 114–15.
82. Power, P., 'Life of St. Mochuda of Lismore', *ITS* (London, 1914), p. 81.
83. Murphy, *EIL*, p. 115.
84. Ibid., pp. 112–15.
85. Greene, and O'Connor, *GTIP*, pp. 137–8.
86. O'Grady, *SG*, II, p. 111.
87. Murphy, *EIL*, pp. 102–3.
88. Stokes, W., 'The Voyage of the Ui Corra', *RC* 14 (Paris, 1893), p. 47.
89. Jackson, *CM*, pp. 288–95.
90. Gwynn, *MD*, IV, p. 5.
91. O'Grady, *SG*, II, p. 142.
92. Gantz, *EIMS*, pp. 82–3.
93. Gwynn, *MD*, III, p. 225.
94. Stokes, *TLP*, pp. 114–15.
95. Gwynn, *MD*, IV, p. 151.
96. Gantz, *EIMS*, p. 63.
97. Power, 'Life of St. Mochuda', p. 81.
98. Gwynn, *MD*, III, p. 379.

99. Stokes, 'Second Battle of Mag Tured', p. 95.
100. O'Grady, *SG*, II, p. 396.
101. Gantz, *EIMS*, p. 67.
102. Tame, D., *The Secret Power of Music* (New York: Destiny Books, 1984), p. 156.
103. Schroeder-Sheker, T., 'Musical-Sacramental-Midwifery', in Campbell, D. (ed.), *Music and Miracles* (Wheaton, IL: Quest Books, 1992), p. 19.
104. Schroeder-Sheker, T., 'Music for the Dying', *Caduceus*, 23 (Warwickshire, 1994), p. 25.
105. Jackson, *CM*, pp. 288–95.
106. Clancy, and Markus, *Iona*, pp. 105–11.
107. Meyer-Baer, K., *Music of the Spheres and the Dance of Death* (Princeton, NJ: Princeton University Press, 1970), p. 353.
108. Scott, C., *Music: Its Secret Influence Throughout the Ages* (Wellingborough: Aquarian Press, 1958), p. 40.
109. Ibid., p. 151.

5

Places

T HE PLACES WHERE MUSIC is heard in this literature are as varied as
the effects. They range from purely supernatural music heard
in an otherworldly dimension to the descriptions of music heard as
part of everyday life, such as the courts of noblemen or kings, the
homes of families and the fairs of the people.

In this chapter, places are divided into three main categories: (1)
places where music is described as part of a purely supernatural
Otherworld dimension; (2) places which are *liminal* – that is, those
certain everyday places which, because of their inherent 'limit' or
'boundary' nature, are natural symbols of transcendence; and (3)
those *everyday* places where music is heard in the normal, mundane
affairs of daily life.

When these categories are placed side by side, there is once again
noticeable a certain parallelism and similarity in imagery and description between the purely supernatural Otherworld locations and
those places described as part of the world of everyday, mundane,
earthly life.

The material in the Christian contexts parallels that of those in the
primal contexts, reinforcing an overall impression of a continuity in
the descriptions of places where music is heard. In the purely supernatural and the liminal places, whether in Christian or primal
contexts, one can see the early Irish felt there was a continuous
awareness of a supernatural presence through music, and particularily at certain special locations. Even in everyday life, if one was
fortunate and the circumstances were right, unusual experiences
regarding music are sometimes described in this literature.

Although in our modern world we have CDs and cassette tapes in our cars, musical performances today tend largely to be relegated to special times and places, that is a ticket is purchased to attend a specific concert at a particular place and time often to hear music performed by specially trained professionals. In our modern world, unlike that of the ancient Celts, things are more compartmentalised and we make clear distinctions between 'professional' and 'amateur' musicians. In early Ireland, this was not the case, as music was a much more integral part of everyday life, and people would sing songs while working in the fields, washing the clothes or entertaining family and friends at home around the fire, for example.

Breandan O'Madagain points out that even up to the nineteenth-century in Ireland, the whistle in everyday life was used to play to the horses while ploughing, to soothe them and cheer them while at work. There were weaving songs, milking songs, lullabies, rowing songs, songs while 'pulling the quern' to grind the barley, religious songs and so on. Although we do not know many details of the daily life of those in the early Irish medieval period, it is possible to surmise that they, too, may have incorporated music into their everyday lives at least as much, and perhaps even more so. O'Madagain states that even for nineteenth-century Ireland:

> Song was an integral part of a whole culture which embraced the life of the community in all its facets, giving it an artistic dimension so that 'art was a part of life, not separated from it.' It has been said that everywhere 'music transforms experience': for the Irish folk mind in the nineteenth century song had esoteric powers of transforming any situation.[1]

So in the material that follows regarding the places where music is heard it is not always clear whether the given place affects the status or quality of the music or vice versa. Even so, we will analyse the relationship and may find influence(s) in either direction.

Supernatural places

The places that are described as purely supernatural or Otherworld dimensions occur in these music references in both the Christian and in the primal contexts, as far as we can distinguish them.

In *Betha Brennain* ('The Life of St Brendan'), we have an example of the genre of the *immrama*, or vision/voyage literature. This literary genre developed out of the religious ideal and practice of pilgrimage overseas, and the necessity of leaving family, friends and country for the love of God. This type of pilgrimage, the *peregrinatio*, is bound up with the ascetic tradition and practice of seeking out deserted places in order to lead a solitary life of prayer and contemplation dedicated to God. In such voyage tales, saints encounter many different countries, islands and adventures in search of the perfect Christian life, and often choose to return home again. These vision/voyage accounts often portrayed how one could search all over the world in many kinds of places for the perfect life, and end up preferring to return home, realising that the ideal Christian life can indeed be lived at or near one's own monastic community. Many of the Irish saints made such voyages around the Continent and Britain, for which they became widely known as good teachers and examples of the ideal Christian life. Seamus MacMathuna, in his work entitled 'Contributions to a study of the voyages of St Brendan and St Malo', says:

> The missionary aspect of *peregrinatio* plays little or no part in the *immrama*, other than in some instances to bring the hero back home. Such is the case, for example, in the second voyage of the *Viti Brendani*: when the voyagers eventually reach the secluded island which has been promised to Brendan, the latter wishes to remain there, but the old hermit on the island tells him to return home and preach to the Irish people. For the unknown hermit on the island, however, it is his place of resurrection.[2]

The places portrayed in this voyage/vision literature may not be meant as actual portrayals of Heaven, the Otherworld or even Hell, as in some other purely visionary literature. But they do represent some form of supernatural ideal, and as such, for purposes of 'placing' the music described in these locations, we may include them in the supernatural section.

In many of the medieval Irish *immrama*, saints encounter various islands on their sometimes perilous journeys out at sea, which often have music or musicians present in some manner. In one such instance, from *Betha Brennain* ('The Life of St Brendan'), St Brendan and his fellow clergymen are told directly by a 'certain old man' on an island of the power of the music of the plains of Paradise, clearly an Otherworld dimension. This aged old man is shown in the literature as very wise, and is most likely a portrayal of a hermit monk. He explains to St Brendan:

'Search ... and see,' says he, 'the plains of Paradise and the delightful field of the land, radiant, famous, lovable, profitable, lofty, noble, beautiful, delightful. A land odorous, flower-smooth, blessed. A land many-melodied, musical, shouting for joy, unmournful.'[3]

Similarly, from *Immram Snedgusa* ('The Voyage of Snedgus'), Snedgus and his men also encounter such an island paradise on their journey out at sea. In this case, Heaven itself is described as having a musical aspect, and birds singing praises to God:

> Melodious was the music of those birds singing psalms and canticles, praising the Lord. For they were the birds of the Plain of Heaven ...[4]

The soul's journey to Heaven is often described in the early Irish literature, and Heaven is clearly portrayed as an Otherworld dimension. John Carey, while analysing the Otherworld concept of Heaven in early Irish literature, points out that the use of Jerusalem as an image for Heaven is commonplace in the more overtly Christian examples, as one might expect. The heavenly city of Revelation 21: 10–27, itself based on Ezekiel, is '"the New Jerusalem", and Paul describes "the city of the living God" as a "heavenly Jerusalem" (Hebrews 12: 22) ... and in *Amra Choluimb Chille* the name *Sion* seems to be used for Heaven', again taking a cue from the 'Zion' of the Old Testament.[5] In this twelfth-century work, the *Amra Choluimb Chille*, Heaven itself as an otherworldly location is described as the dwelling place of the soul of St Columba of Iona and as having inherent musical qualities: 'He reached the plain where they know the custom of music'.[6]

In the following passage from the *Tripartite Life of Patrick*, the Christian Heaven is described as being filled with the music of angels:

> So after founding churches, after consecrating monasteries, after baptising human beings, after preaching the faith throughout the whole country, after so much patience and labour, after bestowing the grace of the Gospel, after destroying idols, the spells and practices of heathenism being made void: after the wizards' arts had been overcome ... he departed to the Lord and slept in peace. And among choirs of angels he rejoices with them in his Lord's presence, deserving to behold Him.[7]

In some instances in the literature of early medieval Ireland, such as the *Saltair na Rann*, the beautiful music of the choirs of angels of Heaven is thought of as coming from the first nine orders of angels, while the 'music' of Lucifer's choirs is thought to emanate from the tenth order of angels–a 'tenth earth grade', that of the human race, the *dechmad grad talman*.[8]

The underworld of Hell, however, is often described as being without any music at all, or as having only the dreadful sounds of the howls of the damned. This is clearly in great contrast to the music of Heaven. For example, from *Fis Adamnan* ('The Vision of St Adamnan'), Adamnan is shown Hell by an angel:

> Now while the saintly companies of the Heavenly Host sing joyfully and gladly the harmonious chorus of the canonical hours, praising the Lord, the souls give forth pitiful and grievous howls as they are beaten without respite by demons.[9]

In Chapter 4, we noted many examples with overtly Christian contexts of supernatural, mysterious music heard continuously around a saint, yet no performer is seen. In one example quoted in full earlier, St Colman, while still a young boy, is described as always having mysterious music surrounding him wherever he went.[10] It appears as if Heaven, the Christian Otherworld, was only inches from his head and always in close proximity to the young Colman at all times.

A recurring feature of Paradise in this literature includes that of the Tree of Life and its musical birds of Paradise. In this example from the twelfth-century *Saltair na Rann*, the Irish Adam and Eve story, the Christian Heaven is described as having musical qualities:

> The King of the Tree of Life with its flowers, the space around which noble hosts were ranged, its crest and its showers on every side spread over the fields and plains of Heaven. On it sits a glorious flock of birds and sings perfect songs of purest grace; without withering, with choice bounty of fruit and leaves. Lovely is the flock of birds which keeps it, on every bright and goodly bird a hundred feathers; and without sin, with pure brilliance, they sing a hundred tunes for every feather.[11]

Described in this way, the Christian view of Paradise or Heaven is clearly a joyful, radiant place, as John Carey elaborates:

> The joys of this peaceful, fertile, musical place are described at length ... the sound of the heavenly rejoicing is like the roaring of waters, the music of harps ... the tree of life scatters its dew throughout Heaven, it nourishes a flock of birds ... each wing sings a hundred songs. In conclusion, God is praised for all His works.[12]

The following example, with an overtly primal context, also uses tree imagery, and is quoted in full here. Cathair, son of Fedilmid, regional ruler of Ireland from Alenn, had a dream and asked the

high king's chief druid to interpret it for him. The druid interprets
the dream as meaning that Cathair will someday himself be king of
all Ireland, and takes note of the symbolism of the music coming
from the crown of a tree:

> 'A tree of gold on the hill free from battle,
> its crown reached the cloudy welkin;
> thence the music of the men of the world
> was heard from the tree's crown ...
>
> This is the storm-tossed tree of gold,
> branching wide, full of fruit –
> thyself in thy kingship over tuneful Banba
> and over every dwelling in Erin ...
>
> This is the stately music
> that was in the crown of the enduring tree –
> thy noble eloquence, lovelier thereby,
> when appeasing a multitude'.[13]

The Otherworld dimension itself is also portrayed in the primal
contexts as having an inherent musical or harmonic aspect.
The following verses, from *Immram Brain*, ('The Voyage of Bran'),
illustrate this belief about the Otherworld as a place:

> Colours of every hue gleam
> throughout the soft familiar fields;
> ranked around the music, they are
> ever joyful in the plain south of Argatnel ...
>
> There is no fierce harsh sound there,
> but sweet music striking the ear ...
>
> Riches, treasure of every colour
> are in Ciuin, have they not been found?
> Listening to sweet music
> drinking choicest wines ...
>
> Listening to music in the night,
> and going to Ildathach,
> the many-coloured land,
> a brilliance with clear splendor
> from which the white cloud glistens.[14]

Although primarily conceived of as a single supernatural realm, the
Celtic Otherworld is often described as having various specific
subdivisions. The references mention particular Otherworld dimensions including 'Argatnel', 'Ciuin', 'Ildathach', 'Mag Mell' and so on.
Most of the various Otherworld subdivisions referred to in this

literature include a musical or harmonic aspect in some way. Proinsias MacCana posits that in *Immram Brain*, the Otherworld place mentioned to Bran from the mysterious *sidhe* woman as 'Mag Mell', could possibly be harmonised with the concept of the biblical *terra repromissionis* ('The Promised Land').[15] This is not surprising in light of the parallel imagery and effects we have already noted in both the primal and Christian contexts.

Another feature recurring in the primal contexts about the Otherworld realm is a musical, shining Otherworld fountain and its streams. This shining fountain is often used in examples that also refer to poetic lore, and especially when also referring to the presence of hazelnuts and salmon. In an example quoted in full earlier, King Cormac visits *tir tairngiri*, 'The Land of Promise', and encounters a shining fountain with five streams flowing out of it; nine hazels grow over this undersea well, and five salmon are in the fountain and eat the hazelnuts which were deemed sacred by the poets.

Another example of a shining Otherworld fountain is the description of the fairy maiden Sinann gazing at the underwater well of Conla, the Well of Segais, considered to be the ultimate source of wisdom. According to the *Dindshenchas*, Sinann walked around the well three times, counter-clockwise, to test its power. After having done so, suddenly three waves came up from the well and drowned her.[16] In Irish folklore, the river Shannon (from the name of the fairy maiden Sinann) traces its origin to this undersea well. The river Boyne, too, was said to originate from a well called the Sidh ('Otherworld dwelling') of Nechtan.

Daithi O'hOgain describes *sidhe* dwellings as 'beautiful places, decorated with precious metals and with sumptuous food and drink and melodious music'.[17] Such Otherworld places are portrayed as supernatural, and are often described as a *sidhe* hilltop, cairn, rath, an undersea world, an island paradise or even a place within a mountain. The fountains, with their musical qualities, are described as features of the same Otherworld dimension.

In this section, then, it seems that the otherworldly status of the place, however it is conveyed, implies the supernatural status of the music.

Illustratory comparative material

In other cultures we also find descriptions of certain supernatural locations or places strongly characterised as musical. Such well-known Otherworld realms as the Christian Heaven, the Seven Heavens of Islam, Shangri-La, Shambhala and the Judaic paradise are often described as having an inherent musical or harmonic quality to them. Generally in such descriptions, angels or *sidhe*-like beings play music and/or sing in these locations, or mysterious music emanates from the Otherworld realm itself, a location believed to be purely supernatural with its own music and harmony.

Celtic myth often makes reference to an undersea Otherworld, such as the folklore surrounding beautiful musical sounds heard from the submerged cathedral of Ys, the sunken Breton community beneath the waves. The folklore tales of the Irish hero Brian tell of his finding an undersea Otherworld dimension while diving down deep into the ocean depths with a crystal diving helmet, to discover red-haired nymphs making music sounding like chimes.[18]

References in world literature to the 'music of the spheres' clearly refer to a supernatural Otherworld that involves planetary spheres, such as:

> The Pamphylian soldier in Plato's 'Myth of Er' saw the system of the seven planets and the fixed stars with a Siren standing on each sphere, 'uttering one tone varied by diverse modulations; and the whole eight of them together composed a single harmony'. Following in Plato's footsteps, Cicero also ended his *Republic* with a cosmic vision, though this time presented as a dream. Scipio Africanus, the Roman hero, saw nine spheres (including the Earth) making a 'grand and pleasing sound'.[19]

Some Jewish rabbis believe that in the world to come, the soul will hear the supernatural musical scale of the Afterlife, 'which is above this physical world ... those who merit reward in the Afterlife will no longer be limited by the dimensions of time and space ... and will retrovert to the supernatural source from whence we came'.[20] This supernatural source is believed to have a musical quality. The writings of the Kabbalah ultimately envision a world in which not only angels sing, but also the stars, planetary spheres, the *merkavah* (chariot-thrones), the trees in the Garden of Eden, the animals and so on, all participate in a portrayal of a singing Universe in praise of God. Martin Buber comments about this special secret melody in relation to the beliefs of the Hasidim, regarding their esoteric custom of working on various Hebrew letter combinations:

> From time immemorial speech was for the Jewish mystic a rare and awe-inspiring thing ... The word is an abyss through which the speaker strides ... He who knows the secret melody that bears the inner into the

outer, who knows the holy song that merges the lonely, shy letters into the singing of the spheres, he is full of the power of God.[21]

It seems that the mystical Jewish tradition certainly acknowledges that a musical or harmonic quality is integral to their holy Otherworld, a 'holy song' of Yahweh. An example of this concept is their view of the heavenly hierarchy of God's choirs and angels, which surround the Throne of Glory – the Seraphim, Cherubim, Thrones, Dominations, Virtues, Powers, Principalities, Archangels, and angels – all in constant song, making this Otherworld dimension very musical indeed.

Sufism, too, has references to the supernatural presence of and power of music in Paradise. The poetic verse of the famous Sufi poet Rumi (1207–73) in his work entitled *Mathnawi* IV, 735–7, comments on the purpose of the *sama* dance of the 'Whirling Dervishes':

> We all have been parts of Adam, we have heard those melodies in Paradise. Although the water and earth of our bodies have caused a doubt to fall upon us, something of those melodies comes back to our memory.[22]

So the Sufi view of Paradise also acknowledges an inherent supernatural musical quality, as 'we have all heard those melodies in Paradise.' Judging by their early medieval literature, it seems that the ancient Irish could not have agreed more.

Robin Gwyndaf, in his informative paper 'Fairylore: Memorates and Legends from Welsh Oral Tradition', was told by an aged Welsh folklore informant recalling his childhood beliefs about a 'green place' where fairies were known to be seen:

> It was in a hollow, and there would be a tremendous amount of mushrooms growing in those places ... And we strongly believed that their home was underneath the ground ... And I don't think anyone saw the fairies during the daylight. I believe that if we had risen early enough in the morning, then we would have seen them dancing. We had come to believe that, of course.[23]

Liminal places where music is heard

Certain places may be described as liminal. Liminal locations are those ordinary places which, because of their inherent characteristic of 'limit' or 'boundary', are natural symbols of transcendence. Examples might be a cave or hillside hollow entrance, a doorway threshold, the edge of a window sill, a certain ford in a river or a certain location where several crossroads intersect.

As one might expect, at liminal places supernatural music is more likely to be heard if the circumstances are right. If and when such a transcendental event might occur, the supernatural music tends to confirm the liminal status, just as the liminal status of a place may also confirm the listener's expectation that the music heard at that boundary is supernatural. For instance, one is more likely to hear supernatural music at the entrance to a special cave or hollow on a certain hillside or mountain rather than on an ordinary hill.

Liminal places are very frequently mentioned in Irish folklore accounts, but less so in this literature of the early medieval Irish period. Nonetheless, we do have a few examples of liminal locations, those places where the normal boundaries symbolise those less visible boundaries which separate our everyday, mundane reality from another supernatural reality, so that the latter cease to exist or are made very flexible. These are places where the 'veil' between this world and the Otherworld is thin or lifted entirely.

But to qualify as liminal *per se*, a 'limit' or specific boundary line of some kind must be present to be crossed over. The early Irish were reluctant to draw an explicit line between exactly where this world ends and where the supernatural Otherworld begins, so these liminal places are important as they seem to serve as special gateways connecting this world to the supernatural Otherworld. They are viewed as especially powerful locations and crossing them is highly significant.

The anecdote attributed to St Brendan regarding the student harper and the appearance of a shining bird at his window, which declared itself to be St Michael, was quoted in full earlier in Chapter 4. As you may recall, the shining bird sang to St Brendan and made the most beautiful music he had ever heard.[24] One may note that, in this instance, the appearance of the shining musical bird was initially at the window's edge, a natural boundary point, much like a doorway threshold. The bird then crosses this window's edge, enters into the everyday world of St Brendan's life and sits on St Brendan's altar. Having done so, he has crossed over from God's otherworldly, shining dimension into our mundane, earthly dimension, the window serving as a 'border' point between the two worlds. This shining bird, stating that he was St Michael in disguise, was located at the place where this world and the sacred Otherworld intermeshed, symbolised by a liminal place.

Another example of a liminal place comes from *Accallam na Senorach*, ('Colloquy of the Ancients'), where a wee *sidhe* harper named Cnu Deroil emerges from the most likely entrance of his Otherworld home, a certain hollow or cave on the side of the mountain named Slievenaman.[25] He belongs with the traditional folklore classification of an Otherworld *sidhe* being who lives within a mountain or hill. The last remaining aged Fianna warriors recount their discovery of this wee musician and the place where he was found, and how the five musicians of the Fianna learned fairy music from Cnu Deroil; this example was quoted in full in Chapter 4. Here, Cnu Deroil says that he clearly comes from the Otherworld dwelling place, Slievenaman, implying that his home is within. In other Old Irish tales, Cnu Deroil's bewitching *sidhe* music is sometimes heard, yet he himself is rarely, if ever, seen. In order to play music for the Fianna, who are portrayed here as being of this world, he had to cross the symbolic border from his Otherworld home into the earthly, everyday world.

Another example of a liminal place is from 'The Voyage of Mael Duin'. It refers to supernatural music heard at the doorway of a noble *sidhe* woman's fort, located on an island out at sea. In the following excerpt, the cleric Mael Duin and his men are in a boat out at sea, see the fort and hear harmonious music coming from the net that is over the entrance of the doorway:

> She went from them and closed the noble pleasant fort: her net, manifesting mighty power, chanted good harmonious music.[26]

Here again, the doorway, like a window's edge, serves as a clear boundary point between the world of everyday reality and the Otherworld of the *sidhe* woman's home. This entrance to the Otherworld realm – in this case her doorway – is covered with a musical net and is a liminal place. It is also described here as being a place of inherent supernatural music.

As scholars continue to debate whether all of the *Immrama* tales are to be interpreted as being entirely in the realm of the supernatural or not, for our purposes here regarding music, I have included this one particular example to illustrate the liminal concept.

Illustratory comparative material

Liminal places are also referred to in the literature of other cultures around the world. One fine example also comes from modern Irish folklore, involving the site of Tory Hole, Slieve Rushen in County Cavan. Tory Hole, a cave in the hillside, is the focus of the following account given by an informant to the Irish Folklore Commission in 1938:

> The Tory Hole – as a certain mountain cavern in the townland of Aughkinnigh is called – is known locally as an abode of the fairies and many are the tales woven about it by the old *seanchaidhthe* of the locality . . . Many years ago . . . one of the fiddlers went in to play a few tunes inside the Tory Hole. He was never seen again. Many a day since, and hundreds of years have gone by, the strains of fiddler's music have been heard coming from the Tory Hole. The fiddler liked the company of the fairies and has never since asked to leave.[27]

Like the mountain home of Cnu Deroil, the Tory Hole is a hillside cavern or hollow, where, once entered, it is believed that a 'line' is crossed into the abode of the *sidhe*. The world inside the hill or mountain is clearly different from that of our mundane, everyday world and, in this case, once this line is crossed, there is no turning back for a mortal.

Legends of music emanating from the caves of nymphs in antiquity are similar to tales from the northern parts of the Netherlands where, according to Corneil van Kempen, such beings were called 'Dames Blanches', the 'White Ladies'. They were believed to live in caves, which are a classic liminal location for occasionally hearing strange, supernatural music.

> They lived in caves, and they would attack people who would travel at night. The shepherds would also be harassed. And the women who had newly born babies had to be very careful, for they were quick in stealing the children away. In their lair, one could hear all sorts of strange noises, indistinct words that no one could understand and musical sounds.[28]

From Scottish folklore, we have a description of the arrival of the musician Thomas the Rhymer of Ercildourne, to the gates of the Otherworld realm of Elfin Land. While resting at Huntlie Bank, at the foot of the Eildon Hills in the Borders, Thomas idly plucked his lute during a break on his journey. Soon, he suddenly became aware of a beautiful lady on a white steed, wearing a green mantle. She asked him to play his lute for her, and he did so, eventually agreeing to go with her to her home in Elfin Land. They rode through the forest, and soon Thomas lost track of where he was, although he thought he knew the area very well as he lived nearby. As Thomas and the Elfin Queen kept riding through the wilderness, the borders between this world and the Otherworld of Elfin Land became flexible; Thomas and the Elfin Queen then arrive:

> At last they reached the gates of Elfin Land, where a thousand faery trumpets proclaimed their approach, and they passed into an enchanted country filled with a splendid light.[29]

This liminal place in the wilderness, the 'gates' of Elfin Land, is a borderline where Thomas crossed from this world into the world of the *sidhe* called Elfin Land. Once he crossed this line, that is actually went through the gates, there was no turning back. He was now in the place of the 'enchanted country' – Elfin Land – and his arrival is announced by a thousand fairy trumpets.

Robin Gwyndaf, a prominent Welsh folklore expert, was told the following tale by an elderly folklore informant recalling his early childhood. It makes reference to the doorway of a cave, a liminal place, and the home of fairies:

> And they lived in many places. They lived in Coed yr Henblas [Henblas Wood], as we say. And in the cave – Ogof Pitar Graen [Peter Green's Cave] we used to call it. Well, the fairies were there. There was no argument about that. But, of course, they wouldn't be out all the time. Sometimes when it was quiet the fairies would play outside the cave's door.[30]

Liminal places are also described in the Breton folktales. The following example describes the activities of the *corrigans*, a race of otherworldly beings similar to the Irish *sidhe*:

> Like the fairies in Britain and Ireland, the *corrigans* find their favorite amusement in the circular dance. When the moon is clear and bright they gather for their frolic near menhirs and dolmens, and tumuli, and at cross-roads ... and they never miss an opportunity of enticing a mortal passing by to join them ... (and, from an informant at Carnac in 1909) ... 'the *corrigans* are little dwarfs who formerly, by moonlight, used to dance in a circle ... They sang a song ... they whistled in order to assemble; where they danced mushrooms grew, and it was necessary to maintain silence so as not to interrupt them at their dance ... the *corrigans* dress in very coarse white linen cloth. They were mischievous spirits ['esprits follets'] who lived under dolmens'.[31]

The *corrigans* live under dolmens in their Otherworld *sidhe* dimension, as described in the above example; they tend to gather at stones like Carnac, to dance and play their music, and also at *crossroads* – clearly a liminal place. That supernatural music might be heard at such a place is not as surprising compared with that of a non-liminal place like an ordinary rock or road.

Everyday places where music is heard

Everyday places in this literature are described as places where music is heard, performed and enjoyed. Such locations might be a king's court, a battlefield, a fair, a monastery, a nobleman's house, a field, a hermit's hut or a hill, mountain, river or earth mound. Such typical everyday places can even occasionally be the site of unusual experiences involving supernatural music, but certainly not very often.

These places in everyday life are distinguished from the liminal category in that they do not have an inherent 'limit' or 'boundary' to them, but simply exist as a location or place in everyday life experience. In these places the presumption is that the music heard is of more mundane source and quality.

However, some places or features of the landscape are natural symbols of the supernatural, either because they are known to be ancient sacred sites or because their physical attributes of height (hills) or depth (wells) make them natural symbols of the divine heights or depths of the reality we all share.

Daithi O'hOgain, in making reference to such everyday locations in early Irish life, lists some of the more common types of such sites, many of which are also described in folklore as being somehow related to the *sidhe*:

> It may be a 'fairy rath' (an ancient tumulus or relic of an earthenwork fort), a riverside (water being anciently associated with Celtic deities), or a cairn or a hilltop. The fact is that ... the locations are the same as those involved in ancient seer-craft[32]

The general presumption is that music heard in such places is itself mundane; however, this presumption may be defeated by some unusual features of the music, and more easily defeated in places of natural sacred significance.

In the clearly Christian contexts, notably the monastic poetry of the hermit monks, great appreciation in everyday life of the 'music' of the natural elements in praise of God is shown. This may be seen with the following reference from the eleventh-century poem attributed to St Columba ('An Exile's Dream') while he was in exile in Scotland, reflecting on his memories of Ireland:

> To Mag nEolairg, by Benevenagh,
> across Lough Foyle, where I might
> hear tuneful music from the swans ...

> The sound of the wind in the elm making
> music for us, and the startled cry of
> the pleasant grey blackbird when she
> has clapped her wings.[33]

These places are simply mentioned here as a normal part of the everyday life and worship of God's creation of a Christian hermit monk, and not as specifically supernatural in any way.

From *Betha Patraic* ('The Life of Patrick'), we have mention of the location of the hill of Cashel as a musical place which occurs in an overtly Christian context:

> Patrick's resurrection in Down,
> His primacy in Armagh,
> On the hillock of musical Cashel
> He granted a third of his grace.[34]

Here the hill of Cashel is simply referred to as a musical place known and appreciated by the Christians in their everyday life; it is not portrayed as being particularily supernatural in any way. However, the hill/mound imagery is interesting to note.

Music in and around monasteries and churches, too, is portrayed in the Christian examples as being highly appreciated in everyday life. The monks would constantly sing the canonical hours and at Mass. Music around a saint and his or her environment is also described in some of the references to music in the Irish saints' lives. For instance, St Moling is described as having a rather unusual 'pet', a musical fly, that was known to always be in his vicinity, and he is portrayed as very saddened when the fly died.

Mountains, and especially mountain tops, are described as places where a saint might go to commune with God and pray. Sometimes certain mountains are also described as places especially conducive to music where saints prefer to go and chant the psalms.

Everyday life in Christian monastic communities is often described as musical, especially regarding chanting in or around the church or monastery itself. Such great appreciation of what is described as the 'music' of the sounds of the smith's anvil while making bells for the church, or the clergy out at sea listening to the 'music' of their hammers as they repair their fishing nets, do not show a supernatural characteristic *per se* as these are places clearly encountered in everyday life. Such places are an integral part of mundane, everyday, earthly life but are described as also having a musical element that is highly appreciated.

The more overtly primal examples also show music being an integral part of everyday life and describe the places where it is heard. Chief among these are battlefields, the courts of kings, fairs, mountains, hills, lakes, forests and so on. Although some of the following primal context examples do not mention anything supernatural about them, others do describe the occasional unusual experience that someone encounters in the course of their everyday business. The imagery is markedly consistent with some of that used in the earlier categories, illustrating a continuity from the everyday mundane examples right through to the supernatural.

Battlefields and the 'music' of the swords are described as being part of everyday life in the following reference to the feats of the hero Conall from *Cath Ruis na Rig for Boinn*, ('The Battle of Ross Na Rig on the Boyne'):

> It is then that Conall drew the sharp long sword out of its sheath of war, and played the music of his sword on the armies. The ring of Conall's sword was heard throughout the battalions on both sides, at that moment of time. However, as soon as they heard the music of Conall's sword, they quaked.[35]

The sound of the anvils of the smiths making weapons at the site of a battlefield is described in this ninth-century poem from the Book of Leinster. It describes activities at the location of the Hill of Alenn, an early Irish site of kingship:

> The music of its bent hard anvils, the sound of its songs from the tongues of poets, the fire of its men at the great contest, the beauty of its women at the high assembly ... Its lovely melodies at every hour.[36]

Kings' courts were popular places in early medieval Ireland for a great variety of everyday musical activities, as one might expect. The court of King Ailill and Queen Medb of Connacht is frequently referred to as the site of much musical activity. From the *Accalam na Senorach* ('Colloquy of the Ancients'), we have the following description of the music of kings' courts, as recalled by Caeilte, an aged, surviving Fianna warrior, while telling St Patrick of the days of old:

> Three sorts of music, and O music of three kinds, that comely kings enjoyed! Music of harps, music of timpans and the humming of Trogan's son Fer-tuinne.[37]

But occasionally in everyday life, albeit rarely, a king could have an unusual experience involving music in some way. We have one sterling example of this phenomenon where, one day, king Cormac and his court received a most unusual visitor from an unknown, Otherworld place. When questioned, the man said he was Manannan, from *tir tairngiri* ('The Land of Promise').[38]

This unusual day results in King Cormac's own court being the place where a supernatural event occurs, as the surprised king receives a mysterious stranger who has with him a magical, musical branch with three golden apples on it. He then decides to go with Manannan to visit *tir tairngiri*, something he obviously had not planned on that day. The musical branch seems to serve as a type of passport to the Otherworld. There are several examples of such interventions by supernatural forces in the everyday life of a king, many of which are musical.

The home of a nobleman was also a place where music was heard as part of everyday life, as illustrated by the reference to the music at a lively party from *Esnada Tige Buchet* ('The Songs of Buchet's House'), which was quoted in full earlier in Chapter 2.[39]

The places where the seasonal fairs were held, such as Carmun or Taltiu, are also portrayed in this literature as being musical environments as part of everyday life experience. From the *Metrical Dindshenchas*, we have the following reference to the 'music' of the chariots at the fair of Taltiu:

> White-sided Taltiu … A fair with gold, with silver, with games, with music of chariots, with adornment of body and soul by means of knowledge and eloquence.[40]

A particular mountain called Slieve Brey is referred to as being 'music-haunted' in the following example from the late twelfth-century poem entitled 'Suibne in the Snow':

> From the Knockmealdown mountains (it is no easy
> expedition) I come to the river in pleasant Gaille.
> From the Gaille river (though it is a long journey)
> I make my way east to music-haunted Slieve Brey.[41]

Trees and groves are sometimes described as places where music might be heard in everyday life, and where musicians would play. Occasionally, they are portrayed as a place where an unusual event might occur, where one may hear mysterious music or perhaps encounter a supernatural musician. One such occasion is from *Cath Maige Mucrama* ('The Battle of Mag Mucrama') which describes Eogan and Lugaid, on their way to visit Art, son of Conn, coming upon a particular 'clump of yew' by a river:

As they came along the flat land by the river, in a clump of yew that overhung a certain rapid water they heard music. Back to [king] Oilioll then they convey a wee man whom they had plucked out of the clump.[42]

Yew trees were sacred to the Druids, and are often associated with the primal society examples; they are very rarely, if ever, mentioned in examples with a Christian context.

Water-based locations like lakes and rivers are also used in some of the overtly primal examples. The waters of Assaroe in south-west Ireland in particular are referred to as being especially musical. As portrayed in *Accalam na Senorach* ('Colloquy of the Ancients'), the waters of Assaroe are featured as being a place where one might have the opportunity to hear the music of the *sidhe*, from *tir tairngiri*, as did the Fianna warriors one day:

they heard a sound, a gush of music, draw near from the water of Assaroe: melody for sake of which one would have abandoned the whole world's various strains'.[43]

In the mid-twelfth century poem about the river Garb ('The Cry of the Garb'), a hermit monk comments that he believes the music of the river Garb is superior to Assaroe:

Though many things be told of the falls
as Ess Maige, at Ess Dubthaige, and at Assaroe
to which salmon run, the voice of the Garb is
more musical ...

The strong prophesied Watercourse, its high
cascade is tuneful! The angelic Tacarda – what
cascade is purer in cry?[44]

The sea is often described as a place in everyday life that has musical characteristics, with most references acknowledging the pleasant sounds of the waves as a special kind of 'music of the sea'. Occasionally, in the process of going about one's everyday business out at sea, the traveller may encounter the music of the mermaids, as in the previously quoted example from the *Dindshenchas* referring to the songs of mermaids heard near Port Lairge (modern-day Waterford).[45]

Lakes and rivers are often designated in the *Dindshenchas* as being everyday places where one might be fortunate enough to hear supernatural music. For example, in the following reference from *Serglige Con Cuchulainn* ('The Wasting Sickness of Cuchulainn'), singing *sidhe* birds from the Otherworld come over a loch where Cuchulainn tells his wife Eithne:

'If in the future any birds come to Mag Muirthemne or to the Boyne, the two birds that are the most beautiful among those that come shall be thine.' A little while after this they saw two birds flying over the lake, linked together by a chain of red gold. They sang a gentle song, and a sleep fell upon all the men who were there.[46]

Illustratory comparative material

The literature of other cultures also attests to the value placed on music in everyday, earthly life at certain locations. For example, the Bible has many references to the enjoyment of music in the everyday life of Moses and the Israelites during their time in the desert. In Exodus 15, the 'Song of Victory' is sung to Yahweh; in Exodus 15: 20, the famous incident occurs where Miriam, the prophetess and sister of Aaron, 'took up a tambourine, and all the women followed her with tambourines, dancing, while Miriam took up from them the refrain ... ' and they all sang praises to Yahweh.

An interesting incident occurs in Numbers 21: 16 where Moses sings at a particular location named Beer to summon up a well in the desert, as part of the everyday life of the wandering Israelites. Music mentioned in relation to battle is often referred to in the Old Testament in particular, for example in Numbers 31: 6 where Moses and the Israelites prepare for war with Midian by 'carrying the sacred objects and the trumpets for the battle cry'. One particular Jewish tradition, 'reported by the Italian Rabbi Moscato (sixteenth century) is that Joshua heard the pleasant melody of the Sun in the middle of battle with the Amorites and was seriously distracted, which is why he said, 'Sun stand thou still upon Gibeon' (Joshua 10: 12), meaning 'Stop singing!'[47] This is an example of supernatural music intervening into earthly experience, even in the midst of battle.

Chinese emperors in ancient China employed very large numbers of musicians to entertain the court as part of normal everyday life. The T'ang Dynasty (AD 618–907)

> kept no less than fourteen court orchestras, each consisting of from five hundred to seven hundred performers ... yet, according to the ancients, to keep so many musicians was far from unnecessary or superfluous, but was the height of wisdom. For the energy invoked by the divinely-attuned tone-patterns of these court orchestras was believed to exert a far-reaching influence into all of the affairs of the nation.[48]

The Chinese historians recorded that for the solstices and other important fairs and festivals, the T'ang Dynasty also brought together an orchestra numbering no less than ten thousand.

The great Highland families of Scotland employed harpists as part of everyday life, and they were greatly valued in carrying on the ancient Bardic tradition.

> It is clear that a harpist would have been an accepted member of any household of rank ... One of these noble households would have been at Kildrummy Castle in Strathdon, the thirteenth-century castle of the Earls of Mar. This was held by Alexander Stewart, the Wolf of Badenoch, fourth son of Robert II. His son, also Alexander Stewart, who lived from c.1375–1435, apparently employed a harper named Duncan ... This man must have been of some standing, since after the fall from power of his patron, in 1438, the Crown awarded him lands at Wester Cloveth, near Kildrummy, to support him in the poor straits in which he now found himself. The King, after all, was also a Stewart, and a close relative of Mar.'[49]

Harpists were obviously greatly valued in everyday life at the castles of the great Highland families.

One instance from the folklore of everyday life in nineteenth-century Wales tells of a place on a particular mountain where a man disappeared for three weeks, his family giving him up for dead:

> A man who lived at Ystradfynlais ... [was] going out one day to look after his cattle and sheep on the mountain and disappeared. In about three weeks, after a search had been made in vain for him and his wife had given him up for dead, he came home. His wife asked him where he had been ... he told her he had been playing his flute, which he usually took with him on the mountain, at the Llorfa, a spot near the Van Pool, when he was surrounded at a distance by little beings like men, who closed nearer and nearer to him until they became a very small circle. They sang and danced, and so affected him that he quite lost himself. They offered him some small cakes to eat, of which he partook; and he had never enjoyed himself so much in his life.[50]

Music as part of everyday life of ancient India

> was divided into three general classes: the classical *raga*, the purely sacred music (vocal chants to deities) ... and folk music ... However, it could be argued that in order to (today) experience the total, committed atmosphere of Indian music, there exists no replacement for hearing it in its natural environment, as the holy men of the hills chant their morning rituals, or as the musicians of the local village spontaneously gather at sunset for the sounding out of the tones of the hour.[51]

Many of these same types of places, like hills or mountains, the local village and so on, are similar to those described in much of world folklore, including that of early Ireland.

Conclusion

As one can see, the places where music is heard vary considerably. The locations in the category of purely otherworldly places range from the Christian Heaven to *tir tairngiri* and the world of the *sidhe*. These supernatural places are described as having musical qualities in them. In the Christian Heaven, there are the angelic choirs singing praises to God, for example.

Many descriptive subdivisions of the primal Otherworld are also described, ranging from the familiar *tir tairngiri* ('The Land of Promise') to *mag mell* ('The Pleasant Plain'), *tir na nOg* ('The Land of Youth'), *tir innambeo* ('The Land of the Living') and so on. The term *sidhe* also applies here to those Otherworld places where the *sidhe* beings might play music or be heard. Thomas O'Cathasaigh, in an article entitled 'The Semantics of *Sid*', shows how, linguistically, the Old Irish term *sid* can mean both (1) an Otherworld hill or mound; and (2) peace/peaceful.[52] As we have seen, the purely supernatural Otherworld is frequently described as having musical qualities, and often such music is described as being an integral part of the Otherworld. This is true whether the context is Christian or primal.

The second category – the liminal places–pertains to certain everyday places or locations which, because of their natural 'limit' or 'boundary' charcteristics, are natural symbols of transcendence. Such places might be a doorway, a window sill, a cave opening at the side of a mountain or a crossroads. Liminality, then, usually implies the possibility of some kind of interaction with the supernatural. Hearing unusual supernatural music at such a place tends to confirm the liminal status of the location. We saw examples from the primal references which spoke of the entrances to the abodes of the *sidhe* beings, those liminal places where such music is heard and where the boundary of everyday consciousness is crossed, providing entry into another reality. Such places serve as a kind of portal or bridge between this world and the Otherworld. Often this border itself is clearly described, that is once entry to the *sidhe* dwelling has occurred and the doorway threshold crossed, another dimension is entered into.

One is here reminded of the well-known Irish tale about Finn mac Cumaill, who got his thumb 'stuck' in a *sidhe* door entrance on a hillside mound. Thereafter, he had his famous 'Thumb of Knowledge', as he had contacted a special boundary point between this world and the Otherworld symbolised by the doorway.

The third category – places where music is heard in everyday life– include a broad range of locations such as kings' courts, the homes of noblemen and at hills, mountains, monasteries, rivers, lochs, trees, fairs and festivals and so on. Early Irish society is portrayed as very highly appreciative of music, and the references are rich with varied illustrations of this attitude. When analysing this material, one gets the distinct impression that in everyday life in early Ireland, one never knows for sure when or where something from the Otherworld might intervene into the affairs of everyday life. When it does, music is portrayed as an especially effective vehicle for this experience. It is as though the early Irish felt that music itself somehow could serve as a direct vehicle to the divine, and sometimes appear to be in awe of its power in this regard.

The theme of water-based places and music occurs throughout this literature. Springs, the sea, lochs, wells and fountains are all mentioned in relation to music in certain instances. The water imagery used is rather consistent, no matter what the context. For example, the Christian clergymen's adventure of hearing the mermaids sing while out at sea is illustrative of a connection between water and music. The sea is also referred to in the ordinary descriptions of music heard around the lochs and rivers of everyday life.

Again, it seems that the early Irish were reluctant to draw an absolutely explicit line between this world and the Otherworld. There are a fair number of such places in reference to everyday life that indicate that they seemed to feel that the supernatural Otherworld permeates in and around our everyday, mundane world in a unique interplay and, as such, one could never be sure exactly when or where one might have an encounter with the Otherworld and its music.

Earth-oriented imagery, too, is markedly consistent throughout the references to music. Such earth-oriented sites might be a hill, mountain, plain or field, mound, cairn, rath, a certain stone or a tree or a grove of trees. In the examples for the supernatural category we have several references to the shining Tree of Life with its musical birds in the Christian Land of the Saints. In the supernatural primal contexts, we have the 'three trees of purple glass' in the Otherworld realm of *mag mell*, as described to Cuchulainn by his charioteer Loeg, and the tree with music at its crown, as seen by Cathair in a dream, for example.

In everyday life, too, trees and music are referred to. In the Christian contexts, the hermits speak of this connection in relation to monastic life. In the primal contexts, yew trees are referred to as where the wee *sidhe* harper Fer Fi was found. The hermit monks often refer to the 'music of the pines' as part of everyday medieval Irish monastic life; 'the Jesuit Athanasius Kircher (1602–80) accepted this idea, as he did so many ancient musical myths, saying that the wind in pine-trees does actually have this effect if the trees themselves are of suitably proportionate heights.'[53] The Book of Lecan, in one of the Irish Apocryphal works entitled 'The Mystical Tree', gives further descriptions of such a tree in the Christian Paradise.[54] This motif of a tree in Paradise is well-known in world literature, and in both classical and post-Latin poetry in particular.[55] The *Saltair na Rann*, the Irish Adam and Eve story, contains references to music in Paradise and the theme of the musical Tree of Life and its singing birds.[56]

One can further note what the early Irish seem to believe about music and their perspective of everyday life from these sources. It appears that they felt that there was a dynamic interplay between this world and the Otherworld, which at the right location and under the correct circumstances could meet and encounter each other. This continuity is seen both in the parallelism of the details in supernatural and mundane places, and in the liminal encounters. For example, the imagery of the Tree of Life of the Christian Heaven with its singing birds is used in some of the examples from everyday life, where the music of the birds on trees is also described in a similar manner in the primal contexts. When these categories are placed side by side there is a certain parallelism in imagery and description between the Otherworld places and those drawn from everyday, mundane life.

It appears that the early Irish believed that music has, more often than not, a linkage or connection to the Otherworld. It seems that because of their belief in the power of music, it was taken more seriously in their society and not regarded as mere entertainment, as is more common in western society today. In the purely supernatural and liminal place categories especially, one can see that there is a good possibility that the early Irish felt there was a continuous connection to a divine or transcendent source through music as the gateway.

Certain types of places do seem to be more predominant among the supernatural places in the Christian contexts that involve music, such as trees, island paradises and so on, while others never appear in those references, such as fountains or the music of the swords in warfare. Often, the Otherworld dimension itself is described as having an inherently musical quality, no matter what the context. John Carey describes the daily living places of the *sidhe* inhabitants, stating:

> Otherworld beings are depicted as living within hills, beneath lakes, or the sea, or on islands in lakes, or off the coast; there are also tales of halls (of the *sidhe* folk) chanced upon in the night, which vanish with the coming of day ... the abodes of the *sidhe* are lakes, rivers, stones, rocks, woods, trees, caves, underground places, bridges, hills or mountains as well as ancient earthworks and ruins; there are also tales of people and countries beneath the sea'.[57]

From the heights of the music of the birds on the shining Tree of Life in the purely supernatural Otherworld, to the 'music of the pines' in everyday life, we see a certain consistency regarding places and music.

Recently in our modern, fast-moving world, the Gregorian chants sung by the Benedictine monks of Santo Domingo de Silos of Spain hit 'number one' on the 1994 music charts, and several years later sales were still going strong. Accounts abound of commuters listening to this music, and certain kinds of New Age meditation music, in their cars every day. We clearly seek in modern times the peace and serenity of spirit that this music seems to provide, and in the process of reclaiming its value are perhaps edging a little bit closer to the early Irish worldview regarding music.

It is now possible to have music with us everywhere, and all the time. With this in mind, we will now explore the times that music is heard from the sources from early Ireland.

Notes

1. O'Madagain, B., 'Functions of Irish Song', *Bealoideas* (Dublin, 1985), pp. 215–16.

2. MacMathuna, S., 'Contributions to a Study of the Voyages of St. Brendan and St. Malo', *Irlande et Bretagne* (Rennes, 1994), p. 46.
3. Stokes, W., *Lives of the Saints from the Book of Lismore* (Oxford, 1890), p. 259.
4. Stokes, W., 'Immram Snedgus', *RC*, 9 (Paris, 1888), p. 21.
5. Carey, J., 'The Heavenly City in *Saltair na Rann*', *Celtica*, 18 (Dublin, 1986), p. 99.
6. Clancy, T. and Markus, G., *Iona: The Earliest Poetry of a Celtic Monastery* (Edinburgh: Edinburgh University Press, 1995), p. 107.
7. Stokes, W., *Tripartite Life of Patrick* (London, 1887), pp. 262–3.
8. Carey, J., 'Angelology in *Saltair na Rann*', *Celtica*, 19 (Dublin, 1987), p. 4.
9. Jackson, K., *A Celtic Miscellany* (Harmondsworth; Penguin, 1971), pp. 288–95.
10. Meyer, K., *Life of St. Colman, Son of Luachan* (Dublin, 1911), p. 15.
11. Jackson, *CM*, pp. 295–6.
12. Carey, 'Heavenly City', pp. 88–9.
13. Gwynn, E., *MD*, III (Dublin, 1913), pp. 177, 183.
14. Jackson, *CM*, pp. 173–5.
15. MacCana, P., 'The Sinless Otherworld of *Immram Brain*', *Eriu*, 27 (Dublin, 1976), p. 98.
16. Gwynn, E., *MD*, III (Dublin, 1913), p. 289.
17. O'hOgain, D., *Myth, Legend and Romance: An Encyclopedia of Irish Folk Tradition* (New York: Ryan Publishing, 1991), p. 186.
18. Rolleston, T.W., *The High Deeds of Finn and other Bardic Romances of Ancient Ireland* (New York: Shocken Books, 1973; reprint of London edn, 1910), p. 47.
19. Godwin, J., *Harmonies of Heaven and Earth* (Rochester VT: Inner Traditions International, 1987), p. 57.
20. Glazerson, Rabbi M., *Music and Kabbala* (Jerusalem, 1988), p. 33.
21. Buber, Martin, *Hasidim and Modern Man*, ed. and trans. Maurice Friedman (New York, 1958), pp. 106f.
22. Godwin, *Harmonies*, p. 67.
23. Gwyndaf, R., 'Fairylore: Memorates and Legends from Welsh Oral Tradition', *The Good People*, ed. P. Narvaez (New York: Garland, 1991), p. 181.
24. Jackson, *CM*, p. 283.
25. O'Grady, S., 'Colloquy with the Ancient Men/Accalam na Senorach', *Silva Gadelica*, II (London 1892), p. 116.
26. Stokes, W., 'The voyage of Mael Duin', *RC*, 9 (Paris, 1888), p. 18.
27. MacNeill, M., 'The Musician in the Cave', *Bealoideas*, 19 (Dublin, 1987), p. 115.
28. Vallee, J., *Passport to Magonia* (Chicago: Contemporary Books, 1969), p. 63.

29. Wilson, Barbara, *Scottish Folktales and Legends* (Oxford: Oxford University Press, 1954), p. 11. Tales based on Campbell's *Waifs and Strays*.
30. Gwyndaf, 'Fairylore: Memorates and Legends', p. 171.
31. Evans-Wentz, W. Y., *The Fairy Faith in Celtic Countries*, (New York: University Books, 1966; 1911 orig.), pp. 207–8.
32. O'hOgain, *Myth, Legend, and Romance*, p. 186.
33. Murphy, *EIL*, pp. 66–9.
34. Stokes, *LSBL*, p. 162.
35. Hogain, E., *Cath Ruis na Rig for Boinn*, RIA Todd Lecture Series 4 (Dublin, 1892), p. 47.
36. Greene, D. and O'Connor, F., *A Golden Treasury of Poetry* (London: Macmillan, 1967), pp. 68–70.
37. O'Grady, *SG*, II, p. 112.
38. Stokes, W., 'Cormac's Adventure in the Land of Promise', *Irische Texte* (ed. with E. Windisch), Series 3 (Leipzig, 1891), p. 212.
39. Stokes, W., 'Esnada Tige Buchet', *RC*, 25 (Paris, 1904), pp. 31–33.
40. Gwynn, E., *MD*, IV (Dublin, 1913), p. 151.
41. Murphy, *EIL*, pp. 138–9.
42. O'Grady, *SG*, II, p. 349.
43. O'Grady, *SG* II, p. 253.
44. Murphy, *EIL*, pp. 116–17.
45. Gwynn, E., *MD* III (Dublin, 1913), p. 191.
46. Cross, T. and Slover, C., *Ancient Irish Tales*, (New York: Barnes & Noble, 1969), p. 178.
47. Godwin, *Harmonies*, p. 60.
48. Tame, D., *The Secret Power of Music* (New York: Destiny Books, 1984), p. 46.
49. Sanger, K. and Kinnaird, A., *Tree of Strings: Crann nan teud*, (Temple, Midlothian: Kinmor Music, 1992), p. 111.
50. Vallee, *Passport to Magonia*, p. 29.
51. Tame, *Secret Power of Music*, p. 177.
52. O'Cathasaigh, T., 'The Semantics of Sid', *Eigse*, 17 (Dublin, 1977–9), p. 149.
53. Godwin, *Harmonies*, p. 16.
54. McNamara, M., *The Apocrypha in the Irish Church*, (Dublin: DIAS, 1975), p. 78.
55. Curtius, E. R., *European Literature and the Latin Middle Ages*, trans. W. R. Trask (New York, 1953), p. 195.
56. Murdoch, B., *The Irish Adam and Eve Story: Saltair na Rann*, (Dublin: DIAS, 1976), pp. 57–8.
57. Carey, J., 'The Otherworld in Irish Tradition', *Eigse*, 19 (Dublin, 1982–3), pp. 40–1.

6

Times

D O THE TIMES AT which music is heard tell us anything about its source or status? Judging from the early Irish literature, they often do. For instance, music is described as being heard continuously in the supernatural Otherworld, where it is viewed as being eternally present. In examples from everyday, mundane life, music is heard at many different times.

In these early Irish references to music, the time music is heard often has parallel characteristics to the place in which the music is heard; for example, if music is described as being heard in a liminal place, it also occurs at a liminal time. A liminal time means a time when the borders are crossed from this world into the supernatural or divine, though it may be difficult to ascertain exactly where the line is to be drawn between the time reality of our everyday life and the 'timeless' realm of the Otherworld.

Like places, the times at which music is heard fall into three major categories: the purely supernatural or Otherworld times; liminal times; and the times music is heard in everyday life.

Supernatural times music is heard

It is not as easy to identify designated supernatural times as it is to locate specific supernatural places where music is heard. 'Eternity' is one term often used to describe a supernatural time state, usually referring to that after death. Another way of identifying supernatural time is by using various adjectives, such as 'immortal', 'infinite', 'perpetual' or 'everlasting'. Likewise, the terms 'continuous' and 'unceasing' are often used to describe the supernatural music heard in such a dimension. A distinct quality of timelessness is implied, as it is also an inherent quality of the Otherworld itself.

As stated, the particular times that music is heard are often similar to the place or dimension the music is heard in. For example, in the supernatural Otherworld, such as God's Heaven or *tir tairngiri* ('The Land of Promise'), the music heard is often described as continuous and unceasing, of being in a 'timeless' realm of eternal harmony. When the Otherworld is reached, the normal laws of time and physics here on earth seem to be suspended and one is in another world altogether. Such a supernatural Otherworld time dimension has its own laws and reality and can be difficult to judge by our earthly standards.

The concept of continuous music heard in a purely supernatural Otherworld occurs fairly frequently in the early medieval Irish literature. One example illustrates this quite clearly, from *Tochmarc Etaine* ('The Wooing of Etain') in which Midir of the *sidhe* folk tries to woo the beautiful maiden Etain with a promise of living in a wonderful land where eternal music is always present:

Fair woman, will you go with me to a wonderful land where music is?[1]

Numerous other examples illustrate the characteristic of beautiful, unceasing music being integral to the Otherworld.

One way of representing the continuous nature of music, especially in the Christian contexts, is to relate its occurrence to the canonical hours into which each monastic twenty-four-hour period of time was divided. These canonical hours were called the Divine Office, and were sung eight times a day – seven during the day and one at night, in which the psalms were sung and holy scriptures read. By doing so, the presence of Christ was believed to be recalled from its invocation in the Mass, in an effort to continually bring God's presence into the monastic environment. So by returning regularly to musical praise at these times, they felt they effectively ensured continuity of music in Heaven and, as we see later, on earth as well.

From *Fis Adomnan* ('The Vision of Adamnan'), we have a reference to the beautiful, eternal music of Heaven in the Land of the Saints, of the singing of the birds of Heaven and of all of the saints together in harmony in praise of God. But there is also the following specific reference to the time of the eight canonical hours in Heaven:

There are three marvellous birds on the throne in the King's presence, and their task is to direct their attention always on the Creator. In praise and glorification of the Lord they sing the eight canonical hours, accompanied by the choir-singing of archangels. The music is begun by the birds and the archangels, and all the heavenly host, both saints and holy virgins, make the response to them.[2]

Likewise, the hour of Vespers and the canonical hours are mentioned in the context of an island paradise in the following reference from *Immram Brennain* ('The Voyage of Brendan'):

When the hour of Vespers had come, all the birds in the tree chanted, as it were, with one voice, beating their wings on their sides: 'A hymn is due to thee, O God, in Zion, and a vow shall be paid to you in Jerusalem.' They kept repeating this versicle for about the space of an hour. To the man of God and his companions, the chant and the sound of their wings seemed in its sweetness like a rhymical song.[3]

In one specific reference from 'The Voyage of Bran', continuous music is portrayed as emanating from a stone through the timeless ages as part of the Otherworld:

Then they row to the bright stone, from which a hundred songs arise. Through the long ages it sings to the host a melody which is not sad, the music swells up in choruses of hundreds, They do not expect decay or death.[4]

The phrase 'through the long ages' implies that the music of this bright stone is always there, eternally musical, constantly singing.

Waterfalls and wells are also described as having continuous music in the Otherworld. From the legend of the origin of the river Shannon (quoted in full in Chapter 5) the *Metrical Dindshenchas* says that the river traces its origin to the well of Connla in *tir tairngiri* ('The Land of Promise'), and describes the moment of the arrival of the *sidhe* maiden Sinann to the underwater well and its seven musical streams.[5]

Illustratory comparative material

The folklore traditions of other cultures also have numerous references to supernatural music heard at certain times. As might be expected, such references often describe the timelessness of the Otherworld and of the music heard there. During such an encounter in the Otherworld, one's normal perception and cognition regarding the passage of time is altered. Often the mortal who returns from this supernatural dimension is completely unaware of the passage of time in this world, a situation of 'missing time' in earthly terms. Such a mortal might be a Christian saint who is described as having visited Heaven, or an ordinary mortal who is portrayed as having been taken to 'Fairyland' or some other purely supernatural Otherworld dimension. What may subjectively seem to a mortal like one hour in the Otherworld of the *sidhe* beings may be a year or more from our everyday, earthly time perspective.

From Welsh folklore, we have the following example which describes the unusual experiences of mortal men being enchanted into 'fairyland' through listening to the sweet song of a fairy bird:

> One such bird sang to a lad called Sion ap Siencyn of Pencader, Dyfed. He had been in the woods, so he thought, merely for ten minutes, but when he awoke the tree upon which the bird sang had withered. When he returned to his home an old man informed him of the words of one Caer Madog of Brechfa: 'She used to say that you were with the fairies and would not return until the last drop of sap in the tree had been dried up.'[6]

The terminology 'with the fairies' implies an Otherworld place. In this example, time in the Otherworld realm is perceived in a different way than in our normal, everyday perception, as in our earthly terms it clearly takes longer than ten minutes for a tree to completely wither and die. Similarly, from the Welsh *Mabinogion*, the supernatural Birds of Rhiannon appear from the Otherworld and sing to selected mortals for a period of seven years.[7] The impression from the Welsh literature is that the singing birds of Rhiannon are always present in Annwyn, a Welsh underworld dimension.

From the nineteenth century, we also have the following tale, told about 1825 in the Vale of Neath, Wales, regarding the supernatural lapse of time in 'fairyland':

> [Here is] the true story of Rhys and Llewellyn ... Rhys and Llewellyn were fellow servants to a farmer. As they went home ... Rhys told his friend to stop and listen to the music. Llewellyn heard no music. But Rhys had to dance to the tune he had heard a hundred times. He begged Llewellyn to go ahead with the horses, saying that he would soon overtake him, but Llewellyn arrived home alone. The next day, he was suspected of murdering Rhys and jailed. But a farmer 'who was skilled in fairy matters' guessed the truth. Several men gathered – among them the narrator of the story – and took Llewellyn to the spot where he said his companion had vanished. Suddenly, 'Hush!' cried Llewellyn. 'I hear music, I hear sweet harps.' ... [Then the narrator], too, heard the sounds of many harps and saw a number of Little People dancing in a circle

twenty feet or so in diameter. After him, each of the party did the same and observed the same thing. Among the dancing Little Folk was Rhys. Llewellyn caught him by his smock-frock as he passed close to them and pulled him out of the circle. At once Rhys asked, 'Where are the horses?' and asked them to let him finish the dance, which had not lasted more than five minutes. And he could never be persuaded of the time that had elapsed.[8]

Time, then, is clearly of a different nature in the Otherworld than in our normal, three-dimensional earthly context. As the inherent nature of the Otherworld is eternal, the music is also portrayed as unceasing.

Among the traditions of the Australian aborigines is found a unique concept of the Otherworld of the shamans. It is referred to as the Dream Time, believed to be the spiritual home of the ancestors. This particular shamanic tradition places great emphasis on the importance of dreams and the instructions obtained in them from the ancestors. Mircea Eliade points out that in many shamanic traditions around the world, it is often in dreams or in the Other-world state that 'historical time is abolished and the mythical time regained.'[9] The ascent to this Otherworld dimension is made by special songs and chants, and by way of the rainbow, mythically imagined as a huge snake, on whose back the master climbs as on a rope. Thus, in the supernatural Otherworld state, the shaman re-establishes the paradisal situation lost at the dawn of time, that is the 'Fall of Man'. In this Otherworld dimension, 'the material limitations and physical restrictions of ordinary people do not exist. The novice returns to his primordial state by contacting the spirits of the ancestors. He thus gets a taste of the sacred nature of being, of a timeless age.'[10]

The Corroboree poets of the Australian Unambal also emphasise receiving their special songs and chants from the Otherworld, where time is 'timeless' by normal, everyday standards. The retrieval of special songs and chants, obtainable only in the Otherworld, is a hallmark of Australian shamanism. Holger Kalweit, in his research on their techniques, states that the poet can 'travel to the Beyond where he can collect songs and chants, which he teaches to the members of his tribe.'[11] That the acquisition of special 'songs of power' and certain chants can come only from the supernatural Otherworld is emphasised in shamanic traditions worldwide, implying that there is a musical or harmonic element to the Other-world, as the continuous music there can apparently be 'accessed' at any time by a trained shaman. In the Australian Aborigine tradition, the Otherworld is described specifically in relation to time as well – the Dream Time.

The motif of melodious music as part of Heaven or Paradise is well-known in world literature. Given the story of the Fall of Man in Genesis and the expulsion from the Garden of Eden, mankind must now attempt, with Christ's help from the Christian viewpoint, to return to the homeland of God's Heaven. Brian Murdoch in his analysis of *Saltair na Rann*, the Irish Adam and Eve story, explains the mention in Irish literature of the theme of the perpetual summer of Paradise and its melodious music, drawing attention to 'the stress on summer as the ideal time in Irish, English, and other northern vernaculars.'[12] Summertime in Paradise, frequently portrayed with the eternal, melodious, sweet singing of birds, is a well-known motif in world literature descriptions of Paradise, with Murdoch commenting that 'the notion of the singing birds, so striking a motif here, is interesting, and seems to be particularily Irish in its intensity, and in the delight taken in it, though perhaps not in intrinsic originality'.[13] Heaven or Paradise is portrayed as constantly 'singing' with beautiful music and harmony, and especially so in the early medieval Irish literature.

From the Bible, Revelation 4: 8 describes the continuous singing of God's Heaven, as the four eternal living creatures never stop singing the chant 'Holy, Holy, Holy'. Similarly, the seven Heavens of Islam are portrayed in the Qur'an as having beautiful, continuous music, especially the rank of the highest angelic choirs, which sing around the throne of God praise and glory to their Lord (sura 40: 7). Judaism, too, has a similar concept in the continuous singing of the angelic orders, also reflecting a belief that the Otherworld has a timeless quality in conjunction with the continuous singing in praise of Yahweh.

In the writings of classical philosophers, the Otherworld was often described as inherently musical or harmonic, with the Golden Age, or Elysium, often portrayed as including the music of the celestial spheres. Its eternal harmony was seen as an integral part of the very fabric of creation itself, an image of the Logos, the unfolding of cosmic Time throughout the universe. The Golden Age is a symbol of the timeless, eternal realm, one of perfect harmony. The return to Arcadia, or Eden, the original Garden of Paradise and its harmony with God, is portrayed in many religious traditions as humanity's overall task, to be reunited with God and the universe.

According to the ancients, we are waiting for this moment, when the 'flaw' of the Pythagorean Comma (as discussed in Chapter 1) can be corrected and we reunite with God to hear again the full harmony of the universe.

Liminal times music is heard

Liminal times, like liminal places, are those times in which the normal boundaries or borders between our usual everyday reckoning of time and Otherworld time are crossed. 'Liminal' is a term derived from the Latin *limen* meaning 'threshold'.[14] At a liminal time, an interplay between earthly time and otherworldly time occurs, with music often described as being heard more often at these times than at others. Examples of liminal times might be dawn, dusk, twilight, birth, death, the exact moment of a sunset, or at one of the four festival points in the ancient Celtic year. Such liminal times are those special moments when one would be more likely to have an opportunity to hear supernatural music or to encounter supernatural musicians in some way.

More specifically, the exact liminal time or moment would be the time(s) *between* the very end of the previous festival time and the very beginning of the new festival time. For example, the twilight time of *Samhain* eve (31 October) is a time when a thin 'crack' in Otherworld time reality would have the opportunity to break through into our earthly, everyday world and be witnessed and/or experienced by mortals. When such encounters are described in folklore, the dilemma raised by extraordinary encounters with non-human entities regarding time is best summed up in the ancient belief that the *sidhe* can only be seen 'between one eye blink and the next'.[15]

Liminal times are part of everyday life and can occur daily, seasonally, yearly or in the human lifespan. But, like liminal places, their boundary nature can signify a crossing-over or transcendence, so the music heard at such times can easily raise expectations of supernatural status. Music performed at these times might be especially sacred or solemn.

Initially, however, we must first take a look at how the early Irish viewed time and divided their annual year. There has survived in Ireland, according to Kevin Danaher,

> from the remote into the recent past, and in many instances into the living present, a body of custom, usage and belief, pertaining to the

observance of certain times, dates, and festivals, which is so extensive and so cohesive as to constitute a folk calendar.[16]

Such a calendar divided the year into four important festival days: *Imbolc*, 1 February, *Bealtaine*, 1 May, *Lughnasadh*, 1 August, and *Samhain*, 1 November.

The term *Imbolc* occurs only in the earliest literature of Ireland and as Daithi O'hOgain states

> its meaning may be either 'parturition' or 'lactation'. Tradition shows clearly that this feast of Brighid was concerned with the birth of young animals and that it was originally under the tutelage of the goddess Brighid. Until recently, it was customary to invoke the protection of her namesake saint on farm animals at this time.[17]

Fairs were held. Danaher adds that, 'On the Eve of the festival . . . the good Saint Brighid, patroness of farm work and cattle, and protector of the house from fire and calamity, was said to be abroad, and steps were taken to bid her welcome and obtain her protection.'[18] In later times, St Brighid was associated with fire and purification rites.

The second of these festival times, *Bealtaine*, 1 May, marked the beginning of the summer season. Cattle were put to pasture, the main dairy season began, the cattle were blessed with prayers for good productivity and songs were sung. Bealtaine originally meant 'bright fire', according to O'hOgain, and tradition has it that often a great fire was lit by various communities, often on a hilltop, 'no doubt anciently derived from a desire to encourage the sun'.[19] The merry month of May also had an association with happiness and love, and as Proinsias Mac Cana put it, 'Indeed, in many societies Spring, and especially the month of May, was the season of love and spontaneous unions, but was nonetheless regarded as an unfavorable time for conventional marriages.'[20]

The unseen supernatural world was also viewed by the early Irish as being especially active on May Eve and during the *Bealtaine* season. The *sidhe* folk of the hills and mounds were at their own revels during this time, and it was believed that humans had to exercise special caution not to disturb or offend them. By watchfulness, prayers and songs, great care was taken to safeguard against the possible machinations of the *sidhe* folk and the evil magic of certain humans. Music and joyful fairs were held around this time, and the hopeful prosperity of the year celebrated.

Lughnasadh, 1 August, was considered to be the beginning of the harvest season. New corn, potatoes and fruit were brought into the household, as were some of the leftovers from the storage from last year's harvest. Many fairs were held at Lughnasadh, later called Lammas time, and included activities of music, dancing, games and storytelling. Maire MacNeill, in *The Festival of Lughsasa*, states that the two great Irish assemblies were the fairs (Old Irish 'oenach') held at Tailten and Carmun: 'Oenach Tailten was held at Teltown in County Meath ... oenach Carmain was associated with the king-ship of Leinster but its site is not known.[21] Some of these traditions have survived down to the present century with the older meanings nearly gone, but the occasion was observed on the Sunday nearest 1 August, called the Sunday of Crom Dubh, also called Garland Sunday or Lammas Sunday. On this day, many times families would climb hilltops for prayers and the gathering of bilberries after Mass. In the collection of music references from this early medieval Irish literature, the joyful fairs of *Lughnasadh*, especially those of Tailten and Carmun, were attended by many different types of musicians, jesters, acrobats and the like to celebrate the harvest.

Samhain, 1 November, meant the time near the end of summer, and the beginning of the winter season. It was considered to be a New Year time, when the veil between this world and the Other-world was particularily thin, that is a particularly liminal time. Being the beginning of the dark winter season, it was associated with the dead and the Otherworld, perhaps the most active time of the year for unusual supernatural events to occur. The dead ancestors were of special importance at this time, and it was believed that one could more likely communicate with them at this time of year than any other. This was also the date of the annual festival of Tara, the ancient centre of Irish kingship, at which time all of the high kings of each province in Ireland would gather. Danaher states that on *Samhain* eve:

> So active were the otherworld beings, that, however, much frightened, nobody was really surprised at any apparition or supernatural mani-festation ... The souls of the dead members of the household returned to the old homestead and were met with tokens of welcome – the open doors, the fire burning on the hearth, and the table set for meal. Special prayers for the repose of the souls of the dead were added to those for protection against danger and evil.'[22]

Fairs at Tara and Tlachta were held on *Samhain*, and often involved much singing and playing of musical instruments. Many scholars believe that later, *Samhain* was called All Saint's Day, a Christianisation of this earlier festival with its primary emphasis on the dead.

These four seasonal points of the year were the major early Irish divisions of time in their society. As to the antiquity of these seasonal festival times, evidence from Irish historical and literary sources indicates that they also had a relationship to one another as liminal times; the festivals themselves were not viewed as totally separate and distinct holiday periods, but as one time of the year flowing into another, all as part of one yearly cycle.

The months of the year were also named for these festivals up to our more modern times. For example, in the modern Irish language May is *Mi na Bealtaine*, August, *Mi na Lunasa*, November, *Mi na Samhna*, and February was popularly called *Mi na Feile Bhride*. Danaher points out:

> The naming of the months from the seasons or the season days clearly points to the conclusion that the season and not the month was the primary subdivision of the year, and makes it probable that reckoning in months was a later introduction, possibly, like the celebration of Easter and the seven-day week, an innovation associated with early Christianity.[23]

A number of the music references from this literature do make reference to a specific season of the year, often related to one of the major four festivals, especially those of Samhain and Lughnasadh.

Regarding the seven-day week, Daibhi O'Croinin concludes that 'the reckoning of time in pre-Christian Irish society was of one, three, five, ten, or fifteen-day periods; the seven-day week was entirely unknown.'[24] D. A. Binchy discusses similar periods of the reckoning of time in early Irish society regarding the time periods allowed for various periods of stay on legal proceedings.[25] However, by the time of our earliest records of the Old Irish period, the seven-day week and the names for each day were commonplace, so some of the music references do reflect these time descriptions, most generally those with Christian contexts.

One of the most favoured liminal times when supernatural music is heard in this literature is that of *Samhain*, 1 November. In one instance at *Samhain*, King Ailill and the poet Ferchess went to pasture their horses and encounter supernatural *sidhe* music:

> Then Ailill went one *Samhain* to pasture his horses on Ane Cliach ... The hill was stripped bare that night and no one knew who stripped it. This happened to him twice ... It was a marvel to him ... Ferchess came to

speak with him, and on *Samhain* they both go to the hill. Ailill waits on the hill. Ferchess was outside it. Then sleep fell on Ailill, listening to the grazing of the cattle. They [i.e. those who had been 'mysteriously' stripping the hill at night] had come out of the fairy mound, followed by Eogabul son of Durgabul, the king of the mound, and Eogabul's daughter Ane, was before him, with a brazen *timpan* in her hand which she was playing for him.[26]

A similar situation occurs at *Samhain* in another reference, where King Ailill and Ferchess are portrayed as going again to a certain meadow with their horses, and wonder who keeps mysteriously stripping the grass bare. They decide to remain there to see for themselves, as follows:

> Ailill took a meadow here in his territory for his horses ... The slender *sidhe* ['elves' or 'fairies'] did not like the intrusion of their territory: they used to destroy the grass every *Samhain* ... 'They are trampling the grass and eating our substance in our despite, singing lovely *sidhe* music which would make the race of Adam sleep' ... [said Ailill].[27]

Probably the most notorious event at *Samhain* every year was the annual destruction of Tara, the centre of kingship, by a blast of fire from the *sidhe* musician Aillen of the Tuatha de Danann, as quoted in full earlier in Chapter 4.[28]

Plagued by such terrorism on Tara every year at *Samhain*, the high King of Ireland was understandably concerned and offered a reward to any man in all of Ireland who could stop this tragedy. All remained silent, as they knew that once the sound of the magical fairy strains of Aillen's *timpan* began, they would be utterly powerless to resist. They would then fall asleep, and inevitably Tara would be burnt:

> Then with a smooth and polished drinking horn that was in his hand the king of Ireland stood up and said: 'if, men of Ireland, I might find with you one that until the point of rising day upon the morrow, should preserve Tara that she be not burned by Aillen mac Midhna, his rightful heritage, (were the same much or were it little) I would bestow on him.' To this the men of Erin listened mute and silent however, for they knew that at the plaintive fairy strain and at the subtle sweet-voiced notes produced by the wondrous elfin man that yearly used to burn Tara.[29]

Finally, it took the resolve of hero Finn mac Cumaill to solve the problem, by the ingenious technique of putting the point of his sword on his forehead to stay awake during Aillen's beguiling music. In this way, he saved Tara from the annual *Samhain* destruction by Aillen's deadly melodies:

[Finn] was not long before he heard a plaintive strain, and to his forehead he held the flat of the spear-head with its dire energy. Aillen began and played his timpan; he had lulled everyone else to sleep, and then to consume Tara emitted from his mouth his blast of fire. But to this Finn opposed ...[30]

The liminal time of *Samhain* in early Ireland is portrayed as a time in which supernatural music might be especially likely to intervene into everyday life. In this case, with Aillen of the Tuatha de Danann, the bewitching music of the Otherworld is featured prominently at the time of *Samhain*.

Samhain is portrayed in a late ninth-century poem by the hermit poet Marban as he describes the atmosphere around his hut:

Bees, chafers (restricted humming, tenuous buzz); barnacle geese, brent geese, shortly before *Samhain* (music of a dark wild one)...[31]

As *Samhain* was considered to be the beginning of the winter season, it is often thought of as 'dark', dangerous or downright menacing at times in this poetry. In sharp contrast, the season of *Bealtaine* signified the beginning of summer, and the descriptions of the music at this time reflect a much more joyful tone:

Woodland music plays; melody provides perfect peace; dust is blown from dwelling-place ... swallows dart aloft; vigour of music surrounds the hill [?]; soft rich fruit flourishes ... the hardy cuckoo sings; the trout leaps.[32]

Lughnasadh (1 August) in particular is mentioned more often in this literature regarding music, with emphasis being on the great fairs of Tailten and Carmun. At these large, joyful, colorful fairs, the young people would dance, while the older folk would tell stories or play various games. Everyone would have feasts and, it would seem, enjoy different kinds of music. As this time of year was the beginning of the harvest, and in ancient times the Fianna warriors would go hunting, signalled by the melodious singing of birds. From *Accalam na Senorach* ('The Colloquy of the Ancient Men'), St Patrick is portrayed as asking the last remaining legendary old Fianna warriors about the time of Lughnasadh:

[Said Cailte of the Fianna to Patrick:] ... on the first day of the trogan month which is called Lughnasadh, we, to the number of the Fianna's three battalions, practised ... to have our fill of hunting until such time as from the tree tops the cuckoos would call in Ireland. More melodious than all music whatsoever it was to give ear to the voices of the birds.[33]

The great fairs of Carmun and Tailten are also mentioned in relation to the time of Lughnasadh. At the fair of Carmun, many instruments, discussed earlier, are described, amidst a general atmosphere of joyful activities:

> Pipes, fiddles, gleemen,
> bones-players and bag-pipers,
> a crowd hideous, noisy, profane,
> shriekers and shouters ...
>
> Tales of death and slaughter
> strains of music ... [34]
>
> These are the Fair's great privileges:
> trumpets, fiddles, hollow-throated horns,
> pipers, timpanists unwearied,
> poets and meek musicians ... [35]

At the Tailten fair at *Lughnasadh*, various games and the 'music' of the chariots is mentioned:

> White-sided Taltiu ...
> A fair with gold, with silver,
> with games, with music of chariots,
> with adornment of body and soul
> by means of knowledge and eloquence ... [36]

Often, the descriptions of the important rites of passage of the birth or death of a saint involve supernatural music in some manner. From *Betha Colmain* ('The Life of Colman') we have the description of beautiful, supernatural music heard all around the church at the moment of his birth, a liminal time.[37]

The moment of the death of a saint is described as being associated with the sacred music of Heaven following his departure from earthly life. From the *Tripartite Life of Patrick*, referring to the time immediately after the saint's death and subsequent burial, is the following is description:

And for the space of twelve nights, to wit, the time during which the elders of Ireland were watching him with hymns and psalms and canticles, there was no night in Mag Inis, but an angelic radiance ... On the first night the angels of the Lord of the elements were watching Patrick's body with spiritual songs. The odour of divine grace which came from the holy body, and the music of the angels, brought sleep and joy to the elders of the men of Ireland who were watching the body in the nights afterwards.[38]

At the moment of the death of St Columba, too, we have a description from the *Amra of Choliumb Chille* of his soul ascending to Heaven accompanied by the music of both heaven and earth (quoted in full in Chapter 5).

At a liminal time such as the moment of death, the music of the Otherworld, in this case that of Heaven, has a better opportunity of intervening in earthly affairs. Of course, with saints, this is portrayed as being even more likely to occur than with ordinary individuals.

Illustratory comparative material

Reports of hearing supernatural music at liminal times such as twilight, dusk, or dawn are common throughout world folklore archives. One seventy-year-old informant stated to Evans-Wentz in 1911 that the area around Tara, the ancient site of the Irish high kings, was still believed to be an active *sidhe* site for hearing supernatural music at certain times, notably at 'the twilight hour':

> At the twilight hour, wondrous music still sounds over its slopes, and at night, long, weird processions of silent spirits march around its grass-grown raths and forts ... 'As sure as you are sitting down I heard the pipes there in that wood (pointing to a wood on the northwest slope of the Hill of Tara, and west of the banquet hall) ... I often heard it in the wood of Tara. Whenever the *good people* play, you hear their music all through the field as plain as can be; and it is the grandest kind of music. It may last half the night, but once day comes, it ends.'.[39]

Likewise from Welsh folklore, tales of the *Tylwyth Teg* and their music reveal a similar belief about the importance of the liminal time element; here, around twilight time and after:

> 'There were many of the *Tylwyth Teg* on the Llwydiarth Mountain above here, and around the Llwydiarth Lake where they used to dance ... they appeared only after dark ... many others ... have seen the *Tylwyth Teg* in these mountains, and have heard their music and song.[40]

The Breton *corrigans* also favoured the twilight hour and were often reported to be seen and heard in earlier times singing and playing their music at Carnac in the evening hours. The *lutins* and the *corrigans* 'only show themselves at night, or in the twilight. No one knows where they pass the day-time.'[41]

From Scotland, we have the great collection of Gaelic verse and prose put together by Alexander Carmichael in the nineteenth century from the Highlands and Islands, the *Carmina Gadelica*.

One excerpt from this collection, by a nurse/midwife from Barra, features the moment of the birth of a child and what she and her assistant watching-women would then do:

> When the image of the God of life is born into the world I put three little drops of water on the child's forehead ... in the name of the Father ... the Son ... the Spirit, and the watching-women say Amen ... All the people in the house are raising their voices with the watching-women, giving witness that the child has been committed to the blessed Trinity. By the Book itself! Ear has never heard music more beautiful than the music of the watching- women when they are consecrating the seed of man and committing him to the great God of Life.[42]

This illustrates a family or community acknowledgement of the special liminal time of the birth of a child and of its celebration by music. It also shows the important role of the watching-women, the midwives, in early Gaelic society.

From Islam, the story of Muhammed's famous night-time journey to Jerusalem features music, where it is stated in the Qur'an that he passed through all of the Heavens, and heard the supernatural singing of the angelic hierarchies. Reference to the liminal time of the twilight hour and the night-time hours being the specific time for his celestial journey is made in the Qur'an, as is the special blessedness of Jerusalem.[43]

The very early morning hours are also believed to be liminal times when supernatural music may be heard, and the exact moment of dawn is often portrayed as when the *sidhe* disappear. The following example comes from the oral Welsh folklore archives of early this century. In it the informant tells of a special green place, a hollow near the water, and, when asked as to *when* the fairies could be seen and their music heard, states:

> I don't think anyone saw the fairies during the daylight. I believe that if we had risen early enough in the morning, then we would have seen them.[44]

This implies that the informant seems to believe that the small morning hours before dawn are a favourable time for seeing the fairies, as once dawn comes with its first ray of sunlight, the fairies tend to disappear. The informant seems to feel that one's opportunity to see and hear the music of the fairies during the daytime hours is practically 'nil', so to speak.

The time of death as a liminal time regarding music occurs in the saints' lives in world literature, as well as in reports from our own day in the twentieth century. One of the best known examples in Musicology is the famous story of the death of the great composer Gustav Mahler:

> Gustav Mahler on his deathbed, when he appeared to be sinking into a final state of shallow breathing, suddenly and with intense, almost superhuman energy, as the legend goes, sat up with eyes wide open and pointed, wildly excited, to a place in the distance. He said with a sense of wonder, 'Mozart!'[45]

At the time of his impending death, it would appear that he perhaps had a vision of Mozart and/or also heard his music. At either rate, it has been claimed that something supernatural involving music did take place at the time of Mahler's death.

Times of music in everyday, mundane life

As portrayed in this literature, everyday life in early Ireland was lively and varied, with many activities that involved the use and appreciation of music. For example, there were work songs, religious songs, weaving songs and so on, all incorporating music into everyday life in a much more direct way than we do now. There was little tendency then to compartmentalise music; instead, it was seen as an integral part of mundane, daily activities. Also, at given points in the week or month, music might be played more often than others. Even the concept of 'continuous music' was prevalent in everyday life as well, with the constant 'music' of the hermit monk's woodland or the wandering poet's 'music' of the rivers described in the references from this literature.

From *Accalam na Senorach* ('Colloquy of the Ancients') we have the following late twelfth-century poem which portrays three Fianna warriors listening to 'wolf-music' in winter time, as recalled by the aged Cailte, a mythological last survivor of the Fianna:

> The stag of Slievecarran of the assemblies
> does not lay his side to the ground; the stag
> of the head of cold Aughty listens likewise
> to wolf-music.
> I, Cailte, and brown-haired Diarmait, and
> keen light Oscar, used to listen to
> wolf-music at the end of a very cold night.[46]

In a poem attributed to Suibne Geilt, while he wanders in exile as a bird he comments on the tuneful cry of the river Garb as part of his everyday life experience:

> I hear melodious music in the Garb at the
> time of its winter splendor; I sleep to the
> sound of great revelry on a very cold icy night.[47]

In contrast, the following excerpt is from a tenth century Old Irish poem, 'Uath Beinne Etair', in which the hermit comments on a very bitter cold winter night and the absence of any music heard at that time:

> The fishes of Ireland are roving, there is
> not a strand where the wave does not dash,
> there is not a town left in the land, not
> a bell is heard, no crane calls.[48]

Rivers are often described as having a kind of 'continuous' music as part of everyday monastic appreciation of God's creation, as do mountains, the sound of the wind through the trees and so on.

The daytime hours are mentioned in many of the hermit poems, as illustrated by this reference from the *Leabhar Breac* manuscript:

> Ah, blackbird, it is well for you,
> Wherever in the thicket be your nest,
> Hermit that sounds no bell,
> Sweet, soft, fairylike is your note.[49]

Similarly, from the late ninth-century Old Irish poem entitled 'King and Hermit':

> Beautiful are the pines which
> make music for me, unhired;
> through Christ, I am no worse off
> at any time than you.[50]

> A hedge of trees overlooks me; a blackbird's
> lay sings to me (an announcement which I shall
> not conceal); above my lined book the birds'
> chanting sings to me.

> A clear-voiced cuckoo sings to me (goodly
> utterance) in a grey cloak from bush
> fortresses. The Lord is indeed good to me:
> well do I write beneath a forest of woodland.[51]

The 'music' of birds is described as being continually heard at night, as in this example from a twelfth-century poem:

The lively linnet does not sleep above the tops of
the fair tangled trees; loud music prevails there;
no thrush sleeps ...

Tonight the curlew does not sleep; high above a storm's
ragings the sound of its clear cry is musical; it
sleeps not between streams.[52]

The time period of 'forty days and forty nights' comes up in the
saints' lives, in particular in the *Tripartite Life of St Patrick*. As quoted
in full previously, in this instance St Patrick is portrayed as banishing evil black birds by singing maledictive psalms at them, after a
period of forty days and forty nights on the mountain of Cruachan
Aigle, in later times called Croagh Patrick.[53]

In the Christian contexts especially, some times set aside as
sacred might be occasions for more than natural music, such as
the Mass or during the canonical hours. One incident from *Betha
Colmain* ('The Life of Colman') refers to the time of Mass and
the miraculous appearance of the bell of St Colman to aid the
priest.[54]

From *Betha Decclain* ('The Life of St Declan'), we have the following reference to a bell being provided by God at the moment of the
beginning of Mass:

Declan was beginning Mass one day in a church which lay in his road,
when there was sent him from Heaven a little black bell ... Declan
greatly rejoiced ... and gave thanks and glory to Christ.[55]

The importance of the time of Doomsday itself, and the music of
the bells of St Patrick and St Columba, are described in the various
versions of their saints' lives. One example in particular is the
description of how St Patrick himself will come for the men and
women of Ireland on the Day of Doom, and summon them to
Heaven with his bell at that time.

The time of the ordination of a priest is portrayed as a special
time in the everyday life of the early Irish saints when supernatural
music might intervene. Such a portrayal is evident in the description of the exact moment of the ordination of St Patrick, when three
choirs mutually responded – the choirs of Heaven, the Romans and
the children from the wood of Fochlad in Ireland, thus designating
this a special time indeed.[56]

The time of the canonical hours in the monasteries were obviously musical times, with much chanting of the psalms and the use
of bells in everyday life experience. From *Betha Colmain* ('The Life

of Colman'), there is the portrayal of St Colman as a young boy, making reference to the canonical hours specifically.[57]

Similarly, from *Betha Mochuda* ('The Life of St Mochuda') St Mochuda as a young boy hears the singing of the clerics at the time of the canonical hours and becomes so inspired that he decides to enter the priesthoood.

In some versions of the Life of St Columba, a man named Enne would not give St Columba an island for his missionary work, so he cursed him, by telling the man of all of the advantages he could have had by donating the island, most notably the beautiful singing of the birds of Paradise and the bells which would miraculously ring by themselves at the time of Mass and at the canonical hours.

Illustratory comparative material

In much of world literature, from saints' lives to folklore, music is explained as being heard in everyday life experience at specific times, often connoting a special religious day, month, year or festival.

From the Bible, and the Old Testament in particular, we have the use of music designated by divine command from Yahweh to be used at certain times as part of everyday religious festivities:

> The trumpets shall be to you a perpetual status throughout your generations ... On the day of gladness, on your feast days and at the beginnings of your months you shall blow the trumpets over your burnt offerings and peace offerings, so that they may be to you a remembrance before your God. (Num. 10: 8, 10)

As part of everyday life in the Temple at Jerusalem, the Levites sang during the offering of the Paschal sacrifice to the accompaniment of flutes, which were sometimes played by non-Levites. As a general description of everyday use of music in Judaic festivals, the following excerpt reveals Talmudic description of the celebration of the Feast of Tabernacles:

> At the liturgical celebration on the seven mornings of the feast those who participated chanted the Hosanna from Psalm 118: 25 while they circled around the altar ... . bending toward it the palm branches which they were holding in their hands. So too, as they retired from the altar at the sound of the trumpet, they cried out repeatedly: 'Beauty be yours, O altar!' At eventide the most distinguished of the people assembled together. Pious men danced with torches in their hands

before the people, singing songs and hymns, while the Levites, arranged upon the fifteen steps (corresponding to the fifteen gradual psalms) which led from the Court of the Men to the Court of the Women, accompanied them with harps, citharas, and numerous other instruments. Two priests with trumpets stood at the upper gate between the Court of Men and the Court of Women. At the first cockcrow they blew the trumpets and continued to do so until they reached the east exit.[58]

It seems that music and singing were an integral part of such festivals, and the great awareness of time in the Judaic tradition is evident from this example.

But one special festival in particular – The Year of Jubilee – stands out in connection with the issue of time and music. We have the description in Leviticus 25: 8, where Yahweh speaks to Moses on Mt Sinai, giving instructions as to how a special ram's horn, the *yobel*, is to be used to summon the people and mark the time of the very special Year of Jubilee (*shanat ha yobel*):

> You will count seven weeks of years, seven times seven years, that is to say a period of seven weeks of years, forty-nine years. And on the tenth day of the seventh month you will sound the trumpet; on the Day of Expiation you will sound the trumpet throughout the land. You will declare this fiftieth year to be sacred and proclaim the liberation of all the country's inhabitants. (Lev. 25: 8)

In the Hebrew, the horn in question, the *yobel*, is a specific type of ram's horn – the more well-known term *shofar* is a more generic Hebrew word for ram's horn. The music of trumpets was sounded during the Feast of Trumpets, the beginning of the seventh month. The music of the *yobel* is to be blown on the Year of Jubilee, a very special occasion as it comes much less often. It is especially unique among the Old Testament Israelite festivals as the title of the festival itself can be translated literally as 'the year which is announced by the blasts of the *yobel*'.

Throughout the life of the Israelites in the Old Testament there are numerous examples of rejoicing, playing musical instruments and singing praises to Yahweh as part of everyday life experience. Likewise, synagogues today carry on these and other musical traditions as part of religious practice.

From Islamic sources, the marking of time in the annual year often coincides with certain festivals that involve singing or chanting. The well-known daily prayers and chants to Allah by Muslims worldwide while facing Mecca is an example of the importance of music in the everyday life of Muslims. The specific practices of Islam comprise the confession of faith (*al-tashahhud*), the prayer ritual, legal almsiving, the annual fast and pilgrimage to Mecca. 'There are several occasions for fasting (*saum*) in Islam; the most exacting fast is that of Ramadan.'[59] This major festival is well-known worldwide, and the twenty-seventh night of Ramadan is especially sacred, a night when it is believed that 'the gates of Heaven are open, and the possibility exists of altering human destinies', as it is thought of as the time of God's revelation to Muhammad. During this time, as might be expected, much popular devotion and enthusiastic veneration of Muhammad occurs, with singing and chanting playing a part in the overall festivities.

Early Christian liturgy emphasised singing, with one musicologist stating:

> The Apostolic Age bears witness to the joyful character of early Christianity, particularly as it was expressed in singing. In Eph. 5: 19 Paul calls upon Christians to 'address one another with psalms, hymns, and spiritual songs, singing and making melody to the Lord in your heart.' Col. 3: 16 also refers to singing 'psalms and hymns and spiritual songs with thankfulness in your hearts to God.' These words clearly express the Apostle's conviction that singing is a fitting way to honor God. There is at the same time, however, a certain reservation in what Paul says. In both passages he adds what seems to be a warning against a purely aesthetic pleasure in singing.[60]

At the time of Christian worship, rejoicing and singing hymns and psalms with a joyful heart was emphasised. At the vigils and feasts of the martyrs, musical instruments were sometimes used, but there was much debate about this among the Church Fathers, however. This was mainly because the early church was struggling against the earlier pagan traditions of music and dancing. St Augustine's second discourse on Psalm 32: 33 illustrates this concept, where he asks his listeners, 'Has not the institution of those vigils in Christ's name caused the citharas to be banished from this place?'[61] A cithara was a stringed instrument similar to a harp and was associated with the worship of Apollo, and several other Greek and goddess traditions.

One of the pseudo-Justinian tracts entitled 'Oratio ad Graecos', written about 400 AD, puts the following words into the mouth of God in a discourse about the use of instruments during the time of the popular feasts of the martyrs: 'I hate your feasts. The gluttony which takes place at them is unseemly, as are the lustful actions provoked by enticing flutes.'[62] Clearly, monophonic singing was preferred by the early Church.

In ancient China, music was performed at very specific times, based on their belief system of the twelve celestial Tones in the universe. The early Chinese believed that the twelve Tones did express themselves individually to a greater degree according to a month of the year, the time of day and so forth. In their view, a particular Tone sounded more prominently in a particular month and during a particular hour of the day. Therefore, the performing of music was coordinated with these special times, often centring around religious festivities. The annual cycle of the year had its own divisions of time:

> Each of the twelve celestial Tones corresponded with an astrological month of the year, during which the Tone was believed to be more prominently sounded throughout the earth. The first six months of the year expressed the six *yang* Tones; the second six months from midsummer to winter solstice expressed the *yin* Tones. The musician performed his music in a key which was associated with the current zodiacal month. The twelve notes, or *lui*, of the Chinese musical system each corresponded to one of the months. The note of each month was, in audible sound, the earthly reflection or 'undertone' of the month's celestial Tone. Therefore each month of the year possessed its own tonic and dominant *lui*, with which all ceremonial music should be performed at that time.[63]

In antiquity, music at the time of the offering of incense to the gods was prevalent. The presence of flutists at the time of the ritual of incense offerings in Rome is confirmed by textual evidence, as Suetonius, for example, speaks of the flutist employed by the Emperor Tiberius at his incense sacrifice. The poet Propertius looked upon flute music as itself a libation for the gods.[64] Likewise, in Greece and other areas of the ancient world, singing and the playing of musical instruments accompanied celebrations and rites to Aphrodite and other gods and goddesses.

Conclusion

Like the places, the times when music is heard vary from the purely supernatural to the everyday mundane. The first category, the purely supernatural Otherworld times, describes the eternal, continuous music of the Christian Heaven or the primal *tir tairngiri*, the Land of Promise. In the numerous references to music from this literature, it appears that the early Irish believed that the Otherworld has an inherent musical quality in it and that this beautiful music is continuous and unceasing.

The second category, the liminal times, are those special threshold times when the boundaries of this world and the Otherworld may be crossed. Such liminal times are considered to be part of everyday life in many ways, yet, occasionally, something unusual may happen regarding music if and when the exact circumstances are right. Such liminal times might be birth, death, dawn, dusk, twilight or one of the four special festival points of the early Irish year.

At such times, intervention from the Otherworld can occur, often transforming the lives of mortals. These liminal times became known in early Ireland as special times when one might possibly hear supernatural music. Such times are special as they serve as time portals or border points, i.e. a very specific 'window of time' in our modern-day terminology.

Again, as with places, it seems that the early Irish were reluctant to draw an explicit line between this world and the Otherworld regarding time. Liminality implies transcendence, and, because of this, there is an inherent potential to experience an unusual event involving supernatural music at a liminal time. At a liminal time, a unique interplay of place and time occurs, creating a situation where the normal boundaries of everyday place and time intersect with Otherworld place and time.

The third category, everyday times, are times mentioned in reference to normal, mundane life. Examples here include the canonical hours in monastic life, the time of a fair or various times of day, such as morning, noon and night. Singing and the playing of musical instruments was enjoyed in everyday life in early Ireland, from the homes and fields of the people at work each day to the courts of the kings and noblemen.

'Eternity' and its characteristic of timelessness always seems to be described or implied among the supernatural and liminal times while it is very rarely portrayed in the everyday references. In the more overtly Christian examples, we often see portrayals of the constant, beautiful music of Heaven or, for example, of the continuous, supernatural music of the special singing stone in the Land of the Saints. In the overtly primal examples, we see references to the unceasing music of *tir tairngiri* ('The Land of Promise') or the continuous beautiful music of *sidhe* birds. In the everyday life examples from this literature, time is generally spoken of in our usual earthly terms.

Much of the material in the overtly Christian contexts parallels that in the overtly primal contexts, creating an overall impression of great commonality in the descriptions of the times when music is heard. Also, it appears that the early Irish believed that music has, more often than not, a special connection or linkage to the Otherworld. It was believed that a person was considered fortunate to have musical talents, or to have had the honour of hearing supernatural music at a liminal time, for example.

In a significant number of cases, descriptions of times in the purely supernatural dimensions use similar imagery to those used in the everyday examples. For instance, the beautiful, continuous music of the Tree of Life in the Christian Heaven and the musical trees in the primal Otherworld are nearly identical to those in the liminal and everyday life descriptions, where we have the constant 'music of the pines' in the everyday life of a hermit monk, for example. Here, all describe time in relation to its continuous quality, be it in everyday life or in the Otherworld.

When these categories are placed side by side, there is a certain parallelism in imagery and description from the Otherworld places and times to those places and times described as pertaining to this world of everyday, mundane life. It seems that the early Irish felt that the Otherworld could occasionally intervene in the everyday affairs of humanity in a musical way, indicating a possible belief in the power of music, especially at liminal times, to connect one to a divine source.

The canonical hours are referred to as part of the usual everyday life of a church or monastery. Vespers and the canonical hours are also specifically mentioned in the Otherworld examples, where the continuous music of the Land of the Saints is heard. Here, the canonical hours and Vespers are also mentioned specifically, as when the birds of the Tree of Life sing psalms and hymns to God. The canonical hours were very important as an integral part of everyday monastic life and

> are referred to as the Divine Office . . . St Benedict speaks of seven offices in the day and one in the night. Eight times a day, then, the monks met to sing the Psalms, listen to scriptural readings, and offer prayers so that the presence of Christ, so strongly evoked in the Mass, was recalled . . . It is highly significant that there were seven services by day and one by night, as we recognize in this number an octave . . . As the movements of

the celestial spheres obey the *musica mundana*, the daily life of the monks follows the *musica humana*, and their voices, the *musica instrumentalis*. As above, so below.[65]

So comments musicologist Dr Katherine Le Mee when discussing the power of Gregorian chant.

Again, we can see an interplay between the everyday setting of the church or monastery and the time of day or night that the chants were sung. In certain references about music from this literature, the canonical hours are also mentioned in exclusively Otherworld contexts, implying that there, too, in God's eternity, the canonical hours are observed.

So the parallelism between the overtly primal and the overtly Christian contexts and the continuity between the otherworldly and the everyday are clear once more when one considers the times in which the music is heard, and perhaps especially at the liminal times. *Samhain* eve, for example, is referred to in the liminal category on several occasions, where, at this special festival time of year, the Otherworld is believed to become more visible or accessible to us in this world. *Lughnasadh* also features, particularily in descriptions of fairs held at this liminal time. The continuous 'music' of the trees as a celebration of God's creation in the everyday life of a Christian hermit can be compared with the mention of the continuous music of the trees in the primal Otherworld, be they from sources with primal or Christian contexts.

So as one examines these references, it seems that although the early Irish perceived day-to-day time much as we do, they also seem to have placed much more emphasis on awareness of the liminal times. It seems they were constantly more aware in the course of everyday life of certain liminal times, such as dawn, dusk, twilight, birth, death and so on, in which the music of the Otherworld might be heard. Generally, it seems that music was seen as integral to all of life, and the times in which it was heard were honoured and observed. They seem to be implying that the ultimate music, so to speak, the beautiful music of the Otherworld, is always present in and around us every day, if only we could be more aware of it.

Notes

1. Jackson, K., *A Celtic Miscellany* (Harmondsworth: Penguin, 1971), p. 172.

2. Ibid., pp. 288–95.
3. O'Meara, J., *The Voyage of St. Brendan* (Mountrath, Portlaoise, Ireland: Dolmen Press, 1985), pp. 21–2.
4. Jackson, *CM*, p. 174.
5. Gwynn, E., *MD* III (Dublin, 1913), p. 289.
6. Gwyndaf, R., 'Fairylore: Memorates and Legends from Welsh Oral Tradition', *The Good People: New Fairylore Essays*, ed. P. Narvaez (New York: Garland, 1991), p. 161.
7. Jones, G. and Jones, T. (trans.) *The Mabinogion* (London: J. M. Dent, 1993; 1949 orig.), p. 31.
8. Vallee, J., *Passport to Magonia* (Chicago: Contemporary Books, 1969), p. 106.
9. Eliade, M., *Shamanism* (Princeton, NJ: Princeton University Press, 1964), p. 103.
10. Kolweit, H., *Dreamtime and Inner Space: The World of the Shaman* (Boston: Shambhala, 1988), p. 102.
11. Ibid., p. 103.
12. Murdoch, B., *The Irish Adam and Eve Story from Saltair na Rann*, vol. II (Dublin: DIAS, 1976), p. 57.
13. Ibid., p. 60.
14. Narvaez, P, 'Newfoundland Berry Pickers "In The Fairies": Maintaining Spatial, Temporal and Moral Boundaries Through Legendry', *The Good People* (New York: Garland, 1991), p. 337.
15. Briggs, K., *The Vanishing People: Fairy Lore and Legends* (New York, 1978), p. 6.
16. Danaher, K., 'Irish Folk Tradition and the Celtic Calendar', *The Celtic Connection*, ed. Robert O'Driscoll (New York: George Braziller, 1981), p. 217.
17. O'hOgain, D., *Myth, Legend, and Romance: An Encyclopedia of Irish Folk Tradition* (New York, 1991), p. 402.
18. Danaher, 'Irish Folk Tradition and the Celtic Calendar', p. 218.
19. O'hOgain, *Myth, Legend, and Romance*, p. 403.
20. MacCana, P., 'The Sinless Otherworld of *Immram Brain*', *Eriu*, 27 (Dublin, 1976), p. 109.
21. MacNeill, M., *The Festival of Lughnasadh*, (London: Oxford University Press, 1962), p. 2.
22. Danaher, 'Irish Folk Tradition and the Celtic Calendar', p. 219.
23. Ibid., p. 221.
24. O'Croinin, D., 'The Oldest Irish Names for the Days of the Week', *Eriu*, 32 (Dublin, 1981), p. 95
25. Binchy, B. A., 'Distraint in Irish Law', *Celtica*, 10 (Dublin, 1973), pp. 22–71.
26. Gray, E., 'Cath Maige Tuired/The Battle of Mag Tuired', *ITS*, 52 (London, 1982).

27. Dillon, M., 'The Yew of the Disputing Sons', *Eriu*, 14 (Dublin 1946), p. 161.
28. O'Grady, S., 'Accalam na Senorach/The Colloquy of the Ancient Men', *Silva Gadelica*, II (London, 1892), p. 142.
29. Ibid., p. 143.
30. Ibid., p. 144.
31. Murphy, G., *EIL*, (Oxford, 1970; 1956 orig.), p. 17.
32. Ibid., pp. 158–9.
33. O'Grady, *SG* II, p. 109.
34. Gwynn, E., *MD* III (Dublin, 1913), p. 21.
35. Ibid., p. 19.
36. Gwynn, E., *MD* IV (Dublin, 1924), p. 151.
37. Meyer, K., *Life of Colman, Son of Luachan*, (Dublin, 1911), p. 11.
38. Stokes, W., *Tripartite Life of Patrick* (London, 1887), pp. 254–5.
39. Evans-Wentz, W. Y., *The Fairy Faith in Celtic Countries*, (New York: University Books, 1966), p. 32.
40. Ibid., p. 140.
41. Ibid., p. 208.
42. Carmichael, A., *Carmina Gadelica*, ed. C. Moore (Edinburgh, 1994; 1900 orig.), p. 189.
43. Musk, B., *The Unseen Face of Islam* (Eastbourne, E. Sussex: MARC Publishers, 1989), p. 227.
44. Gwyndaf, 'Fairylore: Memorates and Legends from Welsh Oral Tradition', p. 181.
45. Hollander, L., 'Will You Join The Dance?', *Music and Miracles*, ed. Don Campbell (Wheaton, IL: Quest Books, 1992), p. 255.
46. Murphy, *EIL*, pp. 154–5.
47. Ibid., pp. 112–15.
48. Jackson, *CM*, p. 65.
49. Carney, J., *Early Irish Poetry* (Cork, 1965), p. 12.
50. Murphy, *EIL*, p. 19.
51. Ibid., pp. 4–5.
52. Ibid., pp. 164–5.
53. Stokes, *TLP*, pp. 114–15.
54. Meyer, *Life of Colman, son of Luachan*, p. 65.
55. Power, P., *Life of St. Declan of Ardmore*, (London: ITS, 1914), p. 19.
56. Stokes, *TLP*, pp. 32–3.
57. Meyer, *Life of Colman, son of Luachan*, p. 15.
58. Quasten, J., *Music and Worship in Pagan and Christian Antiquity* (Washington DC: National Association of Pastoral Musicians, 1983, English trans. of 1973 German edn.), pp. 62–3.
59. Musk, *The Unseen Face of Islam*, p. 218.
60. Quasten, *Music and Worship*, p. 59.
61. Ibid., p. 74.

62. Ibid.
63. Tame, D., *The Secret Power of Music* (New York: Destiny Books, 1984), p. 41.
64. Quasten, *Music and Worship*, p. 11.
65. Le Mee, K., *Chant* (New York: Bell Tower, 1994), pp. 71–2.

7

Conclusion

As WE HAVE SEEN under each of the five chapters on performers, instruments, effects, places, and times, there appears to be a broad continuum rather than a strict division between the other-worldly and the mundane; this is also shown in the examples with Christian and primal contexts. The references in this collection from the early medieval Irish sources seem to indicate a sense of an unbroken line that joins the sacred and the profane regarding music. Examples from other Celtic cultures, particularily those of Scotland and Wales, seem to suggest that this view was more wide-spread.

This unbroken line might be portrayed as a visual continuum, or 'register'. One extreme of the continuum is the most mundane, everyday portrayal of earthly reality; the other represents the most supernatural and otherworldly qualities of reality. The area in the middle, the liminal area, indicates those situations where it is very difficult to conclude exactly, where the world of everyday reality ends and the Otherworld begins.

It is noticeable that the middle area, the liminal, is larger than either of the two ends of the continuum. It would seem that this area represents varying 'shades of grey', so to speak, more than black or white *per se*. Many of the examples from the early Irish literature about music acknowledge this 'grey area' of reality more often, where both the black and the white intermingle with each other, and it is difficult to tell exactly where one begins and the other ends.

As our modern tendency in the late twentieth century is to describe and distinguish reality in very separate categories, it may

[_____ { _____ } _____]

| **Mundane and Everyday** | **Liminal** | **Supernatural** |
| reality | (where the mundane ends and the supernatural begins) | the Otherworld |

initially be quite a challenge for a modern Westerner to thoroughly grasp the concept of the 'liminal'. It makes our rational minds uneasy as it is not strictly a black or white category. We have been so conditioned to a more compartmentalised view of reality that the journey back to the early Celtic mindset is indeed a challenge, but also an opportunity.

Obviously, the early Irish lived in a different era from ours. In order to properly analyse their literary references about music as they pertain to their perspective of reality, we must attempt not only to conceive of the possible existence of a supernatural reality itself, but to go one step further: to accept that this may be *ever-present* in some way in our daily lives. Music is often a favourite medium of an encounter with the Otherworld in these sources.

In other words, at the right time or place, and under the correct circumstances, it appears to have been believed by the early Irish that an unusual encounter could occur, and that this encounter frequently involved music. Again, judging from the other Celtic cross-cultural examples, the literature and folklore of Scotland, Wales, Cornwall, and Brittany also tends to express this belief.

Our modern western perspective tends to be highly dualist – god/world, body/soul, and so on – which is very good for rational thinking and analysis. However, we often tend to shun and fear the categories of the liminal and the so-called supernatural in our modern lives, preferring instead to believe that rational, dualist scientific analysis will be able to solve and make sense of everything 'some day'.

Ironically, the early Irish might say that this mythical 'some day' could well be 'every day', as they appear to have accepted the premise that this inherently mysterious Otherworld is not only real and ever-present, but that it should be acknowledged and celebrated, not ignored. They might even object to the very term 'Otherworld' itself, which was conceived by modern-day western minds and seems to imply that the supernatural, spirit-world is 'out there' somewhere, that it is alien to us, that it is 'other'. They would probably view this outlook as flawed, as it appears that they believed that this world and the supernatural spirit world dynamically interact with each other, often with music as the bridge between the two.

One does not need a final philosophy of the meaning of music in order to see music as something which can be seen as a metaphor which tests the world and registers the reality of early Irish society. These various references to music help illustrate how the early Irish viewed music in their life experience. It also shows how fluid their basic concept of reality seems to have been, judging from the references in the liminal category in particular. We will begin with the Performers, and take a closer look at how the early Irish viewed them.

Performers

In the references to performers from this collection, one can see that there are clearly more performers listed in the supernatural category than in the mundane (see Charts 1 and 2 in the Appendix at the end of the book).

This alone may tell us something about the early Irish viewpoint of music, that it was believed to have some kind of supernatural source, power or influence from the Otherworld much of the time. In the mundane categories, a variety of musical performers are involved in everyday life in early Irish society, such as monks singing the canonical hours, the music at a nobleman's party or court musicians entertaining a king. All of this one might expect for an early medieval society.

However, what one might not expect are the unusual portrayals of supernatural performers like the mermaids discovered by travelling clergymen while out at sea, *sidhe* harpers portrayed as singing to the clergy and putting them to sleep, a severed head entertaining a court after a battle, and the music of three precious stones in the Christian Heaven. Such supernatural portrayals of musical performers and the frequency of them in this literature seem to indicate a value system based on a greater awareness of the spiritual in everyday life or, at the very least, a keen appreciation and awareness of the potential of music to be connected to the supernatural in certain circumstances.

The supernatural performers in primal contexts are mainly portrayed as *sidhe* musicians, usually playing an instrument and/or singing. A key example here is the fairy harper. But a fair amount of this material is not as easy to classify, including such unusual performers as the music of *sidhe* birds, a severed head, the musical streams of *tir tairngiri*, the musical branch and so on. The general type of supernatural performer portrayed in a primal context, if not clearly a *sidhe* musician, is generally portrayed as relating to the natural elements, for example the 'music' of the streams of *tir tairngiri* ('The Land of Promise') or the music of the plains of the Otherworld, a 'many-melodied land'. Trees in the Otherworld are often portrayed with singing birds on them, and even as having a unique harmony all their own.

Within the Christian contexts, the supernatural musical performers are initially what one might expect from portrayals of the Christian Heaven or Paradise, with many angels, archangels and saints, all singing in harmony to God. But there are many more unusual supernatural musicians in the early Irish Christian Heaven, such as birds singing the canonical hours in harmony on the Tree of Life, three precious stones singing of their own accord, mermaids on an island paradise, and the beautiful music of the hills and plains of Heaven, for example. It seems that here, too, as in the primal context examples above, the early Irish felt that such unusual supernatural performers are an important and integral part of Heaven, the Christian Otherworld.

Regarding those everyday music references in a Christian context, one may be surprised to see many references to the more unusual types of performers in everyday life, although not quite as many as those in the purely supernatural category. Examples here might be the music of the wolves, stags, the river and so on.

The everyday Christian world and its supernatural counterpart, Heaven, both favour singers heavily, with not nearly as many portrayals of performers with musical instruments as one might expect. It appears that the Christians, especially the hermit monks in their environment of solitude and prayer, had a deep appreciation of music in their daily lives. Most of the everyday Christian musical performers did so in a monastic environment, whether in a church, in a monastery itself, or out in the wilderness around a hermit's hut, but the emphasis tends to be on the constant singing and chanting of the monks.

In the liminal category of musical performers, we have those few mortal performers with Otherworldly influences of some kind, such as saints who encounter musical performers in Heaven or Paradise, or the talented harper Corainn's music summoning a deadly dragon, for example. Most of these references deal with descriptions of transport to and from the Otherworld dimension. In those with primal contexts, this transport occurred while a mortal musician is playing a musical instrument, or is in a trance-like sleep state or dream.

In those references with Christian contexts, many of the saints reach the Otherworld dimension of Heaven during deep and intense prayer, by having an out-of-body experience while enduring a difficult illness, or while singing psalms or hymns as part of daily worship.

The reader may note that in these special instances of transport between this world and the Otherworld, the performers are portrayed as crossing the boundaries in a very fluid manner. This seems to indicate that the early Irish worldview, as shown by the ready acceptance of such unique experiences, was a more holistic one, incorporating the Otherworld into everyday, mundane life. The early Irish seem to have felt that the performing of music–be it everyday or supernatural–could be done by a multitude of performers, some quite unusual, from this world or the Otherworld.

Thus it is the *music itself* that binds all the members of this continuum together in what appears to be an unbroken line of musical performers, up to and including the ultimate supernatural source of the most beautiful music of the Otherworld.

Instruments

As one might expect for an early medieval Celtic society, harps, fiddles, bagpipes, timpans, trumpets, pipes, whistles, horns and bells are all commonly portrayed. However, everyday objects and tools may also have been perceived by the early Irish as musical instruments, such as chariot wheels, fishing nets, swords in battle, bones, the sounds of water, the wind through the trees, the blacksmith's anvil and so on.

Among supernatural instruments in primal contexts, harps clearly predominate, but with a few surprises, such as the afore-mentioned musical branches, mermaids' voices and the singing of a severed head. The supernatural instruments referred to in those references with Christian contexts are primarily singing voices, featuring the vocal music of angels and saints, birds in Heaven and mermaids (see Charts 3 and 4 in the Appendix at the end of the book). The ringing of bells is also mentioned fairly frequently, but rarely are other types of instruments referred to as being part of the Christian Heaven itself.

Surprisingly, from this particular collection of references from the early medieval Irish literature, not one harp was mentioned as being present in the Christian Heaven! Perhaps this may be due to some lingering suspicions about the harp and its powerful associa-tion with the earlier primal religion of Ireland and/or its association with certain bardic or druidic beliefs by the Christian clerics who wrote these saints' lives. But even so, this is rather ironic, especially given that in the Bible, for example, King Saul was comforted by David's lyre, and in John's Revelation Heaven is certainly portrayed with harps in it – in fact a number of them.

But in these early Irish descriptions of Heaven itself, at least from this selected collection of references from the saints' lives written in Irish, bells and vocal music far outweigh any mention of the harp, which is now the national symbol of Ireland. Of course, this collection is not totally comprehensive, although it does include many, if not most, of the major early Irish sources. This collection does not cover the Irish saints' lives written in Latin, but even so, it is still surprising that not one harp was included in the portrayals of Heaven in the early Irish saints' lives of Sts Adamnan, Brendan, Colman, Coluimb Cille, Declan, Fechin, Fursa, Kieran, Mochuda, Moling and Patrick. As the harp and lyre are referred to in the Bible but are not mentioned at all as being part of Heaven in these particular Irish references written by Christian clerics, it seems that the tendency to exclude the harp from Heaven may have had a cultural basis rather than a biblical one.

This is in great contrast to the portrayals of the primal Other-world, where harps are frequently referred to. But perhaps a great irony here is that these tales, sagas and so on with a primal context were consciously written down by *Christian* scribes and clerics. It is to their credit that we even have such tales of fairy harpers in the

Otherworld with their exquisitely beautiful music. Clearly, they valued these tales enough to write them down for posterity.

However, as far as the harp as an instrument goes, they seem to be saying that they approve of it being portrayed in the primal Otherworld, but not in the Christian Heaven. In addition, there is also a lack of any mention of the harp in the Christian everyday, mundane examples, which describe life in and around monasteries. To corroborate this view, there is also no mention of the 'three strains' motif in the Christian Heaven, a reference that has strong associations with the harp.

A further finding is the total absence of the bell in portrayals of the primal Otherworld. However, many times bells are referred to in portrayals of the Christian Heaven. Perhaps the Christian scribes who wrote down this material felt quite strongly that the bell was a proper 'Christian' instrument while the harp was conceived of primarily as a 'pagan' instrument. One can never know for sure, of course, and can only conjecture.

But in both the primal and Christian contexts, an important and interesting subcategory of supernatural instrument emerges. This I have termed 'mysterious or unknown music', that is where supernatural, ethereal music is heard, yet no performers or instruments are seen. It is as if the instruments, and by inference their performers, are invisible, with the music coming directly from the Otherworld or Heaven.

Regarding the supernatural instruments in the primal contexts, one may again note a preference for musical instruments over voices, with the timpan (*timpan*) and the harp (*cruitt*) predominating. The musical branch and trees also figure. It is interesting to note that the Christian Heaven does show portrayals of musical trees, often in a prominent way as with the Tree of Life, but never shows the musical branch, which had poetic and pre-Christian connotations.

The instruments in the mundane, everyday contexts show no stones at all. Apparently, the concept of a special 'singing stone' as a musical instrument is reserved exclusively for the supernatural Otherworld, whether the context is primal or Christian. As to why, we can only conjecture. Perhaps the idea of a 'singing stone' was so sacred or special to the early Irish that it was viewed as a supernatural musical instrument at times.

This may not be so surprising when one considers the early Irish connection between kingship and the *Lia Fail*, the special upright stone that was said to screech or speak only upon recognition of the proper candidate for king. In Scotland, too, emphasis on the Stone of Destiny and its relationship to kingship echoes a similar belief. It seems evident that the concept of a special speaking or singing stone was viewed as sacred and connected with the Otherworld in a powerful way. This may seem all the more ironic, given the ubiquity of stones and rocks in the everyday, earthly environment. Yet it was believed by the early Celts that certain stones were animate, that is, were alive in some way and had a consciousness of their own, and could speak or sing given the proper time and inclination.

There are many descriptions of swords as musical instruments in the examples with primal contexts, but none at all in the Christian, as the Christian references tend to emphasise spiritual rather than earthly warfare.

Another important category of musical instruments describes those few musical instruments portrayed as having some kind of Otherworld influence, such as when a harp hears a secret or when a saint's bell magically appears from nowhere just in time to begin Mass. Here we find much tree imagery associated with musical instruments, such as when a birch tree grows out of the handle of St Patrick's bell or the wood from a special grove of trees becomes a magic harp. Much of the material in the references within Christian contexts deals with the special power of the saint's bell to serve as a 'bell of wrath' against his enemies, to exorcise demons or to sound on Doomsday. The issue of kingship comes up in the primal contexts, for example in the reference where the double pipes made from a particular grove of tree saplings are directly related to the young man becoming king.

With instruments, as with the performers, there is also a continuity across what would otherwise seem the distinctly separate areas of the otherworldly and the mundane, the supernatural and the natural, and across the divide between the Christian and primal contexts. For example, a single instrument like a bell or a harp can convey through the various references to it a sense of the unbroken line that joins this world and the Otherworld.

Effects

The effects of music from the primal contexts are many and varied, including the ability of music to put the listener into a trance-like sleep state, or to cause great joy, ecstasy or melancholy in the listener. The famous 'three strains', *suantraigi* (sleep), *genntraigi* (joy), and *golltraigi* (melancholy), are portrayed as having especially powerful effects.

Perhaps surprising is the great degree of fear associated with otherworldly music in these references, as such music is also described as having dangerous, melancholic or even deadly effects. The music of the primal Otherworld is mysterious, joyful, trancelike and beautiful, yet it is also portrayed as having the power to summon something (often an animal) or someone (usually a *sidhe* being) to the musician. The music of the Otherworld also has the ability to inspire or teach other musicians, and to be relaxing, healing or protective (see Charts 5 and 6 in the Appendix at the end of the book). Music is also shown to be associated with increased prosperity, the prophecy of a future king's realm, and as a gift to be bestowed upon a selected mortal from the *sidhe* beings.

In the Christian contexts, the effects of music in Heaven are overwhelmingly joyful or ecstatic. Other very positive effects are noted, such as the ability of the music of Heaven to lull one to sleep or the protective effects of the saint's bell. However, the portrayals of the power of the saint's bell, which was used as a curse toward the uncooperative or ungodly, show that the Christian scribes were equally aware of the potentially negative effects of such music. Many references to the phenomenon of 'mysterious or unknown music', where mysterious music is heard yet no performers or instruments are seen by the listener, also occur in this collection.

Further parallels exist between music references within both primal and Christian contexts as regards descriptions of the effect of music to inspire or teach, and be healing or therapeutic.

In both primal and Christian contexts, the vast majority of mundane, everyday effects relate to the natural elements. Not a single Christian everyday example refers to the music of the swords, yet this portrayal occurs fairly often in the primal examples as part of the descriptions of a battle scene. Overall, the heavy emphasis on the natural elements as having a kind of 'music' of their own may tell us something about how much the early Irish appear to have valued nature and the earth.

The liminal category for effects deals with those unusual situations where, for example, a mortal hears otherworldly music on earth, then visits the Otherworld or Heaven and then returns back to everyday life, a situation identically experienced by a royal nobleman (Bran), a king (Cormac), two saints (St Patrick and St Fursa) and Cuchulainn's charioteer (Loeg). Another liminal situation is where a saint from Heaven (St Michael) shape-shifts into a musical bird, visits a mortal saint (St Brendan) and then returns to Heaven. All of these examples portray a fluidity between this world and the next. The music here is both a lure to go to the Otherworld or Heaven, and also a special 'transport' mechanism – the bridge between the dimensions.

But the major issue within the effects category is as follows. It appears that the more dramatic the musical effect described, the more supernatural is the context. This is true whether that context is primal or Christian. The supernatural music of the Otherworld, it would seem, runs right through everyday life, reaching up to the heights (joy and ecstasy) and down to the depths (misery and despair) of mundane, everyday life experienced here on earth. The heights (mountains, hills) and the depths (the sea, wells) of the landscape are also portrayed as having inherent musical qualities of their own in many of the references.

One never seems to know for sure just when or where one might encounter the supernatural music of the Otherworld and its effects. The one certainty seems to be that it is often so powerful and beautiful that its otherworldly origin is not in doubt, and the references make this clear by explicitly differentiating it from more mundane types of music.

It seems that the degree of supernatural influence tends to determine how dramatic the effect is on the listener, both in the primal and the Christian contexts.

Places

The places where music is heard are generally portrayed in and around the daily environment. In the primal contexts, this includes the court of a king, the sites of battlefields, fairs, festivals, cairns and those outdoor places such as hills and mounds. In the Christian contexts, the everyday places where music is heard are around a hermit monk's cell, a monastery or a church. All of these one might expect.

However, the category of liminal places indicates some locations that may seem a bit more unusual, such as a mountain-side entrance to a *sidhe* dwelling, the doorway of a *sidhe*-woman's abode on an island paradise, or at the edge of a window sill (see Charts 7 and 8 in the Appendix at the end of the book). These places suggest, again, a fluidity between this world and the Otherworld. At such locations, the boundaries between this earthly, mundane world and the supernatural Otherworld intersect, creating a special place that may be seen to serve as a portal or entry into another dimension.

The places in the purely supernatural Otherworld feature trees, stones, fields, hills, plains, mountains, birds' abodes like tree branches, which are common to both the primal and Christian Otherworld descriptions that relate to music.

Noticeably absent from the Christian Otherworld in the references from this collection is the motif of an Otherworld fountain with musical streams flowing from it. Generally, it seems, the Christian Otherworld is more likely to feature the Tree of Life and its singing birds than a fountain with musical streams, which is featured more often in the primal Otherworld examples.

Similarly, the location of a battlefield is mentioned mainly in the primal examples as a place where one might hear the 'music of the swords', but this does not occur in the Christian places.

But the greatest number of portrayals of the music of the Otherworld in both primal and Christian contexts is the idea of the Otherworld or heavenly dimension as having an inherent musicality all its own, a place of continuous, beautiful music.

Times

Since terms like 'unceasing' or 'continuous' are the closest those on earth can come to describing the concept of eternity, these characteristics applied to music indicate its quality of timelessness, especially regarding references to music in the Otherworld dimension.

In the references with primal contexts which describe the Otherworld, the concept of unceasing or continuous music is constantly emphasised. The constant music of the plains and land(s) of the Otherworld clearly predominates, followed by music heard continuously at island paradises, and the unceasing, continuous music of trees, birds, wells, streams, fountains, and stones, for example. It is as if all of creation has an inherent musicality, and the music never stops (see Charts 9 and 10 in the Appendix at the end of the book).

Music in the Christian Heaven is also portrayed as being of a continuous, eternal nature. Here, birds are specifically portrayed as constantly singing the canonical hours in harmony on the Tree of Life. Three precious stones continuously sing music in praise of God, and the insects portrayed in the Christian Otherworld are the bees which continuously sing to the flowers on an island Paradise.

The everyday, mundane times when music is heard in the primal contexts are the times of battle, a fair or a festival, or at the party of a nobleman. In the Christian contexts, the everyday, mundane times when music is heard occur mainly during Mass and at Vespers, which one might expect. However, the future time of Doomsday is mentioned quite frequently, with the traditional Old Testament time period of 'forty days and forty nights' referred to especially when speaking of St Patrick. The time of an ordination ceremony and also the season of winter, with its curious absence of music, are mentioned by the hermit monks in their poetry.

But by far the most frequently portrayed time regarding music in everyday Christian life is simply 'continuous', including the 'music' of the natural elements like the wind through the trees, the rivers' torrents, the birds' singing, the sea's waves and so on. It certainly appears that the hermit monks valued this type of 'music' very highly in their everyday life and mention it with such frequency that one cannot help but take note of it.

The liminal times at which music is heard in the overtly primal contexts reveal that the time of *Samhain* eve (31 October) is a particularly special time at which to hear the supernatural music of the Otherworld. Also, *Lughnasadh* (1 August) is mentioned as quite musical overall. Surprisingly, there seem to be no direct early Irish references to music heard at *Imbolc* (1 February) or to *Bealtaine* (1 May). In the literature of the Highlands and islands of Scotland, however, there are more references to *Imbolc*, with a strong Brigid/ St Bride tradition, and the Welsh material has more references to celebrations at *Bealtaine*. Clearly, *Samhain* and *Lughasadh* were regarded as especially liminal in some way in the early Irish society, and were viewed as times when the boundaries between this world and the Otherworld were especially thin and when supernatural music was more likely to be heard.

In the Christian contexts involving times, one can clearly see that the moment of a saint's death is the most frequently mentioned liminal time, followed by the moment of a saint's birth. This is in great contrast to the primal context liminal examples, where no musical references at all occur to the issue of either birth or death, judging from the references in this collection.

Summary

This has been a summary of the general findings that arose from an analysis of the collection of references to the performers, instruments, effects, places and times regarding music and the Celtic Otherworld in early medieval Irish literature.

In this overall effort to collect and catalogue the music references, and to attempt to look at the early Irish and their understanding of music, it is clear that they consistently make reference to music, and especially supernatural music, no matter what the context. There appears to be a continuity in imagery across what would otherwise seem to be the entirely separate areas of the otherworldly and the mundane. There also seems to be parallel imagery used across the divide of the overtly primal and the overtly Christian contexts. There appears to be an unbroken line in the influence of supernatural music in this literature that touches the very heights of existence and, occasionally, also the depths of everyday, earthly life.

The whole of creation seems to radiate a harmony in this literature, from the music of the natural elements all around, to the indescribably beautiful supernatural music of the Otherworld. That music itself seems to be portrayed by this society as the 'great connector', that is as a medium or bridge to either go to, or be visited by, an Otherworldly personage, for example, seems to say something about the early Irish viewpoint of life itself. Rather than see life in black and white or either/or terms as many people tend to do in more modern times, life instead seems to be portrayed here as an ever-moving, ever-changing, ever-shifting reality including both what we now call the mundane, everyday and the supernatural Otherworld.

In such a worldview, it is very difficult, if not impossible, to discern where one begins and the other ends. Its inherent dynamism prevents such limitations; we must instead open up to the mystery of life itself, and to music and harmony as an integral part of it.

In the words of Irish playwright Stewart Parker, play is how a society experiments, imagines, invents and moves forward; play is the means by which people test the world and register its realities. Perhaps, as has been suggested, one could say the same about music. And one could then see from what the early Irish texts say about music, that music revealed to them a reality more like a seamless continuum from the mundane to the heights we now refer to as the 'otherworldly' or 'supernatural', thus offering us an alternative to our hard dualisms. But not only do the early Irish seem to have this view, of course; the other Celtic cross-cultural examples from Scotland, Wales, Brittany and Cornwall also seem to share this perspective in particular, as does the literature of other world cultures.

And even today, in the late twentieth century, we are still able to learn from and marvel at the power of music in our lives. We often fail to notice how music in our environment affects us, or largely ignore it. Perhaps we do so at our peril.

Take, for example, the recent findings at the University of California about children being able to concentrate better and succeed at examinations by listening to music, classical or otherwise. Listening to the works of Mozart, Vivaldi and Bach has helped students with reading, writing and analytical skills, but ironically, so did the well-known rock hit *Another Brick in the Wall* by Pink Floyd. It all depends on the rhythms and number of beats per minute, with a steady sixty beats a minute having the greatest results in producing a calming effect and stimulating creative thinking.[1]

It also appears that chickens appear healthier and happier, and lay more eggs, when farmers play music to them, according to Bryan Jones of the Roslin Institute near Edinburgh, Scotland. In an article from the *Daily Telegraph* (London) in January 1998:

Jones, of Edinburgh's Roslin Institute, said he set out to discover if music could soothe ruffled feathers and boost egg production. 'We wanted to determine whether the mythology was based on fact,' said Jones, whose institute produced Dolly, the world's first cloned sheep. After surveying more than 100 poultry farmers at a British pig and poultry fair, Jones said researchers found that 46 per cent of the farmers routinely played music to their birds. 'The most important question we asked them was whether they had noticed any benefits,' he said. The answer was an overwhelming yes. 90 per cent said birds dosed with music were calmer, 52 per cent said they were less aggressive, 20 per cent reported the overall health of the flock had improved, and 16 per cent claimed increased egg production.[2]

It seems as though the early Irish would have agreed, as they acknowledged that music seemed to help cows produce more milk and so increase prosperity in some of the references.

They also greatly acknowledged that music could be beneficial for a king's realm and important to a nation. Down through the centuries, they have not been alone regarding this belief. Plato and Aristotle believed that music has a powerful role in education, as it can be used effectively for good or ill. The power of music, especially when combined with drama, can be 'terrifyingly impressive. At the Nuremburg rally of 1936, the thunderous cheers of the vast crowd eventually drowned the music of the massed bands which played Hitler in.'[3]

The influence of a national anthem or the traditional folk music of a nation has been well-known for centuries. In seventeenth century Scotland, Andrew Fletcher of Saltoun (1655–1716) expressed a similar sentiment when he said: 'If a man were permitted to make all the ballads, he need not care who should make all the laws of a nation.'[4]

So even in modern times we seem to agree with the early Irish that music does affect us, often in powerful, albeit mysterious, ways. But scientists, medical researchers and others are still trying to find out exactly how music affects us.

Nonetheless, it is very difficult to imagine a world without music. Anthropologists tell us that nearly every society on earth has made music in some way. Even if music were totally banned, it seems as though we would still carry a tune in our minds throughout the course of everyday life. It seems as though music is part of us, and an inherent part of the universe, the rhythm and pulse of life itself. Nietzsche said that for him, music was 'something for the sake of which it is worthwhile to live on earth'.[5]

The early Celts may well have added that music can, at times, bring the Otherworld and its heavenly music down to our home here on earth, to greatly enrich our lives. Even if we don't know why, we still seem to need music in our lives in some way.

The wisdom of an old Gaelic proverb states: 'To him that farthest went away, the sweetest music he ever heard was "Come Home".'[6] Many myths and stories tell of how humanity is still searching for Eden, for a 'Paradise Lost'. Perhaps, then, the Otherworld and its beautiful music is beckoning us to 'Come Home' again, to restore the universal Lost Chord.

Notes

1. Jinks, P., 'Teaching Profession Rocked by Pink Floyd Sound Test', *Scotland on Sunday*, Edinburgh, 11 January 1998, p. 3.
2. Glaskin, M., 'Music Soothes Chickens and Makes Them More Productive', *Daily Telegraph*, London, 24 January 1999, p. 10.
3. Storr, A., *Music and the Mind* (London, 1992), p. 46.
4. Lockhart, G. W., *Fiddles and Folk: A Celebration of the re-emergence of Scotland's Musical Heritage* (Edinburgh, 1998), p. 6.
5. Storr, *Music and the Mind*, p. 188.
6. Nicolson, A., *Gaelic Proverbs* (Edinburgh: Birlinn, 1996; orig. 1881), p. 17.

Appendix

Chart 1 Musical performers: overtly primal contexts

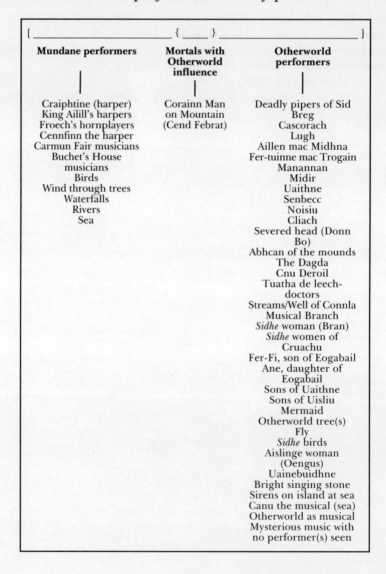

Mundane performers	Mortals with Otherworld influence	Otherworld performers
Craiphtine (harper)	Corainn Man on Mountain (Cend Febrat)	Deadly pipers of Sid Breg
King Ailill's harpers		Cascorach
Froech's hornplayers		Lugh
Cennfinn the harper		Aillen mac Midhna
Carmun Fair musicians		Fer-tuinne mac Trogain
Buchet's House musicians		Manannan
Birds		Midir
Wind through trees		Uaithne
Waterfalls		Senbecc
Rivers		Noisiu
Sea		Cliach
		Severed head (Donn Bo)
		Abhcan of the mounds
		The Dagda
		Cnu Deroil
		Tuatha de leech-doctors
		Streams/Well of Connla
		Musical Branch
		Sidhe woman (Bran)
		Sidhe women of Cruachu
		Fer-Fi, son of Eogabail
		Ane, daughter of Eogabail
		Sons of Uaithne
		Sons of Uisliu
		Mermaid
		Otherworld tree(s)
		Fly
		Sidhe birds
		Aislinge woman (Oengus)
		Uainebuidhne
		Bright singing stone
		Sirens on island at sea
		Canu the musical (sea)
		Otherworld as musical
		Mysterious music with no performer(s) seen

Chart 2 Musical performers: overtly Christian contexts

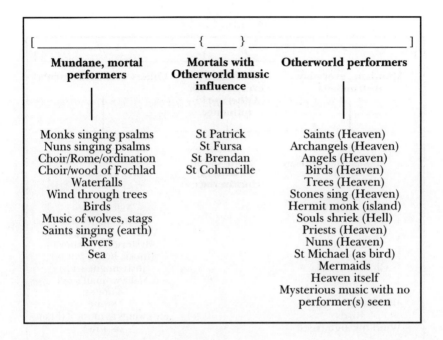

Mundane, mortal performers	Mortals with Otherworld music influence	Otherworld performers
Monks singing psalms	St Patrick	Saints (Heaven)
Nuns singing psalms	St Fursa	Archangels (Heaven)
Choir/Rome/ordination	St Brendan	Angels (Heaven)
Choir/wood of Fochlad	St Columcille	Birds (Heaven)
Waterfalls		Trees (Heaven)
Wind through trees		Stones sing (Heaven)
Birds		Hermit monk (island)
Music of wolves, stags		Souls shriek (Hell)
Saints singing (earth)		Priests (Heaven)
Rivers		Nuns (Heaven)
Sea		St Michael (as bird)
		Mermaids
		Heaven itself
		Mysterious music with no performer(s) seen

Chart 3 Musical instruments: overtly primal contexts

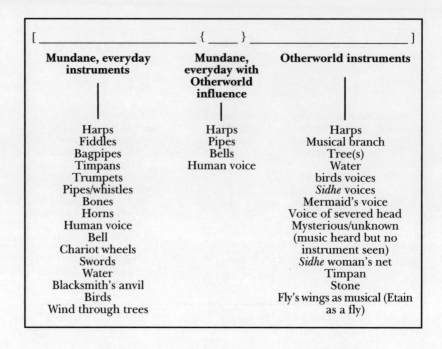

Mundane, everyday instruments	Mundane, everyday with Otherworld influence	Otherworld instruments
Harps	Harps	Harps
Fiddles	Pipes	Musical branch
Bagpipes	Bells	Tree(s)
Timpans	Human voice	Water
Trumpets		birds voices
Pipes/whistles		*Sidhe* voices
Bones		Mermaid's voice
Horns		Voice of severed head
Human voice		Mysterious/unknown
Bell		(music heard but no
Chariot wheels		instrument seen)
Swords		*Sidhe* woman's net
Water		Timpan
Blacksmith's anvil		Stone
Birds		Fly's wings as musical (Etain
Wind through trees		as a fly)

Chart 4 Musical instruments: overtly Christian contexts

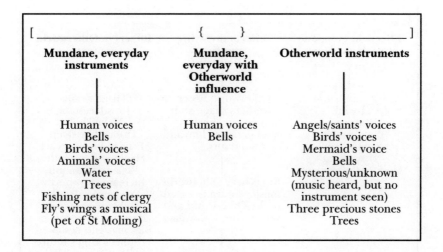

Mundane, everyday instruments	Mundane, everyday with Otherworld influence	Otherworld instruments
Human voices Bells Birds' voices Animals' voices Water Trees Fishing nets of clergy Fly's wings as musical (pet of St Moling)	Human voices Bells	Angels/saints' voices Birds' voices Mermaid's voice Bells Mysterious/unknown (music heard, but no instrument seen) Three precious stones Trees

Chart 5 The effects of music: overtly primal contexts

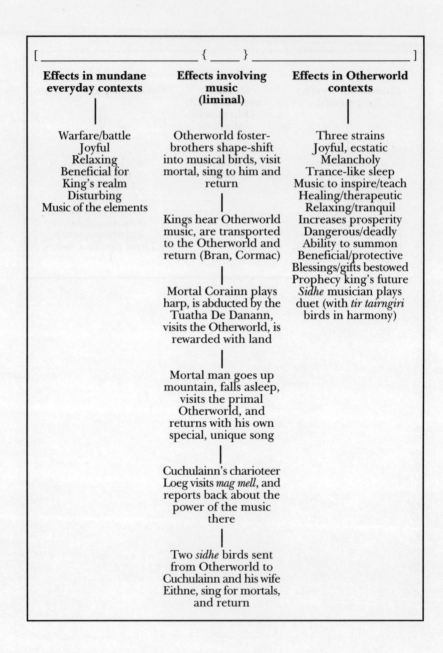

[_____ { _____ } _____]

Effects in mundane everyday contexts

Effects involving music (liminal)

Effects in Otherworld contexts

Effects in mundane everyday contexts	Effects involving music (liminal)	Effects in Otherworld contexts
Warfare/battle Joyful Relaxing Beneficial for King's realm Disturbing Music of the elements	Otherworld foster-brothers shape-shift into musical birds, visit mortal, sing to him and return	Three strains Joyful, ecstatic Melancholy Trance-like sleep Music to inspire/teach Healing/therapeutic Relaxing/tranquil Increases prosperity Dangerous/deadly Ability to summon Beneficial/protective Blessings/gifts bestowed Prophecy king's future *Sidhe* musician plays duet (with *tir tairngiri* birds in harmony)
	Kings hear Otherworld music, are transported to the Otherworld and return (Bran, Cormac)	
	Mortal Corainn plays harp, is abducted by the Tuatha De Danann, visits the Otherworld, is rewarded with land	
	Mortal man goes up mountain, falls asleep, visits the primal Otherworld, and returns with his own special, unique song	
	Cuchulainn's charioteer Loeg visits *mag mell*, and reports back about the power of the music there	
	Two *sidhe* birds sent from Otherworld to Cuchulainn and his wife Eithne, sing for mortals, and return	

Chart 6 *The effects of music: overtly Christian contexts*

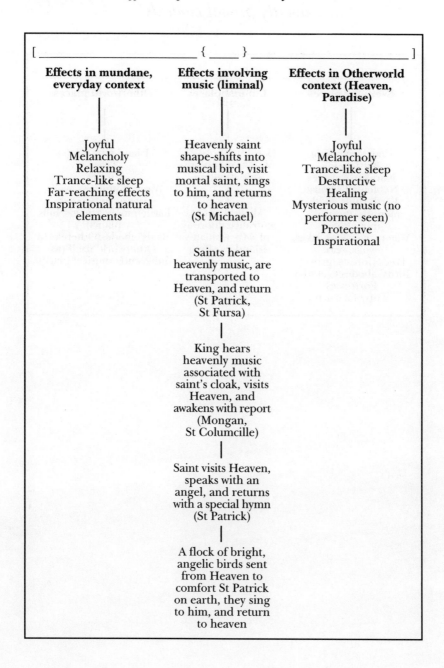

Effects in mundane, everyday context	Effects involving music (liminal)	Effects in Otherworld context (Heaven, Paradise)
Joyful Melancholy Relaxing Trance-like sleep Far-reaching effects Inspirational natural elements	Heavenly saint shape-shifts into musical bird, visit mortal saint, sings to him, and returns to heaven (St Michael)	Joyful Melancholy Trance-like sleep Destructive Healing Mysterious music (no performer seen) Protective Inspirational
	Saints hear heavenly music, are transported to Heaven, and return (St Patrick, St Fursa)	
	King hears heavenly music associated with saint's cloak, visits Heaven, and awakens with report (Mongan, St Columcille)	
	Saint visits Heaven, speaks with an angel, and returns with a special hymn (St Patrick)	
	A flock of bright, angelic birds sent from Heaven to comfort St Patrick on earth, they sing to him, and return to heaven	

Chart 7 Places where music is heard:
overtly primal contexts

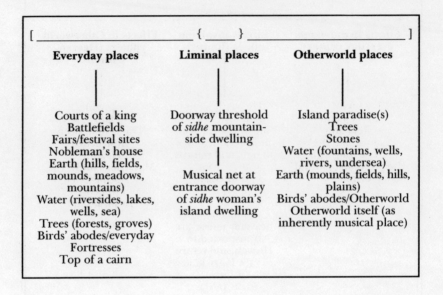

Everyday places	Liminal places	Otherworld places
Courts of a king	Doorway threshold	Island paradise(s)
Battlefields	of *sidhe* mountain-	Trees
Fairs/festival sites	side dwelling	Stones
Nobleman's house		Water (fountains, wells,
Earth (hills, fields,		rivers, undersea)
mounds, meadows,	Musical net at	Earth (mounds, fields, hills,
mountains)	entrance doorway	plains)
Water (riversides, lakes,	of *sidhe* woman's	Birds' abodes/Otherworld
wells, sea)	island dwelling	Otherworld itself (as
Trees (forests, groves)		inherently musical place)
Birds' abodes/everyday		
Fortresses		
Top of a cairn		

Chart 8 Places where music is heard:
overtly Christian contexts

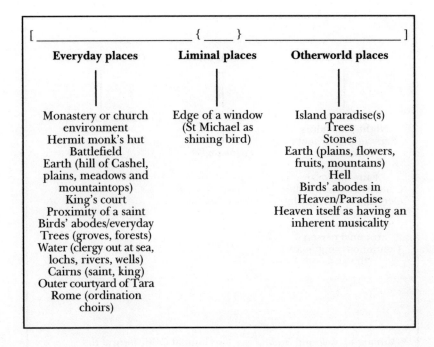

Everyday places	Liminal places	Otherworld places
Monastery or church environment Hermit monk's hut Battlefield Earth (hill of Cashel, plains, meadows and mountaintops) King's court Proximity of a saint Birds' abodes/everyday Trees (groves, forests) Water (clergy out at sea, lochs, rivers, wells) Cairns (saint, king) Outer courtyard of Tara Rome (ordination choirs)	Edge of a window (St Michael as shining bird)	Island paradise(s) Trees Stones Earth (plains, flowers, fruits, mountains) Hell Birds' abodes in Heaven/Paradise Heaven itself as having an inherent musicality

Chart 9 Times when music is heard:
overtly primal contexts

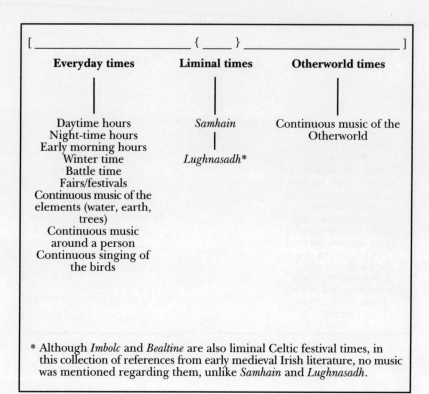

[_____ { ____ } _____]

Everyday times	**Liminal times**	**Otherworld times**

Daytime hours
Night-time hours
Early morning hours
Winter time
Battle time
Fairs/festivals
Continuous music of the
elements (water, earth,
trees)
Continuous music
around a person
Continuous singing of
the birds

Samhain

*Lughnasadh**

Continuous music of the
Otherworld

* Although *Imbolc* and *Bealtine* are also liminal Celtic festival times, in
this collection of references from early medieval Irish literature, no music
was mentioned regarding them, unlike *Samhain* and *Lughnasadh*.

Chart 10 Times when music is heard: overtly Christain contexts

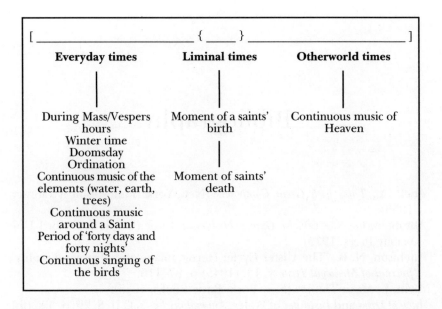

Bibliography

Abell, A., *Talks with Great Composers* (New York: Philosophical Library, 1955).

Abraham, G., *The Concise Oxford History of Music* (London: Oxford University Press, 1979).

Aitchison, N. B., 'The Ulster Cycle: Heroic image and Historical reality', *Journal of Medieval History*, 13, (1945) p. 87–116.

Alvin, J., *Music Therapy* (New York: Basic Books, 1975).

Ancient Laws and *Institutes* of Wales, *Anomalous Laws*, C.II, S. 29, p. 396 (fol. edn).

Anderson, A., 'Tain Bo Fraich', *Revue Celtique* 24 (Paris, 1903), p. 127–54.

Bamford, C. and Marsh, W., *Celtic Christianity* (West Stockbridge, MA: Lindisfarne Press, 1987).

Bannerman, J., 'The Clarsach and the Clarsair', *Scottish Studies*, 30 (Edinburgh, 1991), p. 9.

Barker, A. (ed.), *Greek Musical Writings, Vol. I: The Musician and His Art* (Cambridge: Cambridge University Press, 1984).

Barker, A. (ed.), *Greek Musical Writings, Vol. II: Harmonic and Acoustic Theory* (Cambridge: Cambridge University Press 1989).

Bede and His World: The Jarrow Lectures, Vols 1 (1958–78) and 2 (1979–93) (Aldershot: Variorum, 1994).

Bell, R., *The Qur'an, translated with a critical arrangement of the Suras*, Vols I and 2 (Edinburgh: T. & T. Clark, 1937).

Bennett, M., *Scottish Customs from the Cradle to the Grave* (Edinburgh: Polygon, 1992).

Bergin, O., 'The Death of Conn of the Hundred Battles', *Zeitschrift fur Celtische Philologie*, 8 (London, 1912), p. 275–7.

Bergin, O., *Irish Bardic Poetry* (Dublin: DIAS, 1984).

Bernstein, L., *The Unanswered Question: Six Talks at Harvard* (Cambridge, MA: Harvard University Press, 1976).

Best, R. I., 'The Tragic Death of Curoi Mac Dari', *Eriu*, 2 (Dublin, 1905), pp. 18–35.

Best, R. I., 'The Adventures of Art Son of Conn', *Eriu*, 3 (Dublin, 1907), pp. 149–73.

Best, R. I., 'The Settling of the Manor of Tara', *Eriu*, 4 (Dublin, 1910), pp. 121–72.

Best, R. I., 'Cuchulainn's Shield', *Eriu*, 5 (Dublin, 1911), p. 72.

Best, R. I., 'The Battle of Airtech', *Eriu*, 8 (Dublin, 1916), pp. 170–90.

Binchy, B. A., 'Distraint in Irish Law', *Celtica*, 10 (Dublin, 1973).

Boethius, *The Principles of Music*, ed. Claude V. Palisca, trans. Calvin M. Bower (New Haven, CT and London: Yale University Press, 1989).

Bonwick, J., *Irish Druids and Old Irish Religions* (New York: Dorset Press, 1986; reprint of 1894 orig.).

Bourke, C. (ed.), *Studies in the Cult of St Columba* (Dublin: Four Courts Press, 1997).

Bradley, I., *The Celtic Way* (London: Darton, Longman & Todd, 1993).

Bradley, I., *Columba: Pilgrim and Penitent* (Glasgow: Wild Goose, 1996).

Bradley, I., *Celtic Christianity: Making Myths and Chasing Dreams* (Edinburgh: Edinburgh University Press, 1999).

Breatnach, L., *Uraicecht na Riar: The Poetic Grades in Early Irish Law* (Dublin, 1987).

Breatnach, L., 'The Caldron of Poetry', *Eriu*, 32 (Dublin, 1982), p. 45–93.

Breatnach, L., 'Canon Law and Secular Law in Early Ireland: The Significance of *Bretha Nemed*', *Peritia*, 3 (1984), pp. 439–59.

Breatnach, L., 'The Ecclesiastical Element in the Old Irish Legal Tract *Cain Fhuithirbe*', *Peritia*, 5 (1986), pp. 36–52.

Briggs, K., *An Encyclopedia of Fairies: Hobgoblins, Brownies, Bogies and other Supernatural Creatures* (New York: Pantheon Books, 1976).

Brocklesbury, R., *Reflections on Ancient and Modern Music* (London, 1749).

Buber, M., *Hasidim and Modern Man*, ed. and trans. Maurice Friedman (New York: Horizon Press, 1958).

Buckley, A., 'What Is the Tiompan?', *Jahrbuch für Musikalische Volks und Volkerkunde*, 9 (Berlin, 1978), pp. 53–88.

Budd, M., *Music and the Emotions* (London: Routledge & Kegan Paul, 1985).

Caerwyn Williams, J. E. and Ford, P., *The Irish Literary Tradition* (Cardiff: University of Wales Press, 1992).

Caerwyn Williams, J. E., *The Court Poet in Medieval Ireland* (Oxford, 1971).

Campbell, Don (ed.), *Music and Miracles* (Wheaton, IL: Quest Books, 1992).

Campbell, J. F., *More West Highland Tales* Vol I, eds Watson, W., MacLean, D. and Rose, H. (Edinburgh: Birlinn, 1994; orig. 1940).

Campbell, J. G., *Superstitions of the Highlands and Islands of Scotland* (Glasgow, 1900).

Cannon, R., *The Highland Bagpipe and its Music* (Edinburgh, 1988), p. 7.

Carey, J., 'The Otherworld in Irish Tradition', *Eigse*, 19 (Dublin, 1982–3).

Carey, J., 'The Heavenly City in *Saltair na Rann*', *Celtica*, 18 (Dublin, 1986).

Carey, J., 'Angelology in *Saltair na Rann*', *Celtica*, 19 (Dublin, 1987).

Carney, J., *Early Irish Poetry* (Dublin, 1965).

Carney, J., 'The Invention of the Ogam Cipher', *Eriu*, 26 (Dublin, 1975), pp. 52–65.

Chadwick, H. M. *The Heroic Age* (Cambridge: Cambridge University Press, 1926).

Chadwick, H. M. and Chadwick, N., *The Growth of Literature* (Cambridge: Cambridge University Press, Part I: 1932; Part 2: 1936; Part 3: 1940).

Chadwick, N., *The Druids* (Cardiff: University of Wales Press, 1966).

Chadwick, N., *The Celts* (Harmondsworth: Penguin, 1971).

Clancy, T. and Markus, G., *Iona: The Earliest Poetry of a Celtic Monastery* (Edinburgh: Edinburgh University Press, 1995).

Collinson, F., *The Bagpipe, Fiddle, and Harp* (Blanefield, Stirlingshire, 1983), no pages given. (facsimile of chapters from his earlier book *The Traditional and National Music of Scotland*, London: Routledge & Kegan Paul, 1966).

Cooke, D., *The Language of Music* (London: Oxford University Press, 1959).

Copland, A., *Music and Imagination* (London: Oxford University Press, 1952).

Cornford, F. M., *Plato's Cosmology* (London: Bobbs-Merrill, reprint of 1937 orig.).

Cornford, F. M., *The Republic of Plato* (London: Oxford University Press, 1945).

Cross, T. P. and Slover, C. H., *Ancient Irish Tales*, trans. various (New York: Henry Holt, 1936); reprinted with a revised bibliography by C. W. Dunn (New York: Barnes & Noble, 1969).

Crowe, J., 'The Adventures of Conla Ruad', *Royal Hist. and Archeology Assoc. of Ireland Journal*, 4, Series III (Dublin, 1874), p. 118–33.

Curtius, E. R., *European Literature and the Latin Middle Ages*, trans. W. R. Trask (New York, 1953).

Danaher, K., 'Irish Folk Tradition and the Celtic Calendar', *The Celtic Connection*, ed. Robert O'Driscoll (New York: George Braziller, 1981) pp. 217–42.

Daniel-Rops, P. L. (ed.), *The Miracle of Ireland* (Baltimore, MD, 1960).

Danielou, A., *Introduction to the Study of Musical Scales* (London, 1943).

Davies, O., *Celtic Christianity in Early Medieval Wales* (Cardiff: University of Wales Press, 1996).

Davies, O. and F. Bowie, *Celtic Christian Spirituality: An Anthology of Medieval and Modern Sources* (London: SPCK, 1995).

Dillon, M., *The Cycles of the Kings* (London: Oxford University Press, 1946).

Dillon, M., *Early Irish Literature* (Chicago: University of Chicago Press, 1948).

Dillon, M. and Chadwick, N., *The Celtic Realms* (London, 1967).

Dionysius the Areopagite, *The Mystical Theology and Celestial Hierarchies*, trans. editors of the Shrine of Wisdom (Brook, Surrey, 1965).

Dobbs, M. E., 'The Battle of Findchorad', *Zeitschrift für Celtische Philologie*, 14 (London, 1923), pp. 395–420.

Dobbs, M. E., 'Cath Cumair (The Battle of Cumar)', *Revue Celtique*, 43 (Paris, 1926), pp. 277–342.

Dobbs, M. E., 'The Battle of the Assembly of Macha', *Zeitschrift für Celtische Philologie*, 16 (London, 1927), pp. 145–61.

Dobbs, M. E., 'The Fosterage of the House of the Two Goblets', *Zeitschrift für Celtische Philologie*, 18 (New York, 1930), pp. 189–230.

D'Olivet, F., *Music Explained as Science and Art*, trans. J. Godwin (Rochester, VT: Inner Traditions International, 1987; orig. 1928).

Donnelly, S., 'The Warpipes in Ireland', *Ceol*, V (1) (Dublin, 1981), pp. 19–24.

Dorson, R., *Folk Legends of Japan* (Rutland, VT, 1962), p. 146.

Dunn, J., 'Life of St. Alexis', *Revue Celtique*, 38 (Paris, 1920), pp. 133–43.

Eliade, M., *The Myth of the Eternal Return*, Bolligen Series XLVI (Princeton, NJ: Princeton University Press, 1954).

Eliade, M., *Shamanism: Archaic Techniques of Ecstasy*, Bolligen Series LXXVI (Princeton, NJ: Princeton University Press, 1964).

Eliade, M., *A History of Religious Ideas* (Chicago: University of Chicago Press, Vol. I: 1978; Vol. II: 1982; Vol. III: 1985).

Elliott, R. G., *The Power of Satire: Magic, Ritual, Art* (Princeton, NJ: Princeton University Press, 1960).

Evans-Wentz, W., *The Fairy Faith in Celtic Countries* (New York: University Books, 1966; orig. 1911).

Farmer, H. G., *A History of Music in Scotland* (London, 1947).

Feehan, F., 'Suggested Links Between Eastern and Celtic Music', *The Celtic Consciousness*, ed. R. O'Driscoll (New York: George Braziller, 1981), pp. 333–9.

Ficino, M., *Commentary on Plato's Symposium*, ed. and trans. Sears Jayne (Columbia: University of Missouri Press, 1944).

Finlay, I., *Columba* (London: Victor Gollancz, 1979).

Fludd, R., *The Origin and Structure of the Cosmos*, ed. Adam McLean, trans. Patricia Tahil (Edinburgh: Magnum Opus, 1982).

Fraser, J., 'The Miracle of Ciaran's Hand', *Eriu*, 6 (Dublin, 1912), pp. 159–60.

Fraser, J., 'The First Battle of Moytura', *Eriu*, 8 (Dublin, 1916), p. 1–63.

Gantz, J., *Early Irish Myths and Sagas* (Harmondsworth: Penguin, 1981).

Glazerson, Rabbi M., *Music and Kabbala* (Jerusalem, 1988).

Godwin, J., *Athanasius Kircher: A Renaissance Man and the Quest for Lost Knowledge* (London: Thames & Hudson, 1979).

Godwin, J., *Robert Fludd* (London: Thames & Hudson, 1979).

Godwin, J., (ed.) *Music, Mysticism and Magic* (London: Routledge & Kegan Paul, 1986).

Godwin, J., (ed.), *Cosmic Music: Three Musical Keys to the Interpretation of Reality*, trans. M. Radkai (West Stockbridge, MA: Lindisfarne Press, 1987).

Godwin, J., *Harmonies of Heaven and Earth* (Rochester VT: Inner Traditions International, 1987), p. 72.

Godwin, J., *Harmony of the Spheres* (Rochester VT: Inner Traditions International, 1993).

Godwin, M., *Angels: An Endangered Species* (New York: Simon & Schuster, 1990).

Greene, D. and O'Connor, F., *A Golden Treasury of Irish Poetry A.D. 600–1200* (London: Macmillan, 1967).

Guthrie, K. S. (ed.), *The Pythagorean Sourcebook and Library* (Grand Rapids, MI: Phanes Press, 1987).

Guthrie, W. K., *Orpheus and Greek Religion* (London: Methuen, 1952).

Gwyndaf, R., 'Fairylore: Memorates and Legends from Welsh Oral Tradition', *The Good People: New Fairylore essays*, ed. Peter Narvaez (New York: Garland, 1991).

Gwynn, E., 'The Priest and the Bees' and 'The Three Drinking Horns of Cormac', *Eriu*, 2 (London, 1905), pp. 82–3 and 186–8, respectively.

Gwynn, E., *The Metrical Dindshenchas*, Part IV, Royal Irish Academy Todd Lecture Series Vol. 11 (Dublin, 1924).

Gwynn, E., 'The Life of St. Lasair', *Eriu*, 5 (London, 1911), pp. 73–109.

Gwynn, E., 'De Maccaib Conaire (Of the Sons of Conaire)', *Eriu*, 6 (Dublin, 1912), pp. 144–53.

Gwynn, E., 'Of the Race of Conaire Mor', *Eriu*, 6 (Dublin, 1912), pp. 130–43.

Hamel, M., *Through Music to the Self* (Shaftesbury: Element, 1978).

Healy, J., *Ireland's Ancient Schools and Scholars* (Dublin: Sealy, Bryers & Walker, 1908).

Hennessey, W. M., 'The Battle of Cnucha', *Revue Celtique*, 2 (Paris, 1874), pp. 86–93.

Hennessey, W. M., 'Of the Three Collas', in Skene, W. F., *Celtic Scotland*, III (Edinburgh, 1880), pp. 462–6.

Herbert, Maire, 'The Seven Journeys of the Soul', *Eigse*, 17 (Dublin, 1977–9).

Herbert, Maire, *Iona, Kells, and Derry* (Oxford: Clarendon Press, 1988).

Herbert, Maire, 'Goddess and King: The Sacred Marriage in Early Ireland', in *Women and Sovereignty*, ed. Fradenburg, L. (Gen. ed. Lyle, E., 7) (Edinburgh: Edinburgh University Press, 1992).

Hogan, E., 'Cath Ruis na Rig for Boinn' (The Battle of Ross na Rig on the Boyne), *Royal Irish Academy Todd Lecture Series*, Vol. 4 (Dublin, 1892).

Hollander, L., 'Will you Join the Dance?', *Music and Miracles*, ed. Don Campbell (Wheaton, IL: Quest Books, 1992).

Homer, *The Odyssey*, Book I, trans. T. E. Shaw (Hertfordshire: Wordsworth Editions, 1992), p. 5.

Hughes, K., *The Church in Early Society* (London: Methuen, 1966).

Hughes, K. and Hamlin, A., *Celtic Monasticism* (New York, 1981).

Hull, E. (ed.), *The Cuchulain Saga in Irish Literature* (London, 1898).

Hull, V., 'Eogan Mor and Conn Cetchathach', *Zeitschrift für Celtische Philologie*, 19 (New York, 1933), pp. 59–61.

Hull, V., 'The Seizure of the Fairy Hill', *Zeitschrift für Celtische Philologie*, 19 (New York, 1933), pp. 53–8.

Hyde, D., *A Literary History of Ireland* (London: T. Fisher Unwin, 1901).

Hyde, D., *The Religious Songs of Connacht*, Vol. 1 (London: T. Fisher Unwin, 1906).

Jackson, K. H., *A Celtic Miscellany* (Harmondsworth: Penguin, 1971).

Jackson, K. H., 'The Date of the Tripartite Life of St. Patrick', *Zeitschrift für Celtische Philologie* (Tubingen, 1986).

James, Jamie, *The Music of the Spheres* (London: Abacus, 1993).

Jones, G. and Jones, T., *The Mabinogion*, Engl. trans. (London: J. M. Dent, 1993 revised edn of 1949 orig.).

Joyce, P. W., *A Social History of Ancient Ireland*, Vol. I (London: Longmans Green & Co., 1903).

Kalweit, H., *Dreamtime and Inner Space: The World of the Shaman* (Boston: Shambhala, 1988).

Keating, T., *The History of Ireland* (London: Irish Texts Society, Vol. 4: 1902,; Vols 8–9 1908; Vol. 15 1914).

Kelly, F., *A Guide to Early Irish Law*, Early Irish Law Series 3 (Dublin: DIAS, 1988).

Kendrick, T. D., *The Druids* (London: Methuen, 1927).

Kenney, J., *Sources for the Early History of Ireland: Vol. I, Ecclesiastical* (New York: Columbia University Press, 1929).

Khan, I., *On Music* (Claremont, CA: Hunter House, 1988; reprint of 'The Sufi Message of Hazrat Inayat Khan', Geneva, 1959).

Kinsella, T., *The Tain* (Oxford: Oxford University Press, 1969).

Kinsella, T., *The New Oxford Book of Irish Verse* (Oxford: Oxford University Press, 1989).

Kirk, Rev. R., *The Secret Commonwealth of Elves, Fauns, & Fairies* (Stirling: Eneas Mackay, 1933; reprint of 1815 orig.). *Note*: This edition includes a Commentary by Andrew Lang.

Knott, E., 'Why Mongan Was Deprived of Noble Issue', *Eriu*, 8 (Dublin, 1916), pp. 55–9.

Leahy, A. H., *Heroic Romances of Ireland* (London: David Nutt, Vol. I: 1902; Vol. II: 1906).

Le Mee, K., *Chant* (New York: Bell Tower, 1994).

Lipman, E. A., *Musical Thought in Ancient Greece* (New York, 1964).

Low, M., *Celtic Christianity and Nature* (Edinburgh: Edinburgh University Press, 1996).

Lyle, E., (ed.) *Scottish Ballads* (Edinburgh: Canongate, 1994).

Macalister, S., 'The Life of Saint Finan of Loch Lee', *Zeitschrift für Celtische Philologie*, 2 (London, 1899), pp. 545–65.

MacCana, P., 'Conservation and Innovation in Early Celtic Literature', *Etudes Celtiques*, 13 (Paris, 1972), pp. 61–118.

MacCana, P., 'The Sinless Otherworld of *Immram Brain*', *Eriu*, 27 (Dublin, 1976).

McCone, K., *Pagan Past and Christian Present in Early Irish Literature*, Maynooth Monographs Vol. 3 (An Sagart, Ireland, Maynooth, 1990).

MacCulloch, J. A., *The Religion of the Ancient Celts* (Edinburgh: T. & T. Clark, 1911).

MacDonald, A. D. S., 'Aspects of the Monastery and the Monastic Life in Adomnan's Life of Columba', *Peritia*, 3 (Edinburgh, 1984), pp. 271–302.

Mackey, J. P. (ed.) *An Introduction to Celtic Christianity* (Edinburgh: T. & T. Clark, 1989).

Mackey, J. P., *Power and Christian Ethics* (Cambridge: Cambridge University Press, 1994).

MacMathuna, S., 'Contributions to a Study of the Voyages of St. Brendan and St. Malo', *Irlande et Bretagne* (Rennes, 1994).

McNamara, M., *The Apocrypha in the Irish Church* (Dublin: DIAS, 1975).

MacNeill, E., *Phases of Irish History* (Dublin: M. H. Gill & Son, 1937).

MacNeill, M., *The Festival of Lughnasadh* (Oxford: Oxford University Press, 1962).

MacNeill, M., 'The Musician in the Cave', *Bealoideas*, 19 (Dublin, 1987).

MacSweeney, P., *The Martial Career of Congal Clairinghneach* (London: Irish Texts Society, 1904).

MacSwiney, J. P., 'The Adventures of Condla the Fair', *Gaelic Journal*, II (Edinburgh, 1885), pp. 307–9.

Marstrander, C., 'The Deaths of Lugaid and Derbforgaill', *Eriu*, 5 (London, 1911), pp. 210–18.

Matheson, W. (ed.), *The Blind Harper (An Clarsair Dall), The Songs of Roderick Morison and his Music* (Edinburgh: Scottish Gaelic Texts Society, 1970).

Merriam, A. P., *The Anthropology of Music* (Evanston, IL: Northwestern University Press, 1964).

Meyer, K., 'The Elopement of Emer', *Revue Celtique*, 6 (Paris, 1884), pp. 184–5.

Meyer, K., 'The Combat of Cuchulainn with Senbecc', *Revue Celtique*, 6 (Paris, 1884), pp. 182–4.

Meyer, K., 'The Conception of Conchobur', *Revue Celtique*, 6 (Paris, 1884), pp. 173–82.

Meyer, K., 'The Adventures of Nera', *Revue Celtique*, 10 (Paris, 1889), pp. 212–28 (Part I).

Meyer, K., 'The Adventures of Nera', *Revue Celtique*, 11 (Paris, 1890), pp. 209–10.

Meyer, K., 'The Wooing of Emer (Tochmarc Emire)', *Revue Celtique*, 11 (Paris, 1890), pp. 434–57.

Meyer, K., *Aislinge meic Conglinne* ('The Vision of Mac Conglinne') (London: Irish Texts Society, 1892).

Meyer, K., 'How Ronan Slew His Son', *Revue Celtique*, 13 (Paris, 1892), pp. 372–97.

Meyer, K., 'The Story of Baile mac Buaine (Scel Baili Binnberlaig)', *Revue Celtique*, 13 (Paris, 1892), pp. 220–7.

Meyer, K., 'The Tragic Death of Diarmait's Three Sons', *Hibernica Minora* (Oxford, 1894), pp. 73–5.

Meyer, K., 'The Cherishing of Conall Cernach and the Deaths of Ailill and of Conall Cernach', *Zeitschrift für Celtische Philologie*, 1 (London, 1897), pp. 102–11.

Meyer, K., 'The Birth of Brandub son of Eochu and of Aedan son of Gabran', *Zeitschrift für Celtische Philologie*, 2 (London, 1899), pp. 134–7.

Meyer, K., 'The Colloquy of Colum Cille and the youth at Carn Eolairg', *Zeitschrift für Celtische Philologie*, 2 (London, 1899), pp. 313–20.

Meyer, K., 'Stories and Songs from Irish MSS', *Otia Merseiana*, II (Liverpool, 1900).

Meyer, K., *Cain Adomnain: An Old Irish Treatise on the Law of Adamnain*, Anecdota Oxoniensa, Medieval and Modern Series 12 (Oxford: Clarendon Press, 1905).

Meyer, K., *The Chase of Sid na mBan Finn and the Death of Finn*, Royal Irish Academy Todd Lecture Series Vol. 13 (Dublin, 1906), pp. 52–99.

Meyer, K., *The Death Tales of the Ulster Heroes* [Conchobar, Loegaire, Celtchar, Fergus mac Roich, and Cet mac Magach] Royal Irish Academy Todd Lecture Series, Vol. 14 (Dublin, 1906).

Meyer, K., *Triads of Ireland*, Royal Irish Academy Todd Lecture Series Vol. 13 (Dublin, 1906), p. 9.

Meyer, K., 'The Expulsion of the Dessi', *Eriu*, III (Dublin, 1907), pp. 135–42.

Meyer, K., *The Instructions of King Cormac mac Airt*, Royal Irish Academy Todd Lecture Series Vol. 15 (Dublin, 1909).

Meyer, K., *Life of Colman, son of Luachan* ('Betha Colmain maic Luachain'), Royal Irish Academy Todd Lecture Series, Vol. 17 (Dublin, 1911).

Meyer, K., *Selections from Ancient Irish Poetry* (London: Constable, 1911).

Meyer, K., 'The Guesting of Athirne', *Eriu*, 7 (Dublin, 1914), pp. 1–9.

Meyer-Baer, K., *Music of the Spheres and the Dance of Death* (Princeton, NJ: Princeton University Press, 1970).

Muller, J. (ed.), 'Two Irish Tales', *Revue Celtique*, 3 (Paris, 1878), pp. 351–60.

Murdoch, B., *The Irish Adam and Eve Story: Saltair na Rann* (Dublin: DIAS, 1976).

Murphy, Sr M., *St. Basil and Monasticism* (New York, 1971; reprinted from 1930 edn).

Murphy, G., 'St. Patrick and the Civilising of Ireland', *Irish Ecclesiastical Record* Series V, Vol. 79 (1953), pp. 194–204.

Murphy, G., *Saga and Myth in Ancient Ireland* (Dublin, 1955).

Murphy, G., *Early Irish Lyrics: Eighth to Twelfth Century* (Oxford: Clarendon Press, revised edn 1962; orig. 1956).

Murphy, G., *Early Irish Metrics* (Dublin: Royal Irish Academy, 1961).

Musk, B., *The Unseen Face of Islam* (Eastbourne, E. Sussex: MARC Publishers, 1989).

Narvaez, P. (ed.), *The Good People: New Fairylore Essays* (New York: Garland, 1991).

Narvaez, P., 'Newfoundland Berry Pickers "In the Fairies": Maintaining Spatial, Temporal and Moral Boundaries Through Legendry', In *The Good People* (New York: Garland, 1991), p. 337.

Nettl, B., *Music in Primitive Cultures* (Cambridge: Cambridge University Press, 1956).

The New Grove Dictionary of Music and Musicians, ed. S. Sadie (London, 1980).

Nicolson, A. (ed.), *Gaelic Proverbs* (Edinburgh: Birlinn, 1996; orig. 1881).

Nutt, A., *The Voyage of Bran* (The Celtic Doctrine of Rebirth), Vol. 2 (London: David Nutt, 1897, with appendices by Kuno Meyer).

Nutt, A., 'Tochmarc Etaine', *Revue Celtique*, 27 (Paris, 1906), pp. 325–39.

O'Beirne Crowe, J., *Amra Choluim Chilli* (Dublin: McGlashan and Gill, 1871).

O'Cathasaigh, T., 'The Semantics of Sid', *Eigse*, 17 (Dublin, 1977–9).

O'Cathasaigh, T., 'Curse and Satire', *Eigse*, 21 (Dublin, 1986).

O'Corrain, D. (ed.), *Sages, Saints and Storytellers: Celtic Studies in Honour of Professor James Carney* (An Sagart, Ireland: Maynooth, 1989).

O'Croinin, D., 'The Oldest Irish Names for the Days of the Week', *Eriu*, 32 (Dublin, 1981), p. 95.

O'Croinin, D., *Early Medieval Ireland 400–1200* (London: Longman, 1995).

O'Curry, E., *Manners and Customs of the Ancient Irish*, Vols. 1–3 (London: Williams & Norgate, 1873).

O'Donoghue, N., 'St. Patrick's Breastplate', in *An Introduction to Celtic Christianity*, ed. J. P. Mackey (Edinburgh: T. & T. Clark, 1989).

O'Donoghue, N., *The Mountain Behind the Mountain* (Edinburgh: T. & T. Clark, 1993).

O'Driscoll, R. (ed.), *The Celtic Consciousness* (New York: George Braziller, 1981).

O'Grady, S. H., *Silva Gadelica*, Vols I & II (London: Williams & Norgate, 1892).

O'hOgain, D., *Myth, Legend, and Romance: An Encyclopedia of the Irish Folk Tradition* (New York: Ryan Publishing, 1991).

O'Keeffe, J. G., 'Mac da Cherda and Commaine Foda', *Eriu*, 5 (Dublin, 1911), pp. 21–42.

O'Madagain, B., 'Irish Vocal Music of Lament and Syllabic Verse', in *The Celtic Consciousness*, ed. R. O'Driscoll (New York: George Braziller, 1981), pp. 311–32.

O'Madagain, B., 'Functions of Irish Song in the 19th c.', *Bealoideas* (1985), pp. 130–216.

O'Madagain, B., 'Gaelic Lullaby: A Charm to Protect the Baby?' *Scottish Studies*, 29 (1989).

O'Maille, T., 'Medb Chruachna', *Zeitschrift für Celtische Philologie*, 17 (New York, 1928), pp. 129–146.

O'Meara, J., *The Voyage of St. Brendan* (Mountrath, Portlaoise, Ireland: Dolmen Press, 1985).

O'Neill, J., 'The Battle of the Boyne', *Eriu*, II (London, 1905), pp. 173–85.

O'Rahilly, C., (ed.) *Tain Bo Cuailnge*, Recension I (Dublin: DIAS, 1976).

O'Rahilly, T. F., *Early Irish History and Mythology* (Dublin, 1946).

O'Sullivan, S., *Folktales of Ireland* (Chicago: University of Chicago Press, 1966).

Patch, H. R., *The Other World, According to Descriptions in Medieval Literature* (Cambridge, MA: Harvard University Press, 1950).

Piggot, S., *The Druids* (New York: Thames & Hudson, 1985).

Plummer, C., 'Some New Light on the Brendan Legend', *Zeitschrift für Celtische*, 5 (London, 1905), pp. 124–41.

Power, P., *Life of St. Declan of Ardmore and Life of St. Mochuda of Lismore* (London: Irish Texts Society, 1914).

Purser, J., *Scotland's Music* (Edinburgh: Mainstream, 1992), p. 21.

Purton, W., 'The Parting of Comhdhan and Conall', *Revue Celtique*, 29 (Paris, 1908), pp. 219–21.

Quasten, J., *Music and Worship in Pagan and Christian Antiquity* (Washington, DC: National Association of Pastoral Musicians, 1983), p. 16 (English trans. of 1973 German orig.).

Ranelagh, J., *A Short History of Ireland* (Cambridge: Cambridge University Press, 1983).

Rees, A. and Rees, B., *Celtic Heritage* (New York: Thames & Hudson, 1961).

Reeves, W., (ed.) *Life of Saint Columba* by Adamnan (reprinted from the Historians of Scotland (1874) facsimile reprint by Llanerch Enterprises, Dyfed, 1988).

Rimmer, J., *The Irish Harp* (Cork, 1977).

Rolleston, T. W., *The High Deeds of Finn and other Bardic Romances of Ancient Ireland* (New York: Shocken Books, 1973; reprint of 1910 orig.).

Ross, A., *Pagan Celtic Britain* (London: Routledge & Kegan Paul, 1967).

Ross, A., *Everyday Life of the Pagan Celts* (London: B. T. Batsford, 1970).

Rouget, G., *Music and Trance* (Chicago: University of Chicago Press, 1985).

Royal Irish Academy, *A Dictionary of the Irish Language* (Dublin, 1913–57).

Ryan, J., *Irish Monasticism* (Ithaca, NY: Cornell University Press, 1931).

Sachs, C., *The History of Musical Instruments* (London: Oxford University Press, 1942).

St Jerome, 'Epistle to Dardanus', *S. Eusebii Hieronymi Stridonensis Presbyteri opera omnia*, ed. Abbé Migne, t. xi., p. 213.

Sanger, K. and Kinnaird, A., *Tree of Strings: crann nan teud: A History of the Harp in Scotland* (Temple, Midlothian: Kinmor Music, 1992).

Schopenhauer, A., *The World as Will and Idea*, trans. R. B. Haldane and J. Kemp, 3 vols (Boston: Osgood, 1883).

Schroeder-Sheker, T., 'Musical-Sacramental-Midwifery', *Music and Miracles*, ed. Don Campbell (Wheaton, IL: Quest Books, 1992).

Schroeder-Sheker, T., 'Music for the Dying', *Caduceus*, 23 (Warwickshire, 1994).

Scott, C., *Music: Its Secret Influence Throughout the Ages* (Wellingborough: Aquarian Press, 1958).

Sendrey, A., *Music in the Social and Religious Life of Antiquity* (Rutherford, NY: Fairleigh Dickinson Press, 1974).

Seymour, St J., 'The Eschatology of the Early Irish Church', *Zeitschrift für Celtische Philologie*, 14 (London, 1923), pp. 179–211.

Seymour, St J., 'The Seven Heavens in Irish Literature', *Zeitschrift für Celtische Philologie*, 14 (London, 1923), pp. 17–30.

Shankar, R., *My Music, My Life* (London: Jonathan Cape, 1969).

Sherry, Patrick, 'Mozart, *Amadeus*, and Barth', *New Blackfriars* (Oxford, May 1986), pp. 233–40.

Stokes, W., 'Mythological Notes (Labraid Lorc and His Ears, Cred's Pregnancy)', *Revue Celtique*, 2 (Paris, 1874), pp. 197–203.

Stokes, W., 'Cuchulainn's Death', *Revue Celtique*, 3 (Paris, 1876–78), pp. 174–85.

Stokes, W., 'The Death of the Sons of Uisnech', *Irische Texte, Series 2* (Leipzig, 1887; published in conjunction with E. Windisch).

Stokes, W., 'The Siege of Howth', *Revue Celtique*, 8 (Paris, 1887), pp. 47–64.

Stokes, W., 'The Voyage of Mael Duin (Immram Curaig Mailduin Inso)', *Revue Celtique*, 9 (Paris, 1888), pp. 447–95.

Stokes, W., 'The Voyage of Snedgus and MacRialga (Imrum Snedhghusa ocus Mic Riagla Andso Sis)', *Revue Celtique*, 9 (Paris, 1888), pp. 14–25.

Stokes, W., 'The Voyage of Mael Duin', *Revue Celtique*, 10 (Paris, 1889), pp. 50–95.

Stokes, W., *Lives of the Saints from the Book of Lismore* (Oxford, 1890).

Stokes, W., 'Cormac's Adventure in the Land of Promise', *Irische Texte*, Series 3 (Leipzig, 1891; published in conjunction with E. Windisch).

Stokes, W., 'The Battle of Mag Mucrime', *Revue Celtique*, 13 (Paris, 1892), pp. 426–74.

Stokes, W., 'Boroma', *Revue Celtique*, 13 (Paris, 1892), pp. 32–124.

Stokes, W., 'The Violent Deaths of Goll and Garb (Aided Guill Maic Carbada ocus Aided Gairb Glinne Rige)', *Revue Celtique*, 14 (Paris, 1893), pp. 396–449.

Stokes, W., 'The Voyage of the Hui Corra (Iomramh Churraig Hua Gcorra Annso)', *Revue Celtique*, 14 (Paris, 1893), pp. 22–69.

Stokes, W., 'Da Choca's Hostel', *Revue Celtique*, 21 (Paris, 1900), pp. 149–65, pp. 312–27 and pp. 388–402.

Stokes, W., 'Death of Muirchertach mac Erca', *Revue Celtique*, 23 (Paris, 1902), pp. 395–431.

Stokes, W., 'The Deaths of Some Irish Heroes', *Revue Celtique*, 23 (Paris, 1902), pp. 303–48.

Stokes, W., 'The Battle of Allen', *Revue Celtique*, 24 (Paris, 1903, pp. 41–67).

Stokes, W., 'Death of Crimthann, son of Fidach, and the Adventure of the sons of Eochaid Muigmedon', *Revue Celtique*, 24 (Paris, 1903), pp. 172–207.

Stokes, W., 'The Wooing of Luaine and the Death of Athirne', *Revue Celtique*, 24 (Paris, 1903), pp. 270–87.

Stokes, W., 'Adventure of St. Columba's Clerics', *Revue Celtique*, 26 (Paris, 1905), pp. 130–70.

Stokes, W., 'The Colloquy of the Two Sages', *Revue Celtique*, 26 (Paris, 1905), pp. 4–64.

Stokes, W., *The Birth and Life of St. Moling* (London, 1907).

Stokes, W., 'Tidings of Conchobar mac Nessa', *Eriu*, 4 (Dublin, 1908), pp. 18–38.

Stokes, W., 'The Training of Cuchulainn', *Revue Celtique*, 29 (Paris, 1908), pp. 109–52.

Strunk, O. (ed.), *Source Readings in Music History: From Classical Antiquity Through the Romantic Era* (New York: Norton, 1950).

Sullivan, L., (ed.), *Enchanting Powers: Music in the World's Religions* (Cambridge, MA: Harvard University Center for the Study of World Religions, 1997).

Tame, D., *The Secret Power of Music* (New York: Destiny Books, 1984).

Teillhard de Chardin, P., *Hymn of the Universe*, trans. S. Bartholomew (New York, 1965).

Tomlinson, G., *Music in Renaissance Magic* (Chicago: University of Chicago Press, 1993).

Ui Ogain, Rionach, 'Music Learned From the Fairies', *Bealoideas*, Vols 60–1 (Galway, Folklore of Ireland Society, 1992), pp. 197–214.

Vallee, J., *Passport to Magonia* (Chicago: Contemporary Books, 1969).

Warren, F. E., *The Liturgy and Ritual of the Celtic Church*, 2nd edn, with a new Introduction and Bibliography by J. Stevenson (Woodbridge, 1987).

Whone, H., *The Hidden Face of Music* (London: Victor Gollancz, 1974).

Wilson, B., *Scottish Folktales and Legends* (Oxford: Oxford University Press, 1954).

Yates, F., *Giordano Bruno and the Hermetic Tradition* (London: Routledge & Kegan Paul, 1964).

Yates, F., *The Rosicrucian Enlightenment* (London: Routledge & Kegan Paul, 1972).

Index